Bill Doescher

Dear Folks

Essays and Insights from a Public Relations Leader

Edited by Traci Dutton Ludwig

Dear Folks: Essays and Insights from a Public Relations Leader

Edited by Traci Dutton Ludwig

First edition, 2019
10 9 8 7 6 5 4 3 2 1
Library of Congress Control Number: 2018965570
ISBN 978-0-9990245-7-7

Cover collage: Bill Doescher and Genesee Street, Utica, New York

PUBLISHED BY PRMUSEUM PRESS, LLC, NEW YORK, NEW YORK

THIS BOOK IS DEDICATED to Linda Blair Doescher, my wife of 41 years, without whom most of the accomplishments and storytelling found within these pages would not have been possible. It is also dedicated to our four "kids" and their spouses — Michelle Blair Hammond and her husband Sam Hammond, Doug Doescher and his wife Marie Menna Doescher, Marc Blair and his wife Kimberly Langworthy Blair, and Cinda Doescher Malec and her husband Gregg Malec. And equally important, it is dedicated to our wonderful grandchildren — Sam Blair, Sabrina Malec, Margaret Malec, Noreen Malec, Charlotte Blair, Fiona Rose Blair Hammond and Coco Blair. May their experiences in life be as enlightening and entertaining as the ones Linda and I have had.

Bill Doescher

CONTENTS

FOREWORD

Rarely, if ever, does an assignment to write an article for a special home-design section of a weekly newspaper turn into an assignment for a whole book. But it happened to me about a year ago when interior designer Linda Blair, whom I was interviewing for the *Scarsdale Inquirer*, introduced me to her husband, Bill Doescher. As Linda and I were concluding our meeting in her home, she walked me over to Bill's study and suggested that he consider me as editor for the book he was writing. I had interviewed Linda for various stories over the years and had heard of her husband, Bill, but I had never met him. Bill, like Linda, was a well-known, 40-year-long, active volunteer in the Scarsdale community, where he served on a number of village organizations and where we all lived. As a professional writer for more than 15 years, I had knowledge of village news and had written numerous local features for the *Inquirer* and the digital publication Scarsdale10583.com; but I had not yet encountered Bill directly.

Soon after our introduction, my cell phone rang. It was Bill on the line. "Let's get started," he invited. He warned me that he had already tried two other editors without much success, and that he had frequently started and stopped the book over the last five years. I listened and was not dissuaded. Bill told me he was now more committed to the project than ever before, and I could sense his earnestness. I promised my commitment in return.

Our first official meeting, and many thereafter, occurred at the local Starbucks near the Scarsdale train station. Later, when heavy editing and intense collaboration were necessary, we moved our meetings to Bill's home office. Linda sometimes checked in with thoughts, but mostly, the chapters developed around Bill's ideas related to personal and professional events and recollections. Each chapter was significant because it contained an embedded life lesson that Bill himself had learned and wanted to pass along to readers.

From the beginning, I was struck by Bill's natural gift of storytelling and by his insightful sense of observation. While working at our usual table by the window at Starbucks, Bill often encountered people he knew. Although they were usually just rushing in for a latte, these friends and acquaintances always stopped by our table to be delighted by a few minutes of conversation. No matter what the topic, Bill was always on point with intelligent yet entertaining dialogue. Even the employees of Starbucks were charmed by Bill's spirited banter and genuine interest in what they also had to say.

Bill's stories — captured in the episodic chapters of this book — demonstrate the value of engaging life with authenticity, curiosity and resolve. They also show the immeasurable results of actively paying attention. This translates to rewards, such as being able to decipher people and situations, anticipate outcomes, preemptively take the right actions and give back in meaningful ways. Such characteristics and philosophies mark many chapters in this book and have contributed to Bill's achievements of a rich life and a successful career.

As an esteemed leader in the field of public relations for more than 50 years, Bill has seen the industry grow up with him. Never content with the status quo, Bill has been a pioneer — a brave fellow, with the courage of his own curiosity — dedicated to the pursuit of new, different and better ways.

Maria Russell, a professor of public relations at Syracuse University's S.I. Newhouse School of Public Communications, was one of the first colleagues to characterize Bill this way. She said, "Like others who preceded him in PR, Bill was and is a pioneer in almost everything he does. Whether teaching investor relations at Newhouse, advising CEOs or mentoring students and friends, Bill has always been a counselor's counsel. He was never just an order taker. Importantly, throughout his career, Bill was never afraid to politely express his opinions. In discussions with a client or boss, he never waited to be told what to do, but rather took initiative with forward-thinking ideas that often turned out to be perfect solutions. Bill has helped public relations professionals move away from being order-takers, to respected counselors, to business executives and government leaders." Without being a rabble rouser, Bill has been a change agent, whose ingenuity and exploration of possibility have opened paths for others to follow.

The authentic storytelling in this book provides sound lessons and strong insight into finding success through a life well lived. The accounts are generous, personable, humorous and wise.

Keep reading, and you'll be glad you did. Like me, your life will become richer for having shared some time with Bill Doescher and his stories.

Traci Dutton Ludwig
January 2019

ABOUT THE AUTHOR

Bill Doescher has been a recognized and energetic leader in the field of public relations for more than 50 years. The industry has grown up with him as he dedicated himself to new, different and better ways of communicating messages to a variety of publics.

Whether teaching investor relations at the S.I. Newhouse School of Public Communications at Syracuse University, advising CEOs, publishing a magazine, managing corporate communications departments during changing times, or mentoring students and colleagues, Bill has always been a counselor's counsel.

After graduating with a bachelor's degree in economics from Colgate University, Bill started his professional career by working as a sportswriter for *The Evening Press* in Binghamton, New York. Before that, while serving as the Colgate University sports correspondent for his hometown newspapers — the *Utica Daily Press* and *Utica Observer-Dispatch* — and as the sports editor of the *Colgate Maroon*, Bill had attracted the attention of sports editors in Central New York.

After a few years, Bill moved on from sportswriting to continue his education at Newhouse. He received a master's degree in public relations. His first PR job was at The Chase Manhattan Bank in New York City. Subsequent communications posts included positions at Champion

International and Drexel Heritage Furnishings, where he recommended and supervised the company's sponsorship of a PGA golf tournament, the Heritage Golf Classic, on Hilton Head Island, South Carolina. Bill's longest corporate communications role was with Dun & Bradstreet, where for 22 years he held increasingly responsible positions including senior vice president & chief communications officer and publisher of *D&B Reports* magazine.

A former president of both the PRSA Foundation and PRSA-NY, Bill has received several leadership awards in the field of public relations. In 2014, he was presented with the prestigious John W. Hill Award by PRSA-NY. This award represents the organization's top honor for outstanding professional achievement in the practice of public relations. Named for the founder of one of the world's preeminent PR firms, the award has been presented annually since 1977. Recipients exemplify Hill's belief that experience, quality, integrity and judgment are the cornerstones upon which the public relations profession has been built.

Bill has been passionate about giving back to society and has been an important member on several nonprofit boards including the Jackie Robinson Foundation and the Newhouse Board of Advisors. He is active in the Hitchcock Presbyterian Church in Scarsdale, New York, where he is an elder and a member of the Session and Chancel Choir. Bill also serves as treasurer of the Hudson River Presbytery, a group of 79 Presbyterian congregations in New York State.

Bill is a resident of Westchester County, New York.

Dear Folks: Essays and Insights from a Public Relations Leader

INTRODUCTION
CONTINUING A FAMILY LEGACY

On June 19, 1986, my father, Frederick W. Doescher, had a stroke that took his speech, paralyzed his right side and impacted his ability to focus and type. His days of writing a weekly family letter, "Dear Folks," on an old Royal typewriter with plenty of carbon copies from his home offices in Utica and Hamilton, New York, were over. He died three years later on June 6, 1989, at the age of 84.

Dad began his writing career for college publications and sports publicity at Colgate University, where he received a bachelor's degree in 1926. Following graduation, he honed his skills by working as an advertising copywriter for the Wicks and Greenman clothing store in Utica. For more than 55 years, however, he was a manufacturer's sales representative for furniture and furniture-related companies, who traveled throughout New York State and Canada, presenting his various lines to the owners and managers of furniture and department stores.

Dad became the family's main letter writer after his own father, Charles Doescher, passed away on May 29, 1966, at the age of 90.

My grandfather, affectionately known as Papa, was always a man of words. According to family legend, it was Papa's great ability as an observer and storyteller that attracted my grandmother, Mary Elizabeth Darby, to him. They married on June 11, 1902, in Waterbury, Connecticut.

In 1937, before I was born, Papa started the Doescher family tradition of letter writing. When I was old enough to comprehend his typed chronicles, I found his letters to be well-written, full of positive stories and advice. What I especially liked about Papa's letters was how they diminished the space between us. Papa lived far away but his words on those pages kept me immediately involved with that side of the family.

My grandmother died on February 26, 1949, when I was 11 years old. Her absence did not diminish Papa's letters. In fact, he was even more motivated to write them, as if they were a way to keep the conversation alive with her, at least in spirit.

I learned things about Papa from his letters that I hadn't noticed before. As a child, my vantage point was naturally rather myopic. Reading the family letters, however, required concentration and encouraged everyone to slow down and pay attention. From Papa's weekly epistles, I discovered that he worshipped every Sunday at the First Congregational Church of Waterbury and belonged to the Masonic Order and the Concordia Singing Society of Waterbury. I also realized he was a teetotaler, exercised at the local YMCA, and enjoyed Italian food at DiOrio's, his favorite restaurant, located on Bank Street. Later in life, when he was not spending weeks of retirement in Maine or Florida, Papa continued to take his main meal — lunch — at

DiOrio's, even though it was several blocks away from his house and down a steep hill. To stay in top physical shape, he walked both ways.

While employed for more than 40 years as a machine-shop supervisor at Scovill Manufacturing Company in Waterbury, Papa managed to write a number of articles about industry tool and dye strategies for McGraw-Hill magazines. He was proud to say he got paid for those pieces. And probably just as important, he was proud to tell his grandsons that he always wore a white shirt and tie to work, setting a high standard for the other supervisors.

Because of his accomplishments and worthy way of living, Papa was quite a role model for the family. He never had a drink in his life, and at the celebration of my brother's graduation from Colgate, he reminded us that no good could ever come from drinking. He was so earnest in his conviction that he had tears in his eyes when he said it. When the conversations from the graduation celebrants got louder in the living room at the Delta Upsilon house, he said, "You see, people begin to talk louder when they're drinking."

Following my father's stroke, Elsie M. Doescher — my father's sister and my maiden aunt — strongly suggested I take on the weekly family writing of "Dear Folks." As a school teacher and my devoted fan, Elsie believed I was the logical choice to carry the tradition forward.

As a communications practitioner with an esteemed career in public relations, I had succeeded in becoming the nearest thing to a professional writer in the family, sometimes using the pseudonyms of William Fredericks and H.O. Kipp, which was my maternal grandfather's name. Nevertheless, I declined. I told Aunt Elsie I had neither the time nor the interest. Elsie, however, was persistent and often tried to cajole me into accepting the letter-writing assignment. But her efforts did not prevail.

Or did they?

In many ways, I realize I have been drafting those family letters for a long time. I've been collecting stories, reflecting on experiences and sharing lessons, without actually putting anything on paper — until now.

Dear Folks, a title borrowed from the salutation in my father's and grandfather's weekly epistles, is an homage to my family's tradition of letter writing, my professional and personal roles and my commitment to passing along life lessons that have had a profound effect on me.

In writing this book, I realize I have been using storytelling, the social and cultural activity of sharing experiences, to build connections and engage community throughout my 57-years-and-counting communications and public relations career. I've taken the same approach in personal conversations with friends, relatives, acquaintances, fellow golfers, college students, mentees, waiters and even strangers.

The *Dear Folks* stories include lessons that have inspired me, caused me to reflect, motivated my decisions and guided me through life. Many of these lessons were learned or inspired by examples seen in my business roles in public relations, marketing, communications, publishing and related fields, as well as through experiences gained through college teaching, mentoring, volunteering, serving on college advisory boards and boards of directors, and participating in charitable and industry-related organizations. Remarkably, I've found that what works in business often works in real life, and vice versa.

Looking back on these stories has also inspired me to look forward. I am more mindful than ever about recognizing the power of connection, the beauty of continuity, the importance of productive learning and the magical simplicity that results from getting to the heart of things. The lessons I am sharing have gotten me this far, and I hope they will work for you, too.

Bill Doescher
January 2019

Frederick Doescher, 1984, left, and Charles Doescher, 1960, right

1.
THANK YOU, UTICA, NEW YORK

Bill outside of John F. Hughes Grammar School in Utica, New York, 1949

"The Pent-up City" (19th century)
"The Handshake City" (1970s)
"The City of Possibilities" (2002)
"The Renaissance City" (2008)
"The Town That Refugees Love" (2014)

— Popular slogans for Utica, New York

Judging from the list of nicknames above, Utica, a city in upstate New York, has meant many things to many people. But, in all the descriptions, there is a strong identification of place and a distinct sense of home.

While we're at it, we could even add another slogan to the list. How about "Bill Doescher's Hometown City?" Sounds good to me, particularly since it was a great place to first call home.

Growing up in Utica, New York, in the 1940s and 1950s was magical. It was the setting for an ideal childhood and a great launching pad for growth, success and survival. It seemed like my friends and I never had a worry or a care in the world. Or at least that's how our parents, teachers, friends and community members made me feel all the time.

And, I mean all the time!

We were special — no matter what anybody else might have said to the contrary. If a criticism was uttered, it was never taken personally.

We surely didn't have any reasons to be upset about anything because local crime waves and combat war zones were for other cities in far-away places. CNN and the other 24/7 radio and TV networks hadn't been invented yet, and racial hate crimes seemingly didn't exist, at least where we lived.

Really bad news never made it to our houses.

The news about the passing of a grandmother, a grandfather or aunt or uncle was sad, but not earthshaking because our parents and clergy, whatever their religion, could always explain that passing was inevitable and therefore understandable.

Even a high school friend's broken arm or leg or hamstring injury that caused us to lose a game didn't matter. My own episode of scarlet fever in the fifth grade, which left me with a heart murmur that disappeared before the U.S. Army came calling, didn't seem like the end of the world. I did, however, have trouble with the new math — whatever that was — when I returned to school after the illness had passed.

A flat tire on my new English bicycle ... now that was something else.

Our parents, relatives and friends' parents protected us with all kinds of shields, physical and mental, from the bad things and bad people. They made sure we were always safe and happy, no matter the cost or circumstances.

Sometimes, to be just one of the guys, I'd find myself in an adventure that my parents might not have approved of. That meant I'd later have to answer one of my friends' mother's truth questions. In particular, I remember Mike Foley's mom, Mrs. James Foley as she was referred to back then, setting up to quiz me about certain events. She'd always implore, "Say honest, Doesch." Moments like those were among the worst things to ever happen.

My friends were everywhere — school, church, on the court, off the field, next door, down the street, around the corner, and across town — South Utica, North Utica, West Utica, East Utica, and in the suburbs of New Hartford, Clinton, Whitesboro, New York Mills, Waterville, Inlet and Old Forge.

Back then, as a high-school student, I occasionally visited the public library on Genesee Street when I was feeling studious, rode my bike for miles and could seemingly go everywhere, played all kinds of sports, skied down hills without proper lessons, participated in a number of activities at a variety of local organizations including Catholic and Protestant churches and a few synagogues. I didn't know about diversity or inclusion or being ecumenical back then; it all just seemed natural.

World War II didn't affect me directly because it wasn't close enough to actually see. The broadcasts about the horrific things going on in Europe and Japan from that big Philco radio in the living room never really penetrated my radar screen as a kid. Only such radio programs as *Tom Mix*, *Hopalong Cassidy*, *The Shadow* and *Inner Sanctum* had my ears.

No matter what, Utica, New York, with a population of about 100,000 in the 1940–50s, with plenty of economically viable businesses and distinct ethnic neighborhoods, was a great place to grow up. Today, although its population has diminished by about half, due to the closing of manufacturing facilities and people moving away, Utica is still a special place. On the outside, the city may be struggling, but its community spirit remains strong.

Part of that spirit comes from the rich identities of Utica's population in my day. Growing up, I got to know the Italian, German, Polish and Irish immigrants, who were driving the economy by working in the mills and opening their own businesses and whose children were my friends. I still remember Marino's Italian restaurant in East Utica, and the generous family that ran it. During World War II, the owners were somehow able to give Hershey chocolate bars to all the kids after every meal.

Utica retains its international flavor, although the demographics have changed. Described as "the town that refugees love," today's population includes people from Bosnia, Vietnam, Syria, Kenya, Burma, the Soviet Union and other foreign countries. According to an article in *The New York Times* in August 2014, "[Utica's diverse residents] have helped transform this once fading town by keeping the economy alive." Adding a comment about the current economic scene, Anthony J. Picente, Jr., the executive of Oneida County, said: "We're like every other upstate city. Our infrastructure is old. Our housing stock is old. But the refugees have renovated and revitalized whole neighborhoods."

I still have a warm place in my heart for Utica and visit occasionally. For sure, it's quiet — more so than I remember. It seems like now on any evening, weekends included, you could shoot a cannonball down Utica's central Genesee Street and not hit anyone. The sidewalks have been rolled up. Everybody's gone home.

It's not like it used to be, but I am sure glad I started out there.

Good luck, Utica. As a popular town bumper sticker says: "Last one out of Utica, please turn out the lights."

DOESCHER LESSON: *Remembering your roots is more important than you think. While you can't get those early moments back, those very experiences helped make you who you are today. They formed the foundation for your future and started laying the path that brought you to the present day.*

2.

MY FATHER, THE SUPERHERO

"The best kind of parent you can be is to lead by example."

— Drew Barrymore

Think of some of your strongest memories — the ones that remain vivid, no matter how much time has distanced you from the actual event. I bet they feel as real today as they did back then, still able to spark their original emotions — whether fear or pride or love or shock or joy. Looking back on my own store of childhood recollections, one memory stands out. It is significant because it involved spontaneous, quick and decisive actions by my father that saved someone's life. It's one of the memories that defined his character for me and made me believe my dad was truly a superhero.

When I think back, suddenly I'm there again....

It was around 1 p.m. on a quiet Sunday afternoon — September 30, 1945. The place was my family's middle-class Utica neighborhood called Ridgewood. Kids were out playing sports or games in their yards. Moms and dads were going about their business. It was just another normal day. Then, something happened. Suddenly, shrill screams for help erupted and reverberated throughout the streets. Everyone stopped what they were doing and listened. They were trying to figure out what was going on and where the panic was originating. To me, it sounded like somebody was getting killed, and it was right across the street at 125 Arlington Road.

My older brother Robert, then almost 12, and his friends were playing a makeshift football game in our backyard. I was standing by, watching the big boys in action. At almost eight, I was deemed to play the role of spectator, although I was secretly hoping to get into the game. When the screaming started, my brother just stood there holding the ball. The other players, and I, likewise remained frozen.

Amidst the screaming, two teenage girls from the neighborhood just happened to be walking by our house. One was the daughter of the then Utica Public Safety Commissioner from nearby Edgewood Road. The girls were the first to notice my father, Frederick W. Doescher, as he was making his way out our front door. They pointed to the house across the street and told him that the yells for "Help!" and "Police!" had seemed to come from over there.

Almost without thinking, my father sprang into action. He ran across the road and jumped over a large hedge. He landed in the neighbor's backyard and bolted toward the screaming. There, he encountered a knife-wielding assailant who was in the process of attacking Francis P. Peters, president of the local N.D. Peters Company, and his wife, Florence.

Florence's mother, who was visiting from England and not familiar with the American telephone system, was hiding inside the house. She didn't know how to call for help.

After his NFL-like leap over the hedge, my father tried to tackle the assailant, who was a man named Martin DeCarlo. DeCarlo had been a trusted employee of the Peters' cement company for more than 10 years and also did gardening at their home. DeCarlo lunged at my father and then continued his assault on the Peters.

My father was not dissuaded. As soon as he saw another chance to get hold of DeCarlo, my father disarmed him and held him on the ground near the garage until the police came. In the meantime, two football players from nearby New Hartford, Dick Daiker and Eddie Monahan, who had been driving through the neighborhood, heard the ruckus and rushed into the backyard to help my dad with the assailant.

During the commotion, my mother, brother and I stood paralyzed on the front lawn. As we were waiting for my father to return, I felt like my feet were stuck in cement. My brother wanted to run to the neighbor's yard to help our dad, but my mother ordered him not to go.

Our next-door neighbor, a New York State senator, was so upset about the developing situation that he got into his Cadillac and exited the area. I guess he did not want to get involved or be anywhere near a possible violent crime.

When the police and ambulances arrived, the Peters were whisked away to St. Elizabeth Hospital. They were in critical condition but eventually recovered and went on to live full lives.

DeCarlo was taken to the Utica jail. While collecting evidence on the scene, it took police a long time to find the large butcher knife, used by DeCarlo as a weapon, because my father had thrown it as far as he could into the empty field beside the Peters' home.

"He's got a lot of guts," Daiker, one of the student footballer players, said about my father to the *Utica Daily Press*. "He really didn't need any help, though, because the man did not struggle at all, and Mr. Doescher had the situation under control." The story about the incident was published on October 1, 1945.

According to the *Utica Observer-Dispatch*, Utica Public Safety Commissioner Stevenson said, "I believe Fred Doescher acted with unusual bravery and presence of mind and that his prompt action in disarming the knife-wielding attacker yesterday near his home may have saved the lives of Mr. and Mrs. Peters."

Members of the Peters family and neighbors were demonstrative in their praise of my father and his role in subduing the Peters' assailant. But my father remained modest.

When local reporters and photographers arrived at our house to interview my dad, he refused to be photographed and was quoted as saying, "I am no hero. I did only what anyone else would have done under the circumstances."

A motive for the attack was never established, but it was rumored that a union dispute was involved. DeCarlo was the union representative for his fellow workers, and he had just returned from attending union meetings in Washington, D.C., two days prior to the incident.

With no previous criminal record, DeCarlo was sentenced to a jail term of up to 15 years. After serving his time, he returned home to the same house where he lived prior to the attack, and he resumed a somewhat normal life. He died in 1982.

I continued to have nightmares about the event for many years.

In what presumably can only happen in a small town, I graduated from high school with the assailant's daughter and worked closely with the Peters' son-in-law in the 1970s when I was vice president of advertising and public relations at Drexel Heritage Furnishings, in Drexel, North Carolina, and he was an account supervisor on my account at DeGarmo, Inc., in New York City.

I sometimes wonder how our lives might have been different if my father had not acted as he did that day, with incredible bravery that prioritized helping others over his own safety.

DOESCHER LESSON: *"Honor thy father and mother" (Exodus 20:12) and learn from them.*

3.
MOM'S STYLE

Bill, Mom and brother Robert dressed for church, 1946

"Always listen to your mother."

— Unknown

My older brother, Robert and I were the only kids in the Ridgewood neighborhood of Utica, New York, that had their khaki pants pressed regularly. It didn't go unnoticed back in the 1950s, and many years later two of my boyhood friends, Johnny Ligas of Eastwood Avenue, and Dickie Scala of Farmington Road, would often chide me about it.

But since they knew my mother well, and spent years devouring her delicious chocolate chip cookies, fresh out of the oven, and often waited at the doorstep for a piece of her famous chocolate cake with vanilla frosting, I could always come back at them with, "As you know, my mother has high standards, and this is one of them." They'd always laugh and say, "We know." As a buyer for Doyle Knower, a prestigious women's store on Utica's Genesee Street, during the 1930s, my mother's high standards regarding fashion were known throughout town. In fact, you could recognize her from a distance, just by the tailored silhouette of her coat and her fine leather shoes.

Katherine Kipp Doescher, my mother, was born in 1906, in Oswego, New York, the only daughter of Horace Olin and Lillian Buchanan Kipp. When it came time to discuss my mother's future, her father, H.O. Kipp, who was general manager for the Swift & Company office in Utica, and her mother, gave my mother a choice. They informed her they could only afford tuition and room and board at any given college of her choice, but not the fancy clothes she dreamed about taking with her. Mom demurred and decided to pass on college. Instead, she went into fashion. I never heard her say she regretted that decision.

In fact, Mom might have never met my father had she gone to an out-of-town college. Dad, a native of Waterbury, Connecticut, and a graduate of Colgate University in 1926, was two years older than Mom and already working as a successful copywriter at Wicks & Greenman, a fine clothing store in Utica. They were married at the Little Church Around the Corner in New York City on January 8, 1931. My mother, of course, wore an exquisite handmade woman's suit for the occasion — a very small wedding.

When my brother and I were kids, my mother's sense for fashion took a new direction — us. Whether we wanted to or not, my brother and I were forced to try on new garments at Wicks & Greenman, a men's clothing store, before every momentous occasion. These included the start of the new school year each August, Easter, Christmas and before we went on vacation. Mom had a favorite salesman, a young-looking man, at Wicks & Greenman. If he happened to be busy with another customer upon our arrival, we had to wait until he finished before we could proceed. Mom never wanted to trust anyone else to help outfit her boys. Sometimes we had to wait 30 or 40 minutes for the salesman to be free. This felt like an incredibly long time for us to wait, especially since we were young kids who didn't want to be there in the first place. We would have rather been outdoors playing sports.

Showing her deep love and pride for us, Mom wanted the best clothes for her two boys. Although my brother and I didn't realize it at the time, this was the reason behind our family's clothing shopping rituals. When it finally became our turn with the young salesman, Mom relished the process of picking out beautiful shirts and trousers for us, then matching them to jackets, ties, caps, sweaters and shoes. After conferring with the young salesman, he would first bring out four or five outfits for each of us. If the shopping experience followed the norm, we knew there would be at least six or eight more outfits for each of us to try on.

These shopping trips always occurred on Saturdays, which meant Dad was able to take part in them. Long mornings turned into afternoons, as we kept trying on clothes — one outfit after another, sometimes swapping out different shirts and adjusting color combinations. The shopping trips did not end until Mom was satisfied. Dad let her direct the process, make the final decisions, and he never discussed the prices, at least not in front of us. Invariably, we were the best dressed kids on the block, and that pleased Mom.

As an important part of her fashion sense and genuine love of people, Mom took up knitting and knit argyle socks by the dozens for my brother, my father and me. Relatives in our extended family and many other people also benefited from Mom's generosity. They included close family friends, such as Ted Lortz, owner of the New Hartford Pharmacy; Dr. Jeff Folley, our dentist in New Hartford, New York; Fred Parkinson, the husband of one of Mom's closest friends, and Bob Gilliland, a gadfly from the Yahnundasis Golf & Country Club in New Hartford, where they belonged. Mom also knitted other warm and cozy things, but it was the argyle socks that brought her fame in the community.

Despite inspiring devotion to her chocolate chip cookies and chocolate cake, Mom was not a particularly good cook. We enjoyed her vegetable soup and special holiday dinners, such as traditional roasted turkey on Thanksgiving and Christmas, but everyday meals were mediocre. Nevertheless, she always tried to take care of us in the kitchen, and she never gave up trying. In August 1977, on her deathbed in the intensive care unit at St. Luke's Memorial Hospital Center in New Hartford, Mom reminded us there were steaks in the freezer that we should warm up for my father's and our dinners. She seemed more concerned with feeding us than worrying about her own heart attack.

In addition to her knitting and cooking, we loved Mom for all the motherly things she did, including cleaning, handling doctors' and dentists' appointments, answering teachers' questions and pushing us out to school each weekday morning. When I contracted scarlet fever in the fifth grade, I was hospitalized for 10 days. Mom nurtured me back to health during a six-week stay at home.

By this time, my father had transitioned out of his job as copywriter and was well established as a manufacturer's sales representative for a number of home furnishings, mattress and table pad companies. His job required frequent traveling, up and down the New York Thruway, between Canada and Yonkers. This meant Mom essentially manned the fort and was the constant presence in our home life. She created a warm and welcoming environment, and she never failed to join in conversations when our friends came over to visit. She even played the piano for all of us to sing. *Deep*

Purple, made famous by Percy Faith & Orchestra, was her favorite.

Mom was one of the first people who taught me the importance of giving back. She made it a way of life in our household, where we were taught never to complain about something we didn't like, but rather to get involved and do something about it. Mom was active with the PTAs at our schools and the local American Cancer Society. She volunteered her talent as a pianist to the Westminster Presbyterian Church in Utica, where she often played for various Sunday School classes.

Mom was also known for being direct, and this prompted her to give us the kind of feedback known today as a "reality check." Her comments and questions were anything but subtle, and they didn't always feel loving at the time. Nevertheless, I knew it was important to listen to them. The stern expression on Mom's face said so.

I remember one of those interactions like it was yesterday. In 1971, when I phoned Mom to say that I would be moving to Hickory, North Carolina, to become vice president of public relations and advertising at Drexel Heritage Furnishings at the age of 34, she asked me, "What do you know about the furniture business you little pipsqueak? Your father has been in that business since forever."

Somewhat startled I could only say that the company wasn't hiring me for my furniture knowledge but rather my communications skills. "Oh," she said, without apologizing.

Later, I realized she was most likely speaking from a position of protection, albeit somewhat misguided. I think she wanted to protect the status of her husband's career that fed and clothed the family, and she also wanted to protect me. Without truly understanding the nature of my job, she was concerned I might be entering the deep waters of an unknown business.

Even when my mother said things I didn't want to hear, her love was unconditional. Her love was not measured by making my brother or me happy. It was an attitude, a way of life, and a long-term journey of caring and protecting us from evil and unjust things in the world.

DOESCHER LESSON: *No one loves you like your mother. She knows your strengths and vulnerabilities, and she accepts the best and worst of you. She remembers you before you even knew yourself. While her actions and words might falter, the devotion of a mother's love is perfect. While you might not understand her methods, your mother is always looking out for your best interests. A mother never stops caring for her child, worrying about her child and trying to protect her child. During difficult moments, try to see yourself through your mother's eyes.*

4. FRIENDS FROM THE NEIGHBORHOOD

"The Utica Boys" on Lake Winnipesauke, New Hampshire;
Pictured left to right: Bill, Tom Zagaroli, John Ligas, and Dick Scala, 1996

"You don't have to have anything in common with people you've known since you were five. With old friends, you've got your whole life in common."

— Lyle Lovett

Friends come in all sizes, forms and characters. Some friends become longtime companions, while others are more temporary. Sometimes, if you're lucky, the friendship itself is so central that it builds natural connections that are not dependent on either proximity or shared experience. Other times, the friendship is more circumstantial and may even depend on a common activity or occupation. So, how do you define friends of any kind? I think, carefully or not at all — especially since, by defining your friends, you are also defining yourself.

Early on, in the Ridgewood section of Utica, my childhood friends were everything to me. Together, we felt invincible. We imagined we could take on the world, or at least our corner of Utica, no matter what kind of outrageous ideas our young brains were concocting. My original group of childhood friends included Johnny Ligas, Dick Scala, Don Oberriter, Dick Abend, Susie Washeim, Bobby Flack and others whose names I can no longer remember but whose faces and idiosyncrasies I'll never forget.

Later our fiercely devoted pack grew to include other pals. Cal Jones and Tom Zagaroli were two of those new friends. They each moved into the neighborhood about the time I was in the eighth grade, and almost immediately, we embraced each of them as one of us.

This was the friend group with whom I played baseball and other sports, meeting up after school and on weekends every chance we could get. We gathered on neighborhood playgrounds, at the Hugh R. Jones School and on the Crestway field, which we used as a baseball diamond, a few blocks away. Someone always brought the bats; someone always brought the balls; and others seemed to supply everything else we needed. Somehow, we seemed organized without having any formal structure. But since it was important to us to play these games, our loose coordination worked.

Our baseball team was called the Ridgewood Raiders. We were competitive and close-knit, both on and off the field. I started out playing right field and then advanced to first base and shortstop. It was the normal progression for players just beginning the sport, and especially so, if you were one of the youngest members on the team, which I was.

Since we were all part of the same neighborhood, it was natural for us to become friends. We knew each other's parents and brothers and sisters. We often were included to join family dinners cooked by our friend's mothers, and it was at these tables that I got to experience some of the best Italian and Polish home cooking of my life.

Susie Washeim was one of the few girls on our block of boys. Nevertheless, we always included her in our group, without any exception. She was like a sister to us, or alternatively, just like one of the guys. And for me, you could even say she was my first "girlfriend." In reality, this meant we enjoyed riding bikes around the neighborhood together when we were in grammar school.

Later, at Utica Free Academy high school, my friend group expanded to include members of The Phi Delta Sigma Fraternity, a social club that met Friday evenings and organized dances with the girls' sororities. This fraternity included kids from outside Ridgewood, such as Mike Foley,

Dale Everett, Dave Reilly and Dick McNaney. Taking an early interest in leadership, I was elected president of Phi Delta Sigma in 1954. At my request, my friend Mike Foley succeeded me as president in 1955. This helped Mike accomplish one of his goals, and I was pleased to pass along the position to him.

Throughout high school, I continued to have various pockets of friends. I preferred to associate with different groups, rather than limiting myself to a singular and possibly insular clique. I was equally comfortable making friends with peers from various church groups, sports teams and other parts of the city. I guess you could say I was always a proponent of diversity, intuitively tuned in to the value of being involved with all kinds of people.

Following graduation from high school, I didn't know what would happen to that core group of friends. I knew we would all move on to other social groups in college, as well we should. But I surmised we'd at least have each other on our "home field" again during holiday breaks and summers. Or, so I thought.

My parents, however, had a different idea. When I was a sophomore at Colgate, they decided to sell their house in the Ridgewood section of Utica and move to Lower Woods Road in New Hartford, New York. I believe they wanted to downsize to save on taxes and have only a smaller property to manage. I couldn't blame them for their practical decision. The three bedrooms in their New Hartford house seemed adequate enough for the comings and goings of our family, particularly since my older brother, Robert, had married Diana Brown and permanently moved out.

Fortunately, my parents' relocation to New Hartford did not break up the "Utica Boys." This was the name we had proudly given ourselves — the foursome of Ligas, Scala, Zagaroli and Doescher.

Not only did we all manage my family's relocation; we succeeded in maintaining close friendships with each other throughout our entire lives. We have celebrated each other's milestones and supported each other through life's challenges, tragedies and joys. Dick Scala was the only attendant to be in both of my wedding ceremonies, in 1961 and 1977. Approximately four decades later, after Dick's death, I returned the favor when I walked his oldest daughter, Lisa, down the aisle, in 2015, to become Mrs. Lisa Scala McGuire. I knew he would have been proud of her.

In college, my friendships included people I knew from Delta Upsilon Fraternity, fellow writers from the school newspaper *Colgate Maroon* and basketball players from a semi-professional team called Victory Body Works, with whom I played in area league and non-league games.

My best friend in college was my roommate and fraternity brother Mert Hersh. Mert and I lived together in Mrs. Dickerson's private home on Kendrick Avenue, in Hamilton, New York, and at the fraternity. We became good friends from the first day we met, as freshmen, in West Hall at Colgate University in 1955. After graduation, Mert was in my first wedding, and I was a groomsman in his only wedding. We have stayed in touch for more than 50 years although we are now separated by great distance. Mert now lives in Phoenix, Arizona, where he moved to be near his two daughters after he retired from a successful executive recruiting firm that he ran in Kansas City, Missouri.

When I think of all these friends from the past, the time does not feel so far away.

Of course, most of today's friendships started more recently. Friends have been gathered from the places I have lived, new business relationships, boards on which I have served, volunteer organizations, mentoring opportunities and my country club's golf course.

I'll take them all — the old friends and the new friends. For a rich existence, you can never have enough good and reliable people in your life.

DOESCHER LESSON: *Friendships are hard to maintain, but they are worth the effort. True friends provide unvarnished advice anytime you need it. They know you so well that you don't have to start at the beginning when explaining yourself.*

5. EVERYONE SHOULD HAVE AN AUNT ELSIE

Aunt Elsie and Bill in front of Bill's parents' house in New Harford, New York, 1960

"There is no greater power and support you can give someone than to look them in the eye, and with sincerity and conviction say, 'I believe in you.'"

— Ken Poirot, author

Why Aunt Elsie? For starters, she wasn't one of my parents, so like most kids, I would listen to her more than them. Also, since she lived hundreds of miles away and only occasionally visited our home in Utica, she was fortunately never there when I messed up.

Aunt Elsie was my father's unmarried sister. She worked as an elementary school teacher near Hartford, Connecticut, but she was so much more. Over the years, she had a significant impact on my life, education and career. She pushed me to heights I had no idea I could conquer. Without her belief and encouragement, I'm convinced I would not have become the person I am today. Many of my successes, I owe to Elsie. She would always inquire, "What and how are you doing?" And I was always sure to have a good answer ready. She kept me on my toes and never failed to cheer me on. I can still hear her voice, passing on her familiar and sound advice: "Remember, you can do anything you set your mind to, as long as you stay focused on the end goal — whatever that may be."

Elsie was my number one fan, and I think of her a lot. She would be pleased to know that I often ask myself, even today, "What would Elsie recommend in this situation?"

I wasn't ready to lose her when she died of heart failure on Thanksgiving Day, 1991, at the age of 83. My wife, Linda, and I had been hosting a Thanksgiving meal at our house in Scarsdale, New York, when the call came in. Elsie had suffered a heart attack and was being taken to Hartford Hospital. As she was being wheeled into the ambulance, she instructed a neighbor to "Call Bill."

Leaving behind the turkey, sweet potatoes and pumpkin pie, as well as trusting a house full of guests to fend for themselves, Linda and I rushed to Elsie's bedside at the hospital. As soon as we entered the room, Elsie said to me, "I was wondering when you'd show up." I think she was waiting for me, and I now feel lucky that we were able to spend a few hours together one last time. We talked about things as though everything was normal — even though we all knew it wasn't.

After some time, Linda and I left Elsie at the hospital and headed back to our Thanksgiving guests. Not more than 30 minutes after we arrived home, a second call came in. This time, it was a nurse ringing from the hospital. She was calling to tell us that Elsie had died.

Elsie's funeral was held at the First Church of Christ in Wethersfield, Connecticut, where she had been a parishioner for many years. A day before the service, I talked with the minister, Reverend Donald W. Morgan, so he would be able to best describe how important Elsie was to our family. He already knew she had been a devoted elementary school teacher and a devout Christian lady. He knew she often volunteered her time at the church and Hartford Hospital, where she was appreciated and adored. What he might not have known was that Elsie's family was extremely important to her. She had often told me she prayed every night asking God to bless her relatives and friends. Her prayers were her "power line to God," she said.

I reminded the minister that Elsie's favorite hymn was "The Church's One Foundation," and her favorite verses in the Bible were Psalms 12:1–2, "I will lift up mine eyes unto the hills from whence cometh my help. My help cometh from the Lord, which made heaven and earth." These were also her father's favorite verses. She knew this because she took care of him for many years during his old age.

In June of 1989, when my father died, Elsie requested the minister use those verses at his burial at Riverside Cemetery in Waterbury, Connecticut. A little over two years later, she was buried next to her brother with those same words.

Before the burial, Reverend Morgan gave Elsie a proper Christian send-off with thoughts about her life. He said:

"Elsie Doescher had a wonderful spirit. She was warm, friendly, caring, outgoing. She always had a certain sparkle. She was independent, determined, well programmed and organized. She knew what she wanted to do and did it. She loved reading, had a keen interest in politics and biographies, and traveled extensively. Family, friends, and church were the most important pieces of her life. Here at her church she was involved in many ways — the art class, the senior book club, and the United Church Women of which she was president at one time. In the book club, she gave some of the best reports. She performed many acts of service to others, like faithfully going to the hospital every week to take books around to the patients or knitting for underprivileged children. There was clearly something of the teacher in her, having been for many years a wonderful elementary school teacher. She encouraged everyone to do the right thing and strive to be their best. She would hold you accountable, because she wanted the best for you. But she was never critical, just wonderfully concerned and caring and helpful.

"We have spoken of her devotion to her family. She kept close contact with them through the years, by telephone or by sending cards to everybody. She was always 'there.' Her most recent family outing was for her great-nephew Grant's wedding in Allentown, Pennsylvania, in September. That would be her last.

"One of her favorite haunts was Ocean Park, Maine, where for many years she would go every summer. The setting, the spirit of the place, the eternal seas were appealing to her. We can understand that. She was an altogether good woman, greatly loved. 'If anyone is going to heaven, it's Elsie Doescher!' said one who knew her well and long, her nephew Bill."

At the conclusion of the minister's speech, he recited a poem that the Elsie had given to my daughter, Cinda, with instructions for her to keep in her Bible. I think that poem well describes the kind of woman Elsie was, so it is worth repeating here:

I said a prayer for you today
  And know God must have heard.
I felt the answer in my heart,
  Although He spoke no word.

I didn't ask for wealth or fame
  I knew you wouldn't mind.
I asked Him to send treasures
  Of a far more lasting kind.

I asked that he'd be near to you
  At the start of each new day
To grant you health and blessings
  And friends to share your way.

I asked for happiness for you
  In all things great and small,
But it was for His loving care
  I prayed the most of all.

And just like that, with the minister's recitation of that poem, we said goodbye to Elsie.

After Elsie's funeral, the family had the task of cleaning out her house. It was a bittersweet process to go through all of the objects and mementos left behind. As we handled them, they constructed a document of Elsie's life, and so, we got to know her again, on her own terms. Even mundane household items lost their ordinary character in the stories they whispered about Elsie and in the unfiltered glimpses of personality they revealed.

In Elsie's Bible, I found a frayed ribbon pinned with a note in Elsie's handwriting. It said, "Part of my Easter orchid corsage, given by Bill D., to wear April 22, 1973, in Hickory, North Carolina." Although the flowers had dried up and disintegrated into dust many years before, the fact that Elsie had held onto that ribbon for almost two decades told me I meant as much to her as she did to me.

She didn't have any children, so I believe I was like her child. She remained close with her brother, who was my father, and talked to him every week. They were dedicated to following a financial television program which was produced by a PBS station in Maryland and aired on syndicates every Friday evening. Both Elsie and my father watched the show from their respective homes, and afterward, either that night or the following morning, they would discuss the segment. They carefully listened to the show's commentators and earnestly debated the advice that was presented. Elsie and my dad played their roles as if they were financial geniuses. I think it was a sort of game between them that they each enjoyed. They relished the interaction, and I enjoyed watching their discussions. Their conversations really showed the power of their sibling relationship and the importance, for both of them, to nurture it.

With similar dedication, Elsie went out of her way to build and sustain a relationship with me. My father's weekly family letters kept Elsie abreast of her nephews' lives, and she made an effort to show that she was paying attention to the news by reacting to it. Sometimes, she answered my dad's "Dear Folks," letters, even going as far as to directly address different family members.

I'm not absolutely sure why Elsie took a liking to me, but I reasoned long ago that it must have been because I paid attention to her and often answered her letters — bad penmanship and all. Another possibility was that I looked a lot like her brother — my father — and I therefore reminded her of him. A third possibility was that she simply liked my personality and saw potential in me.

Elsie and I communicated mostly by phone or mail throughout my life. No matter how long the conversations or letters were, she definitely had my ear. Even when I was an adult, Elsie continued to share advice. She would often send me copies of articles she thought I should read. These included numerous health articles over the years, mostly cautioning against the dangers of cigarette smoking and explaining their adverse effects on the body. As Elsie continued her information campaign, she was quietly communicating her steadfast concern for my health. While I read all the articles, I basically chose to ignore them. That is, until Elsie's persistence finally paid off. Following a 10-day hospitalization for a ruptured appendix in the 1980s, I decided I no longer needed cigarettes and quit smoking. Needless to say, Elsie was delighted.

During my childhood, Elsie did special things she didn't have to do. She organized adventures, experiences and treats that would have gotten any nephew's attention, and which certainly captured mine. While visiting the family one winter in 1951, she took a bus and slogged her way through several blocks of snow in order to attend my first basketball game as a starter. I was an eighth grader at John F. Hughes Elementary School in Utica at the time. Elsie also took me on my first train ride, from Utica to Syracuse and back. This occurred before I was a teenager, and I clearly remember the thrill of walking through the cars with Elsie close behind. She probably would have rather watched the outside view pass by from our seats, but she instead got up and accommodated my boyhood zest for adventure. It's a good thing she did, because we stumbled upon an unexpected highlight. Passing through the cars, we encountered the Utica College basketball team. Excited to meet them, I spoke to the players and told them I was a huge basketball fan. I learned they were staying on the train past our destination in Syracuse, in order to travel to an away game.

Exposing me to another mode of travel, Elsie took me to an airport when I was about eleven years old. We weren't actually going anywhere, but that didn't matter. It was a time period when airline travel was new and exciting, and Elsie thought the experience of being at an airport would edify my reservoir of knowledge. So, she organized a trip to Oneida County Airport, where we sat down to drink soda and watch planes from Mohawk Airlines take off and land.

When I was 13, Elsie planned an even longer adventure. With my parents' permission, she took me on a summer vacation to New England, with an itinerary centered around history. The trip included destination landmarks such as the Henry Wadsworth Longfellow House, Plymouth Rock and Boston's Old North Church, where Paul Revere began his famous midnight ride. Caring much more about sports than history, I was instead excited by the idea of watching a baseball doubleheader that matched the Philadelphia Phillies against the New York Giants at the old Polo Grounds in New York City and then, while we were in "Beantown," the Boston Red Sox versus the Chicago White Sox at Fenway Park. Of course, Elsie accommodated this wish, and we saw all three games.

Elsie was there for many firsts in my life. I remember her watching over me as I took my first swim in the Atlantic Ocean. I think I said something like, "Elsie, this water has salt in it!" Later in life, I wondered why I had been so surprised. Hadn't I learned about salt water oceans in my early science classes? Maybe I just wasn't paying attention in class.

In addition to exposing me to new experiences, Elsie always found ways of letting me know she believed in me. At an early age, she encouraged me to have my own personalized stationery. She rationalized that I would become famous one day, and the girls who received my early letters would cherish the correspondence and show my letters to their grandchildren. Of course, Elsie's predictions weren't quite accurate, but they weren't totally wrong either. At my 50th high school reunion, a female friend from grammar school actually told me she still had some of the letters I posted to her from Camp Dudley, in Westport, New York, when I was a boy.

Through her charitable actions and words, Elsie was always thinking of ways to make others better, including me. Without anyone asking, she offered to send me to prep school, at her own expense, for two years. She suggested my family take a look at two schools — The Taft School, a coeducational boarding school in Watertown, Connecticut, and Mount Hermon, which was then an all boys' school in Northfield, Massachusetts. In 1972, Mount Hermon merged with Northfield, an all-girls school, and the school is now known as Northfield Mount Hermon. To attend prep school, I would have had to repeat my junior year and spend five years total in high school. Concerned about prolonging my education, I declined Elsie's offer. Looking back, I've often wondered if I might have made the wrong decision. Being wiser today, I believe I should have taken advantage of Elsie's offer to send me to prep school. My life's pursuits, including the undergraduate college I attended, might have been different had I gone to one of those schools she suggested. But you can't turn back the clock.

Even with the prep-school turndown, Elsie remained committed to my education. Her ultimate gift of love was encouraging me to go back to school for a master's degree in public relations and providing me with a much-needed loan to make it happen. Elsie's money was not attached to any obligation to pay it back, but, of course, I did. Although I was not even close to being Phi Beta Kappa when I graduated with a bachelor's degree from Colgate University, Elsie's belief in my ability to succeed in graduate school was steady. Her loan made me feel that I wasn't just studying for myself; I was also doing it for her.

When I arrived at the School of Journalism at Syracuse University, now known as the now S.I. Newhouse School of Public Communications, in 1960, to begin a master's degree program, I had only $80 from my last paycheck as a sportswriter at Binghamton's *The Evening Press*, my manual Royal typewriter and my 1951 Pontiac. The Pontiac — you guessed it — had been Elsie's old car.

With the exception of hounding me with anti-smoking literature, Elsie never lectured me. She was never judgmental. She was never intrusive. She never grilled me on one subject or another. Instead, she was a voice of reason, wisdom and encouragement. I cherished her for this, and I always relied on her advice. Because she let me know she believed in me, I was able to believe in myself.

For all these reasons, Elsie's positive presence was always on my mind, and it still is today. She really made a difference in my life, and I hope that one day someone will say the same about me.

DOESCHER LESSON: *Never underestimate the power of believing in people and encouraging them. It might be the motivation that changes lives.*

6.

GOING FOR THE NO-HITTER RECORD

"Winning doesn't always have to be the end goal."

— Unknown

In 1938, a 23-year-old left-handed pitcher by the name of Johnny Vander Meer pitched two consecutive no-hitters for the Cincinnati Reds. The games occurred on June 11 and 15, barely six months after I was born, making Vander Meer the only Major League pitcher to throw back-to-back no-hit, no-run games.

Fast forward to nine years later.

I was 10 years old and suddenly confronting the reality that I might be in the midst of a possible third consecutive no-hitter, underway at the small baseball diamond above Cub Alley at Camp Dudley. Camp Dudley was a boys camp with plenty of sports and fellowship, in Westport, New York, and the place where I spent five summers as a kid.

Obviously, the field wasn't even close to resembling Cincinnati's Crosley Field or Brooklyn's Ebbets Field, where Vander Meer accomplished his most enduring feat.

Nevertheless, we had a possible third consecutive no-hitter underway. And I was that pitcher.

I already had two consecutive no-hitters under my belt. I had eaten a healthy breakfast, a camp requirement, and I was ready. Probably too ready.

As opposed to the many thousands of fans in the stands at Major League games, our spectators numbered maybe six — the two teams' coaches, an extra player for each team and perhaps two Cubbies who weren't playing a game at the moment.

But none of that mattered. In my swelled, youthful confidence, I was going for my third no-hitter in a row. The Vander Meer record was all that mattered to me, and I was about to break it. Or so it seemed.

Regardless of my plans for greatness, the situation didn't end well. While pitching for that possible third no-hitter in a row, a funny thing happened. Despite plenty of encouragement from my catcher, Tommy Walton, I just couldn't seem to get the ball over the plate. As a result, I was unceremoniously relieved by my third baseman, Pete Willmott. Handing the ball over to Pete, I muttered something that our coach, Paul Lutz, didn't like. It was a curse word, and I shouldn't have said it. Soon to be an ordained minister, Coach Lutz showed his disapproval by sending me — neither to the bench nor to third base to take Willmott's place — but rather, to my cabin.

It was a rude awakening but an important lesson on good sportsmanship. Coach Lutz reminded me of the strict behavior expected of all Dudley campers, and he instructed me to apologize — not only to my teammates and the opposing team, but also to everyone who happened to be watching the game in Cub Alley. Coach Lutz emphasized these apologies would be necessary if I wanted to continue my twice-daily, swimming privileges at "Swim Point" for the rest of the season.

I thought about the consequence of not being able to swim with my friends in the lake, which was an activity I really enjoyed. I only needed a few minutes of reflection before I was determined to apologize and move forward. I waited for the game to end and talked to the players, the other campers and everyone else involved.

I have never forgotten the lesson.

It was at that moment that the camp's motto, "The Other Fellow First," truly began to take hold. For me, the lesson has been lifelong, and I continue to act with consideration for others today.

Many years after that failed no-hitter, I read a *Wall Street Journal* article about my third baseman from long ago. It was reported that Peter Willmott, then described as a Williams College grad out of Glen Falls, New York, and a former president of FedEx, was retiring as chairman of Carson Pirie Scott and taking millions with him as severance.

I sent him a note that said, "Pete, I wouldn't pay you $5 to be my third baseman."

It didn't take long for the phone to ring.

DOESCHER LESSON: *Never forget good manners. Using "The Other Fellow First" philosophy is always appropriate in real-life situations. It will always steer you in the right direction and will avoid words and deeds you might later regret.*

7.
STILL TRYING TO MAKE THE VARSITY

Bill (second from left in back row) with Victory Body Works basketball team after winning the YMCA championship in Utica, New York, 1959

"If your dreams do not scare you, they are not big enough."

— Ellen Johnson Sirleaf, President of Liberia (2006–2018)

Sports have always been a big part of my life. Not only have I been an avid fan, I have also enjoyed playing sports recreationally and competitively. Although I am probably more talented at golf, basketball is the sport I approached with the most ambition. I liked the challenge and never gave up trying to be successful in basketball.

I remember feeling a certain surprise when I arrived for the first tryout of the Colgate University freshman basketball team in the fall of 1955. Coach Bob Dewey pulled me aside and asked, "Do you want to play basketball here or graduate?"

"What do you mean?" I thought but didn't say out loud.

I had graduated that previous June from my local high school, Utica Free Academy (UFA), 30 miles down the road. In that community, only 24 percent of the graduating class went on to college. Coach Dewey knew that if I was going to make it at Colgate academically, I would need to devote a good amount of time to my studies. I was smart enough but had not yet learned the value of good study habits. In high school, countless other things had always gotten in the way — and basketball was one of them.

During my entire school career, I managed to stay involved with basketball because I loved everything about the game — the camaraderie, the competition and the excitement of winning (when we did). Even though I had failed to make the UFA varsity basketball team in my sophomore, junior and senior years, I stayed close to the sport by volunteering to be the team's manager in my senior year. This way, I was able to attend all the games and play in all the practices. At the same time, I continued to play on organized club and church basketball teams, including those sponsored by the YMCA, Fran's Restaurant, McGuirl's

Tavern, Phi Delta Sigma Fraternity, the Ridgewood Raiders and Westminster Presbyterian Church.

All the time I was playing, I was convinced that someday I would make the varsity — either in high school or college. Realistically I knew I would never rise to the level of playing in the National Basketball Association. However, I did get close to this dream when, in my business career, I did some executive recruiting for David Stern, who was then Commissioner of the NBA. Nevertheless, the hope of making a school's varsity team was real enough for that ambition to stay alive. I wanted to repeat those highlights of being a starter and the top scorer on a school team, just like when I was at John F. Hughes Grammar School in Utica.

My interest in basketball started early, even before my successful shots in the grammar school gymnasium. As a boy, I often practiced on a dirt court in a lot next to our house at 116 Arlington Road. I would dribble and shoot balls alone, with my brother Robert or with others in the neighborhood. Our collective passion for the game prompted us to form an informal neighborhood team, which we named the Ridgewood Raiders. We took ourselves very seriously and organized games against other teams around town. Sometimes, we played against teams from The First Presbyterian Church or Temple Beth El in Utica, and we were able to use their gyms. Other games occurred in community spaces and church basements. Some were organized a week before we played; some were held according to a seasonal schedule we developed, and others were spontaneous. I was the high scorer for my team in one memorable game against the Presbyterian Church team in which we ultimately lost 106–105. Six-foot-nine Gary Evans, former UFA and future Syracuse University star who was on the opposing team for that game, had 36 points, and I had 35.

My brother Robert and I didn't play on many organized basketball teams together, although we often shot baskets one-on-one outside our house. Robert was four-plus years my senior and a City of Utica foul-shooting champion at one time. Once, however, I asked him to suit up with us in a Westminster Presbyterian vs. First Presbyterian church league game. It paid off. He scored 26 points; I scored 24 points; and our team won, 61–55. It was a remarkable comeback, since we were losing at halftime. Our parents, who had never seen us play together, had come to watch the game, but they didn't see the win. At halftime, seeing our lagging score and fearing their presence would jinx the game, they decided to leave.

In one of the last games as manager of the high school basketball team, I almost got to play. It was at an away game my senior year and the UFA players, led by Bill Metzger and Wayne Decker, tried to persuade Coach Fred Collins to allow me to change into uniform at halftime and join the action. All of the players knew of my aspiration to play in a varsity game and wanted to help me accomplish that goal. For a moment, I imagined myself dribbling down the court in a breakaway to score in my first varsity game ever.

However, Coach Collins was not on board with the team's idea. I watched his facial expression as my friends tried to persuade him, and I could see he was giving it a lot of thought. But in the end, I never made it into the game. Or any other varsity game for that matter. Feeling disappointed, it was a long bus ride home.

Nevertheless, from my position as team manager, I was able to take part in some major victories. UFA won three conference basketball championships that year — Central-Oneida League, City, and Central New York Conference. Of course, I wished I had been an active player in those games, but it was still fun to be part of the team — especially when we won. Those were important victories for us because we all really loved the game.

It was that same love and dedication to sportsmanship that motivated us to celebrate our losses, too. Once, in 1955, after losing in the playoffs at the War Memorial in Syracuse, some members and fans of the UFA team "celebrated" by renting a hotel room. By celebrating, I mean we stayed overnight and probably jumped on the beds. Bill Metzger, Mike Foley and I were among the celebrants who stayed, and we hitchhiked home to Utica the next day.

In fact, hitchhiking to basketball games and school was a regular part of my teenage years. Most days, my friends and I hitched a ride to UFA. We'd often get into a neighbor's car at the corner of Arlington Road and Oneida Street. Three of us could easily fit into the backseat of the large cars of that era. Usually, our rides consisted of cars in which the husband was driving himself to work, with his wife in the passenger seat, ready to drive the car back home afterward. In the evenings, my friends and I often took a bus home because it was already too dark for drivers to easily see us trying to hitch a ride .

Some of our morning rides became regulars. One neighborhood husband who picked us up was the regional manager of New York Telephone Company. He lived about five blocks from my house, and my friends and I socialized with his daughter, who went to another high school. Our driver would say the same thing each morning as we got out of his big black Cadillac, "Take care; have a nice day." Since this was before those words became ubiquitous, we boys could hardly contain ourselves each time he said it. We would wait for his parting words and — in the way kids sometimes find ordinary things funny — we could hardly keep from laughing every time he said them.

Another of our regular drivers was the morning man on the WTLB radio station headquartered nearby. Since he was driving in the car with us and not speaking into the radio microphone at that time, we asked him, "How do you do it?" He cleverly told us he had everything on tape, which worked out fine. Until it didn't. One day the tape broke, and the morning man got fired. I guess it was a lesson to us about how things worked in the real world, how one mistake, one oversight or one bad decision could be decisive enough to change your world. On the basketball court, we saw it too. One shot could mean winning or losing the game. But, in basketball, even when we lost, we kept our eyes on the next prize and learned from our mistakes. We were committed, after all.

In my third year of high school, with college on the horizon, I hoped to take basketball even more seriously. On a Saturday, my Dad drove me to Colgate University to show off my skills to the Colgate Raiders' head basketball coach, Howie Hartman. I was not alone on the court that day. At Hartman's request, Dad and I shared the drive to Colgate with fellow UFA student and basketball player Gary Evans. This was the same Gary Evans who scored 36 points, when I only scored 35, in a First Presbyterian game played back in Utica. I was only a junior, but Evans was already a senior, and at 6-foot-9, he stood out on any court. Hartman wanted Evans for the team and tempted him with a partial scholarship. However, since Syracuse offered him a full scholarship, Evans matriculated there and became the second-string center.

Nevertheless, my ambition to make the varsity continued. Even sharing the court with Evans, I played my best that day. I desperately wanted to believe that Coach Hartman was really interested in me. Even without lettering at UFA, I thought I'd finally have a chance at playing varsity if I went to Colgate. Of course, I did not want to admit to myself that Hartman was most likely more interested in looking at Evans that day than he was in looking at the barely 6-foot-1 me.

The following year, when I was a senior at UFA, I was accepted to Colgate — and basketball had nothing to do with it. Nevertheless, when I arrived on campus in 1955, I still hoped to play on the varsity basketball team. That's why Coach Dewey's words stunned me at tryout. I can still hear his question echoing today, as if he were standing in front of me on that basketball court: "Do you want to play basketball here or graduate?"

I was disappointed, but I took Coach Dewey's words to heart and followed his advice. I temporarily put my basketball in the closet and made my way to the Everett Case library instead. I attended all my classes and even sought help from the college's superb tutorial system when needed. I immersed myself in academic and college life, majored in economics, became a member of the Delta Upsilon fraternity and served as sports editor of the *Colgate Maroon* and the *Salmagundi* yearbook. I also covered Colgate sports for the *Utica Daily Press* and *Utica Observer-Dispatch*. I continued to do all this until I graduated in 1959.

And what about that basketball in my closet? Somehow, I couldn't quite let go of its temptation.

With freshman year behind me, I completed a stint of summer school at Utica College to improve my progress with academic requirements, study habits and grade point average. Feeling confident about being on the right academic track, I pulled the basketball out of the closet when school started up again in the fall.

In my sophomore year, I joined some fellow Colgate students on the semi-pro Victory Body Works team that played in the Utica Municipal League. Victory Body Works, our team's sponsor, was an automotive body shop. We played exhibition games against a variety of Utica organizations, such as the Knights of Columbus and the YMCA, but many of our games were against teams in nearby Rome, Little Falls, Poland, and other Utica suburbs. Yes, there are suburbs of Utica.

Players for Victory Body Works during my three years on the team included friends named Jack Nichols, Phil Bisselle, John Maurer, Harry Mariani, Dick Capitani, Jim Riday, Bob Purple, Bill Fitzgerald, Jim Elston, Bill Eldridge, Jay Metz, Ron Colwell, Dave Herpy, and Fred Woodruff. There was at least one non-Colgate player —Joe Altongy, a star player from Utica's St. Francis de Sales High School . Our coach was Fred Woodruff's father, Clarke Woodruff. Coach Woodruff graduated from Colgate with my father in 1926 and was employed by the Utica Insurance Company. He often referred his accident clients to Victory Body Works for repair work, and I suppose that was the connection between our team and our sponsor. Coach Woodruff paid for our team's entry fee for the Municipal League, bought our uniforms and paid for our dinners after each game.

Over the years, some of the Victory Body Works team members came to be treated like family members at the generations-owned Victory Body Works establishment. One summer, following a minor car accident, I rehabilitated and painted my 1949 green-colored Ford at Victory's location on the Seneca Turnpike in New Hartford, New York. The guys in the shop taught me how to fix my car's dents, sand down the car's surface and repaint it. The owner of the body shop had me do all the work and did not charge me a dime for the supplies. During the midday breaks, I was often invited to sit down and have hamburgers with the family.

The Victory Body Works basketball team was a rather organic organization. We rarely practiced. We were all busy students, and some of us had part-time jobs. Many of us had girlfriends who also wanted our time, so it was difficult to coordinate a training schedule. All of us were basically playing for the love of the game. Sometimes, we'd discuss certain plays during the time-outs, but there wasn't much more organization than that. At one time or another, each of us was the high scorer for our team.

In one game, I was designated to be the defensive guy, so I didn't score at all. My goal was to stop one of the opposing team's main scorers, Dick Miller. Since I already knew Miller from his days as a superstar at UFA, I was familiar with his moves. My strategy was to just guard him closely and basically stay with him at all times. At one point I was so focused that I accidentally ran Miller into the gym wall, and he missed both foul shots. He ended up with only three points, and our team won the game.

As a team, Victory Body Works was pretty successful. We were young and in fairly good shape, so we were able to get up and down the court faster than most teams we played against. We also didn't drink or smoke as much as the other guys in the league, and that was a definite advantage. In the three years I played for Victory Body Works, I was high scorer in a number of games, including one 29-point game. In the 1957–58 season, I even led the division in scoring.

But I still hadn't made the varsity.

Victory Body Works finally showed its mettle and captured the first annual Utica YMCA basketball tournament title when I was a Colgate senior in the winter of 1959. We defeated Utica State in the finals, with a suspenseful 71–62 win. The win was spectacular, especially since the Utica State team was comprised of former Utica high school standouts and star college players from such schools as Ohio State, Utica College and Syracuse. Among the stars of the Utica State team were: Gary Evans, my 6-foot-9 friend who then had finished playing for Syracuse; Mike Damsky, a former Ohio State cager, who years later would join me on the Utica College Board of Trustees; Nonnie Pensero, a former UFA and Utica College player; and Chuck Stevesky, a former Syracuse and Sampson Air Base star.

Likewise, my Victory Body Works team also consisted of incredible talent, with many great players from Colgate. Jack Nichols, who was then the all-time leading scorer for Colgate, was one of the team's stars. He had broken former New York Knickerbockers' Ernie Vandeweghe's Colgate scoring record in 1957. In the YMCA championship game,

Nichols was high scorer with 25 points, followed by Phil Bisselle with 21. Bisselle, a former captain of the Colgate cagers, won the Milt Nelson most valuable player award, and the Victory Body Works' team won the sportsman trophy. Other Victory squad members in the tournament included Charlie Hagenah, captain of the 1958–59 Colgate basketball team, John Maurer, a two-year veteran on the Colgate varsity, Harry Mariani, Jim Riday, Dick Capitani, Joe Altongy, Fred Woodruff and me.

Shortly after Victory Body Works' championship title victory, I graduated from Colgate and took a job as a sportswriter for *The Evening Press* in Binghamton. I was covering the amateur golf wars, the Binghamton Triplets farm team of the New York Yankees in the Eastern League, high school football and the boxing great Carmen Basilio when he played in a charity softball game. All the while I kept waiting for a potential opening to get back in the game of basketball. I was looking for a spot on any team in the Binghamton Municipal Basketball League.

Then one evening in the fall of 1959, an opportunity materialized. While at a local restaurant, I encountered Sandy Stone, the top woman amateur golfer in the area and a physical education teacher at Chenango Forks High School. I had previously met her while covering women's golf for *The Evening Press*, and she was well connected to many amateur sports personalities in the area. She introduced me to Tom Rugala, a member of the DiLascia Bakery basketball team in the Municipal League, and I signed on. I saw a lot of minutes with that team and started a few games, but I was never the high scorer.

Nevertheless, by playing in the Municipal League, I had natural opportunities to become more familiar with the league's players and to write about them in my job as a sportswriter. Halfway through the season with DiLascia, it was predicted that my number on the draft board was nearing the top, so I chose to enter the U.S. Army as a reservist for six months of active duty as part of a six-year commitment. I was then replaced in the DiLascia team line-up by Ron Luciano, a former All-American tackle on the Syracuse University football team who later became an umpire with Major League Baseball. I never played another game for DiLasica's, but my basketball career was not quite over.

After graduate school, I joined the public relations department of The Chase Manhattan Bank in New York City as an editor and press relations associate. Chase had a basketball team that played in the New York City Bankers League. I inquired and was soon added to the squad. I took part in about 14 games before I decided my job in public relations was more important than playing in the New York City Bankers League.

I guess you could say my basketball career was over, but my passion for the sport never died. In my dreams, I am still trying to make the varsity.

DOESCHER LESSON: *Find and pursue something you really enjoy. You don't have to be excellent at it, but you should love it. Be rigorous in your pursuit and involvement. Be open to developing your skills. Your hobby may become a rewarding, lifelong passion.*

8.
FINALLY DRIVING MOM'S 1962 BUICK

Bill and Mom's 1962 Buick, 1998

"The great American road belongs to Buick."

— Buick slogan

It was a dream of mine to one day drive my mother's 1962 Buick. In good weather, usually from May to October when the sun was shining, and the temperature was at least 60 degrees, Mom would proudly cruise the road in her gorgeous car — a white, two-door 1962 Buick Special convertible, with sparkling red interior and a black top. In particular, she loved driving it from her home in New Hartford to the beauty parlor in East Utica, New York. In total, it was a ride of approximately 16 to 18 minutes when she traveled at her comfortable speed of 30 mph.

Other than these trips, which were important to my mother, the Buick stayed inside our family's garage at 13 Lower Woods Road. Especially during rain or snow, she insisted that the car remained sheltered. That meant someone else had to drive Mom to appointments and the beauty parlor in another car. Usually it was my father or our next-door neighbor, Jeanie Prime, a retired school teacher from nearby Chadwicks High School.

Feeling the excitement of pleasing the woman he loved, Dad was thrilled to purchase Mom's "cute little car" in the late 1960s. The transaction was carried out by McRorie Sauter, Dad's all-time favorite Buick dealer in Utica. The car was so handsome, it could have been an anniversary gift or a Valentine's Day surprise, but it wasn't.

Mom was the third owner of the car. However, since the car looked as "clean as a whistle," as Mom always said, it felt like she was its first owner. I imagine that car must have inspired devotion from all its owners because it had been cared for exceptionally.

Dad had his own motivation in buying that car for her, which he said he fell in love with on one of his regular visits to the dealership. It was unusual for him to purchase a used car, since he had bought all of his other cars new. As a home furnishings salesman who called on customers up-and-down the New York State Thruway from Montreal to Yonkers and everywhere in between, my father put a lot of miles on his cars' odometers and had to change his vehicles often. His preference for buying new cars lasted for approximately 50 years and helped my father maintain a permanent seat at the "shoot-the-bull" table at the dealership.

When he decided to purchase the Buick for my mother, no other car would do. As part of the deal, my dad traded in my maternal grandfather H.O. Kipp's four-door, black Buick Roadmaster which he had helped my grandfather originally buy in the 1950s.

My grandfather, whom we called Papa, willed that Buick to his daughter, my mother, when he died. He documented his wishes with a handwritten note in green ink on a yellow pad that he left in the top drawer of a maple desk positioned in the dining room of his South Utica rental apartment. The one provision was that either Bob or Bill, Papa's only grandchildren and his daughter's only sons, would occasionally take their Nana for a ride "around the horn." That meant we were supposed to drive our grandmother on a pleasurable scenic route from South Utica, through Waterville, into West Winfield and back. Sadly, Nana passed away before we could satisfy his wishes.

While I was allowed to drive Papa's old Buick and even accompany him on rounds to area meat distributors as the City of Utica's official meat inspector, it was a different story when it came to my mother and that precious 1962 white Buick convertible. Driving her car was not even a consideration. That automobile was my mother's baby. It was her pride and joy, and she was not about to let me or anyone else, except maybe my father, drive that car for any reason, any time. She made her wishes clear, and that was that. Period.

Although I thought about it, I never tested her resolve with a fake emergency just so I would have an urgent need to drive her car. She feared I would put a scratch on it, ruin the interior or perhaps even burn out the motor by forgetting to check the oil. As a consequence, my brother Robert and I could only admire Mom's car vicariously as it sat in the garage. We didn't even go for a ride in it.

My mother kept the car until she died on August 18, 1977. I was living in Hickory, North Carolina, at the time. After Mom's passing, I thought I might finally have a chance to drive her car, but my father sold the Buick "out from under me" to the guy who had been mowing their lawn regularly from the time he was 16 years old. He told my father he had been "lusting for the car for many years." I don't think Dad even knew that I was also interested in it.

Some years later, the lawn-mowing guy decided to sell Mom's car back to us. He needed money to pay for his daughter's college tuition and was sentimental about keeping the Buick in the Doescher family. He asked around the old neighborhood in Utica, and one of my old friends gave him my telephone number. I was then living more than five hours away in Scarsdale, New York.

I didn't hesitate when the lawn-mowing guy called on a Saturday morning one day in the fall. Before I even knew the asking price of $9,000, and without pausing to negotiate a good deal, I said, "Yes." All that mattered was that I would be able to buy the 1962 Buick and finally have the chance to get behind the wheel of Mom's car.

Shortly thereafter, Mom's car arrived on an auto carrier from Utica to my home in Scarsdale. I became the Buick's fifth owner. I had the car checked by a mechanic, installed a new muffler, performed other necessary repairs and started enjoying that Buick immediately. It was a beauty on the road, and I was proud to be driving Mom's special convertible. My first passengers were our kids, Doug and Michelle. Of course, we put the top down and zoomed up the Bronx River Parkway and back.

That car was more than just a toy for me, as many collectible cars are for their owners. It created continuity with the past and connected me with my mother. For a period of several years, I drove it in the local Memorial Day parade. It was one of the featured classic cars used to carry military veterans along the village parade route. With the car's top down, those chauffeured heroes could wave to admiring onlookers while I drove in the front seat.

I also loved showing off that car at fall car shows, such as at Scarsdale's annual Concours d'Elegance event. The 1962 Buick never won an official prize, but it attracted plenty of admirers; and it was *my* prize. Even though Mom never let me drive it originally, I know for certain that she would have been pleased to know I finally did.

After several years of maintaining the car, the thrill of ownership wore off, and the expenses kept mounting. I was even paying a considerable storage fee for a permanent spot at a Mobil gas station garage in the village. Shortly thereafter, I made the practical decision to sell the car, letting it go for even less than I paid for it.

The buyer was a nice man, Anthony DeLorenzo, who, for years, has been employed by the local police department to monitor parking meters in the village of Scarsdale. With only 54,000 miles on that 1962 Buick when he got it, DeLorenzo became serious about restoring the car and showing it off. In particular, he has frequented all the classic auto shows in areas such as Thornwood, Bear Mountain and around Iona High School.

"People have always been thrilled to see what great condition the car is in," DeLorenzo has told me. "So far, in addition to the many compliments, we've won five trophies at the shows." Mom's car has thus left our family and, instead, become an integral part of the DeLorenzo family. With passion for the car spanning the generations, Anthony's grandson Justin likes to claim the car as "his" even though it is really is registered under his father Richard's name.

So, there you go, Mom, your Buick has kept a lot of people happy over the years. It has even given some of them a sense of history and purpose, and I'm sure this is something that would have pleased you.

Just one more thing ... Thanks, Mom, for the chance to finally drive your car. Although I wasn't able to get your permission to drive it when I was young, I was compelled to sit at the wheel of your iconic Buick and care for it with all the tender love I could muster. Those experiences gave me insight into the confidence you must have felt when the car was yours. I can imagine you sitting behind the wheel with the top down, your hair tied back in a scarf, feeling the freedom of the wind rush by and all the possibilities of the open road ahead.

DOESCHER LESSON: *Never give up hope if you really want something to come your way or happen in your life. If you have enough patience and are able to wait long enough, that dream may just come true — and, if so, it will probably happen at a better time.*

9. SPEAKING FROM THE PULPIT

"If we had more hell in the pulpit, we would have less hell in the pew."

— Billy Graham, American Christian Evangelist

I have always embraced the possibilities life has given me and been open to recognizing them as they have appeared. Some have presented themselves unexpectedly. Others have emerged as hard-earned results. And, perhaps most special, some have felt like manifestations of things I have always wanted to do, like delivering a sermon — three sermons as of this writing.

The mere idea of giving a sermon as can be downright intimidating to a lay person. After all, you need to have not only faith and passion, but also good writing skills, excellent public speaking abilities and the willingness to properly prepare. Even though I could check off all these boxes and have delivered speeches and lectures all over the world, the idea of delivering sermons at my church, Hitchcock Presbyterian, in Scarsdale, New York, did not just happen overnight.

First, I had to convince myself that I was qualified to speak to the congregation. Before delivering my first sermon in 2015, I wasn't so sure. It took the encouragement of a friend and fellow choir member, Merrell Clark, to build my confidence. Convinced I had the wisdom, personality and character to guide others, Merrell suggested I should not stop at delivering a sermon but should even consider pursuing the requirements and education needed to become a minister. He mentioned this on several occasions as we stood together in the choir loft and even referred me to online divinity schools. Merrell's own father had been a minister, and Merrell had previously studied religion and earned a master's degree at the Yale Divinity School. Although he eventually pursued a business career, Merrell has delivered five sermons at Hitchcock and at other churches in Westchester County, New York, and in Philadelphia, Pennsylvania.

Like Merrell, I have always been active in the church. However, I never considered giving a sermon until Merrell prodded me to consider it. I have often served as a reader, and I was part of a team that collaborated on a Father's Day sermon years ago. While I was confident that I could speak well in front of the congregation, I also knew I had no experience in writing and delivering a sermon on my own.

So, I started at the beginning. The first step was to research a theme and identify scripture lessons to go along with it. I then presented my ideas to Rev. Jack Lohr, an interim pastor at Hitchcock, who gave me the green light to proceed. I then got to work writing a script of what I would say, making sure to identify the sections I wanted to emphasis. When the draft was almost done, I showed it to

Rev. Lohr. He provided valuable guidance, including a reminder not to speak for too long. "We have to serve communion," he cautioned, "and our goal is always to finish the service in 60 minutes.

With Lohr's suggestions in mind, I went home and wrote the remainder of the sermon. The ideas flowed, and it was easy to finish — partly because I had been thinking about the concept for the last 40 years. I was inspired by the simple phrase of three magical words — "God loves you" — that Rev. Gordon Sperry said to conclude his benediction every Sunday at the Corinth United Church of Christ, where I attended, in Hickory, North Carolina, in the 1970s.

At that time, I was president of Corinth's Brotherhood Group; I sang in the choir, and my children attended the Sunday School. But it was those words "God loves you" that kept bringing me back to church every week. It was powerful to believe that God loved me, and I thought this message would be powerful for a sermon, too.

As magnanimous as they were, those three words were just a starting point. From the concept of "God loves you," I had to develop a structure for the sermon that would tell a story and give clarity to the message.

In order to create such a structure, I researched best strategies for writing a sermon and adopted the following guidelines: First, the writer must establish the sermon's objective and identify the audience; Next, the sermon's introduction and conclusion should be developed, while taking care to keep the message impactful, because people remember the first and last things they hear. Between the important introduction and conclusion, the rest of the sermon's content should be structured to maintain fluidity and engagement. I have been told by ordained ministers that the ideal sermon should be approximately 12 to 15 minutes long. This time frame supports average attention spans and works within the duration of the service.

In terms of content, it is important to draw out connections that make the sermon's topic relevant to a contemporary audience. Personally, I like to consider how the revelation of God in a particular historical context applies to the church's life today. Then, I select scripture lessons from the Bible that relate to the theme. By following this structure, even a novice sermon writer can quickly be on the way to crafting a meaningful sermon.

How long will it take to write a sermon? Obviously, less than 40 years, but I would recommend dedicating several hours to its preparation — and even more to practicing out loud. Some professional ministers have been known to reshape or entirely change their sermons in the early morning hours of a Sunday. But that approach would be stressful, and possibly disastrous, for a lay person.

I had no real expectations for my first sermon, except that I wanted to deliver it to the congregation — which I did. My family came to church to hear me speak. This included family members who do not normally attend church and others who are Jewish. After the service, 25 people approached me to compliment the sermon. The pastor was hoping my initiative would encourage other lay people to deliver occasional sermons, but this never materialized. I think it was not because of lack of interest, but rather fear of public speaking.

To this end, I can only advise people who lack the confidence to speak before any kind of audience to find a community college or local service group that offers public speaking coaching. Trust me, with a little bit of training and practice, self-assurance will come, and you will be pleased with the results. Of course, if it's a sermon you're developing, speak to your minister or clergy for advice.

The success of my first sermon was followed by a second. Delivered on July 13, 2017, it addressed the theme of "The Other Fellow First." Lohr had since left Hitchcock, so this second sermon occurred under the blessing of Rev. Pete Jones, who became the senior minister at Hitchcock. He introduced my sermon by saying, "Bill Doescher has long had a passion about the subject of his sermon today."

Those words were indeed true because the topic of that second sermon was inspired by a motto I learned as a 10-year-old camper at Camp Dudley on Lake Champlain, in Westport, New York. Dudley campers, then and now, learn that important life lesson — "the other fellow first" — through direct experiences of fellowship. This lesson has remained with me and served me well throughout my life. As such, I thought it would be beneficial to share it with others who may not have had a similar Camp Dudley experience in their youth.

My third sermon, delivered in August of 2018, was entitled "Why Diversity Matters." As someone who has been involved with diversity and inclusion programs for many years and who had been a board member of the Jackie Robinson Foundation for 22 years, this sermon proved easier to write than the first two. The main point was that everyone should be involved with diversity and inclusion because it's the right thing to do, and equally important, it's the Christian thing to do.

Preparing and delivering each of the three sermons was a long process, but in the end it all felt very natural. Speaking at the pulpit was a little like talking to a student group, a chamber of commerce or members of a Rotary Club, but with an obvious religious overtone.

Looking out at the congregation from behind the pulpit, I was pleased to see faces engaged and awake. Conversations following my sermons confirmed that people were indeed interested and that my topics had direct meaning to their individual lives.

"I came to church today just to hear your sermon, and you didn't disappoint," one parishioner told me after my third sermon. Other appreciative feedback came from young people who were not obligated to praise my sermons. Their attention told me they had been listening and that my words had impacted their developing minds and attitudes.

It's powerful and amazing to realize an individual and his or her words can impact another human being's life.

These sermons satisfied my lifelong interest in positively influencing people through counsel and inspiration.

Looking back, I now see that the paths leading me to the pulpit began decades before I started writing those three sermons. They began in eighth grade when I first thought about becoming an Episcopal priest. I had serious conversations with an ordained brother at Grace Episcopal Church in Utica, New York, who was involved in running a church basketball league in which I played. This brother wisely recommended that I think about such a serious decision somewhat later in life, perhaps while in college.

In high school, I was elected president of the Junior Deacons at Westminster. This position led me to a similar conversation with Rev. P. Arthur Brindisi, who had originally been a Catholic. The same conclusion was reached: Wait until you're older.

At Colgate University, said to have been founded by 13 men with 13 dollars and 13 prayers in 1819, religion surfaced again. This time, it was a part of a philosophy and religion core curriculum course that I was required to take during my freshman year. I remember one of the course highlights was learning about Martin Luther, a seminal figure in the Protestant Reformation.

The idea of becoming a minister remained on the back burner while I was in college. Instead, I finished my studies, became a sportswriter, attended graduate school, started a family and began building my professional career.

Religion did not resurface until I started attending the Corinth United Church of Christ in Hickory, North Carolina. That's where I listened to Rev. Sperry's powerful Sunday benedictions. When I moved to Scarsdale, New York with my second wife and a growing family that included four children between us, I briefly joined Hitchcock and sang in the choir. However, I was soon drawn to the Scarsdale Congregational Church where our kids were actively involved in the Senior Youth Fellowship Program.

When our kids graduated and moved away from home, I returned to Hitchcock to sing in the choir. I immediately felt welcomed by the community there and became involved in the Session. There, I connected with Merrell, and the sermons just seemed to develop naturally.

The message behind the first "God Loves You" sermon had been personally important to me, and I earnestly wanted to share it. That was my original objective. However, giving the sermon accomplished even more than that. It was rewarding that my message touched people in the pews and left them with a meaningful message. It was truly a bonus because I hadn't expected such broad acceptance.

Although I was a seasoned public speaker, I was nervous to speak from the pulpit for the first time since I had never before spoken alone in God's house. But, once I started talking, the attention and acceptance of the congregation made it easy. They came away with one important thought — "God loves you." This had been a guiding concept for me for more than 40 years, and I am thrilled to have passed it along to amplify its place in the world.

DOESCHER LESSON: *We are at all times both students and teachers. Be open to new information and new voices. Share your knowledge and wisdom. Words are as powerful as actions and can create positive change. Remember this when you speak, because you might be making a great impact on another person's life.*

10.

SERMON: GOD LOVES YOU

This Sermon, by Bill Doescher, was delivered at Hitchcock Presbyterian Church, in Scarsdale, New York, on November 2, 2014.

God loves you. God loves you in the balcony. God loves you in the choir loft.

God loves Pastor Elizabeth Smith-Bartlett, Pastor Jack Lohr, and me, too.

This talk today had its genesis more than 40 years ago in Hickory, North Carolina. That's where I first heard "God loves you" at the end of a benediction by the late Reverend Gordon Sperry, pastor at the Corinth United Church of Christ.

I have long understood the meaning of church and been an involved member of various congregations.

I thought I wanted to be an Episcopal minister when I was a youngster but was encouraged to think about it somewhat later.

I was president of the Junior Deacons, sang in the choir, and led the processional by carrying the Christian flag while in high school at the Westminster Presbyterian Church in Utica, New York.

I taught 8th grade Sunday school at the Congregational Church in Briarcliff Manor.

In Hickory, I was president of my church's Brotherhood Group. I sang in the choir, and my children were enrolled in the Sunday school.

My relatives were regular churchgoers and leaders in their respective churches.

But, honestly, back then — more than 40 years ago — I really didn't know why I was going to church on Sundays.

Perhaps it was to hear the pastor's last words every Sunday and try to believe that God loves me.

I kept going.

Some of you may have had similar thoughts. You might have thought:

Do I go to church on Sundays to reach out to God, and church seems like the safest place to do that?

Do I go because that's what's expected of me?

Do I go to hear the music, listen to the sermon and prayers or to greet my fellow parishioners?

Do I go because God loves all of us unconditionally?

Do I go to hear John 3: Verse 16 speaking to me, "For God so loved the world, that he gave his only son, that whoever believes in him should not perish but have eternal life?"

Back in the early 1970s, this is what I heard at the end of church in Hickory, North Carolina: "Go forth into the world of peace, be of good courage; hold fast to that which is good; render to no one evil for evil; strengthen the fainthearted; support the weak; help the afflicted; honor everyone; love and serve the Lord, rejoicing in the power of the Holy Spirit. God Loves you. Amen. "

Powerful words indeed!

According to Pastor Jack, in *The Presbyterian Book of Common Worship*, there is a very similar benediction.

But no "God Loves You." And that is what I needed to hear. That's what we all need to hear.

To prepare for this talk, I reached out to a number of people, including ministers, a rabbi and an expert on the late C.S. Lewis, author of more than 30 books and *Mere Christianity.*

According to many, Lewis, a former atheist, was one of the intellectual giants of the 20th century and arguably the most influential Christian writer of his day.

In *Mere Christianity,* Lewis noted, "Don't think God will love us because we are good; God will make us good because he loves us; and the majority of humanity believes in some kind of God or gods."

My late Jewish mother-in-law believed that there was indeed a God for everybody. With Christian in-laws, that was her way, I believe, of providing family unification for an ecumenical family.

That was an important comment for her, and she said it often. Today, we still repeat that and her other worthy thoughts.

If Magda Bierman had been a scholar of Judaism, she might have gone on further to explain more about it to her

Christian relatives. Unfortunately, she was not such a scholar, so we are left to our own devices.

Scholars note that Jewish tradition says that humans are created in the image of God.

Judaism does not have a formal mandatory set of beliefs. Judaism is more concerned about actions than beliefs. My wife, Linda, taught me that. In the Jewish faith, each individual's relationship with God is unique and deeply personal, and in that regard not too different from what Christians believe.

God and his love are everywhere.

Some of you may have taught your children this bedtime prayer:

> Now I lay me down to sleep,
> I pray the Lord my soul to keep:
> If I shall die before I wake,
> I pray the Lord my soul to take.

Beautiful! There are other versions, but the prayer, no matter how it is said, is clear evidence that you don't have to be in church to talk to God.

And, you also don't have to wait for the annual Thanksgiving Day prayer to talk to God.

I don't, and neither did the now retired New York Yankees shortstop Derek Jeter, who often prayed on the field at Yankee Stadium.

A few years ago a very good friend of mine introduced me to the Men's Golf Fellowship in Naples, Florida, and I attended numerous breakfast meetings.

The organization is dedicated to helping men, mostly retired, take a fresh look at their goals, relationships and faith.

Over the years, Steve Silver, the organizer and author of *New Man's Journey,* has recruited impactful speakers who openly talk about their faith. Each speaker talks about his or her faith in a most personal way and about accepting God at certain defining moments in life.

I was moved by one speaker — Tom Monaghan, former owner of Domino's Pizza and the Detroit Tigers' American League baseball team and founder of Ave Maria University near Naples, Florida.

Seeing himself in C.S. Lewis's description of "pride" while reading *Mere Christianity* in 1990, Monaghan became convinced that he needed to root out that "greatest of sins" (his words) by turning away from ostentation and serving God.

When he sold most of his possessions, including Domino's, he decided that pro-life causes and Catholic education were where he wanted to invest the rest of his life.

Nearly 25 years later, he's given most of his fortune away and is now living a different kind of dream — working for the university he built, where he lives in a 10-foot by 12-foot student dorm room during the week.

He's a man who has seen and had it all and concluded his own life was worthless outside of what he could do for Christ. "I'm working harder than I ever did at Domino's," he told the men's group gathering.

To me, Monaghan indeed understands that God loves him.

At another breakfast, Bernhard Langer, a Champions Tour professional golfer, a Masters champion on the regular PGA Tour and a very nice man, told me and others, that after studying the Bible he turned his life over to God.

"Now," he said, "I have true peace here and an assurance of Heaven. When I turned my life over to Him, everything changed drastically. The void in my heart was filled."

If you believe the teachings in the Bible, like Langer, you know regardless of your past, God loves you.

I truly believe God loves me. I can feel it in my heart whether here in church or not.

Regardless of your experiences, God loves you.

Regardless of your fortunes or successes, God loves you.

Regardless of your disappointments, God loves you.

He has always loved you, and his love is unconditional.

God loves you and me because of who God is, not because of anything you or I did or didn't do. Consider this thought, and be inspired by something Saint Paul wrote, as per a translation in the *New Jerusalem Bible*: "God is love and whoever abides in love abides in God, and God abides in them."

Love seems to be the ideal and the dream, in some manner of expression, for every person.

We seem more fulfilled when we are in a state of spiritual love and, somehow, emptied when our focus moves elsewhere.

Is it possible that love becomes the purpose of our existence?

Although billions of words have been written and spoken about love in its many expressions, not one, or all, of them can fully capture the essence of love.

God loves you.

Amen.

11.
SERMON: THE OTHER FELLOW FIRST

This sermon, by Bill Doescher, was delivered at Hitchcock Presbyterian Church, in Scarsdale, New York, on August 20, 2017

The seeds for this sermon, which were placed in my youth, came from experiences, beginning at age 10 as a camper at Camp Dudley on Lake Champlain in Westport, New York.

Back then my parents did what many parents here at Hitchcock do, and took me to Sunday school and church at Westminster Presbyterian Church in Utica, New York. I still have my Bible that that church's Session gave me on June 9, 1946, as part of my promotion to the Junior Department.

However, I didn't learn about this "Other Fellow First" philosophy that I am extremely passionate about until I got to Camp Dudley a year or so later. I have never forgotten it.

For you and I today, it can be said that this motto is just another way of urging us into action, bringing God's call to life. More broadly, God calls us to grow in faith, serve the church and transform the world.

Today, the Dudley motto and mission are the same as they were when I was a camper, and it was a camp only for boys. Today, it comprises a camp for boys, located in the heart of New York's majestic Adirondack Mountains, and another camp for girls, on the peaceful shores of Lake Champlain in Vermont. The camp population, today, includes campers from all around the world representing different races, religions, socio-economic groups and ethnicities.

The camp mission statement says: "We strive to develop moral, personal, physical and leadership skills in the spirit of fellowship and fun, enabling boys and girls to lead lives characterized by devotion to others."

The emphasis here is devotion to others.

The Other Fellow First

The Bible, no matter which version you read, is brimming with God's call stories on this subject. For example:

In Philippians 2: Verse 4, "Do not merely look for your own personal interests, but also for the interests of others."

In Romans 12: Verse 10, "Be devoted to one another in brotherly love; give preference to one another in honor."

In Acts 2: Verse 45, "They sold property and possessions to give to anyone who had need."

And Matthew 22: Verses 36–40 interprets "The Other Fellow First" motto in an all-encompassing way. It says:

"Master, which is the great commandment in the law?

"Jesus said unto him, thou shalt love the Lord thy God with all thy heart, and with all thy soul, and with all thy mind.

"This is the first and great commandment.

"And the second is like unto it. Thou shalt love thy neighbor as thyself.

"On these two commandments hang all the law and prophets."

There are plenty of other examples to consider regarding "The Other Fellow First."

Indeed, there are four most caring examples, among many, right here at Hitchcock.

One: Midnight Run. Rudy Whyte and his dedicated band of volunteers provide the homeless on the streets of New York City with clothing, blankets and personal care items once a month, on the last Saturday of each month. They also manage the Hitchcock Breakfast Runs for the homeless.

Two: Living in America. This most impressive outreach program, in its 42nd year, provides weekly English conversation classes at the church for international adults. Volunteer teachers, those currently involved and those who have taught previously, are mighty proud — beat the chest proud — of their service with this organization. Diane Gismond, Linda Camp and Eleanor November are the current leaders of this organization.

Three: The Hitchcock Thrift Shop. The Hitchcock Thrift Shop is manned by 25 dedicated men and women volunteers, many from Hitchcock, who sort, price and prepare merchandise for sale. The $30,000 raised annually benefits local and international outreach organizations that provide assistance to women and children in need. Our very own Lee Maiden, Rene Thiel and Alma Whyte are the Thrift Shop Managers.

Four: Haiti Marycare. Hitchcock's Tracey Tsai is executive director of this program and brings her passion about it to our church 24/7. It's not an official organization of the church; it just seems like that because of Tracey's enthusiasm. She has taken six humanitarian trips to Haiti within the last two years. Tracey has also worked with Jack Binder, a local dentist who sometimes sings in the Chancel Choir, to help provide dental care to residents of Haiti. No doubt you will be hearing more from Tracey about her pet project in the days and weeks to come.

Caring services from Hitchcock is just part of our DNA.

The Other Fellow First

Then there's the Jackie Robinson Foundation (JRF), founded by Rachel Robinson, now 95, in 1973, the year after the death of her husband, sports and social justice icon, Jackie Robinson. In addition to four years of generous financial assistance, as a board member for 22 years I know firsthand that JRF also offers a comprehensive set of support services that has led to a consistent, nearly 100 percent graduation rate among its scholars, more than twice the national average for African-American college students.

Helping educate minority college students is an example of putting the other fellow first.

The Other Fellow First

Then there's the Sopranos actress Jamie-Lynn Sigler, best known for her role as Meadow Soprano on the mega-hit HBO series, who lives with a relapsing-remitting multiple sclerosis diagnosis and uses her star power to advocate for others living with the disease.

She's teamed up with Biogen as an ambassador and blogger for a special promotional campaign to encourage others living with MS to make small but impactful changes in their lives.

As the father of a daughter who has MS, I know how important such a campaign can and must be.

Encouraging others with MS is putting the other fellow first.

The Other Fellow First

And who can ever forget the incomparable and six-term U.S. Senator John McCain from Arizona, who is without question a hero for all time. He's recently been diagnosed with irreversible brain cancer and very much in the news. But long before his work in Congress, he was a war hero and a war prisoner in Hanoi who had been shot down as a Navy pilot and refused to be released early without his comrades. That's bravery!

Standing by his comrades is putting the other fellow first.

As you probably surmised by now, I am a staunch believer in the motto, "The Other Fellow First," and I make it a point to give back by, among other things, mentoring JRF scholars, college students, graduates, colleagues and, yes, even executives. Personally, it's extremely rewarding, and I get much more back in return from those experiences than I give. It's my pleasure to be on other side of the desk so to speak.

Giving back is putting the other fellow first.

The Other Fellow First

Then there's this well-known verse we remember from the Bible:

"For God so loved the world, that he gave his only begotten Son, that whosoever believeth in Him shall not perish, but have everlasting life."

For sure, that qualifies as the other fellow first. Is it loving thy neighbor as thyself?

Is it being an advocate for others?

Is it providing caring services for others?

Is it enabling educational services for minority college students?

Is it selling property to support anyone who had need?

Is it standing by your military comrades?

"My friends, it's all of the above and much more. Perhaps "The Other Fellow First" idea can be helpful to us now and in the future, and especially as we continue to search for answers regarding the Charlottesville tragedy. We must remember "The Other Fellow First" as we attempt to counter the kinds of bigotry and hate that the world witnessed in last week's scenes of horrific and unnecessary violence."

Bottom line: As was posted on the Hitchcock community website last Sunday, "The ideology of white supremacy is evil and against the will of God." Of course, this is 100 percent correct. White supremacy, bigotry and racism have absolutely no place in our society. No place whatsoever! It should not be tolerated.

Silence on matters of such hatred and bigotry is antithetical to the gospel. We desperately need moral leadership in this country and should demand that we get it. Fortunately, I don't stand alone in this demand.

Let's hope and pray that the dark days will soon be behind us and the future ahead will be bright.

The "Other Fellow First" lesson is pretty simple but, sometimes, not easy to follow.

Perhaps you have your own motto or one taken from a meaningful experience that can bring about similar thoughts.

Or a personal call from God that fits your soul.

No matter which direction it comes from, chances are you will be doing God's work ... important work for God, and equally important, for yourself.

The late Audrey Hepburn of Hollywood fame closes the curtain for me today with a most pointed summation: "As you grow older, you will discover that you have two hands — one for helping yourself, the other for helping others."

Indeed, a perfect saying to live by — and one that puts the other fellow first.

Stay Strong. God loves you. Amen.

12.

SERMON: WHY DIVERSITY MATTERS

This sermon, by Bill Doescher, was delivered at Hitchcock Presbyterian Church, in Scarsdale, New York, on August 12, 2018

In the book, *Moving Diversity Forward* by Verna Myers, a nationally recognized expert on diversity and inclusion in the field of law, it says, “Diversity is being invited to the party. Inclusion is being asked to dance.”

Think about it. Yes, it’s cute, innovative and attention-grabbing, but it’s also one way of describing my topic this morning, “Why Diversity Matters.”

So, if you don’t mind, I will be dancing with all of you, so to speak, for a few minutes this morning.

Make no mistake, diversity was God’s idea. Even a study of science will tell you about a variety of plant and animal life. People, God’s final creation, are diverse, too. He did not create us as clones or robots. According to Mark, chapter 10: verse 6, He created two different genders.

As someone who has been privileged to be involved with diversity and inclusion programs for many years and for 22 years a member of the board of directors of the Jackie

Robinson Foundation that provides college and graduate school scholarships as well as leadership development opportunities for highly motivated students of color with limited resources, I believe I am able to present an objective and educated point of view on the subject.

With that preface, you won't be surprised that I firmly believe everyone should be involved with diversity and inclusion as the "right thing to do" no matter your station in life, ethnicity or religious affiliation.

And equally important, it's the Christian thing to do.

Other than the scriptures that we read this morning by Margaret Black and me, there are plenty of other passages in the Bible to back up that statement.

Human diversification receives its first mention in Genesis, chapter 1: verse 27. It says, "So God created the human race in his own image ... male and female he made them."

In Galatians, chapter 3: verse 28, it says, "There is neither Jew nor Gentile, neither slave nor free, nor is there male and female, for you all are one in Jesus Christ."

In Acts, chapter 10: verses 34–35, it says, "Truly I understand that God shows no partiality, but in every nation anyone who fears Him and does what is right is acceptable to Him."

You and I know intuitively that diversity matters. From a business perspective, it has become abundantly clear that the more diverse companies and institutions are, the more they achieve better financial performances.

McKinsey & Company, a global management consulting firm, says companies in the top quartile for racial and ethnic diversity are 35 percent more likely to have financial returns above their respective national industry medians. Also, companies in the top quartile for gender diversity are 15 percent more likely to have financial returns above their industry medians.

Now, I am not suggesting achieving greater diversity and inclusion is easy. It isn't. But we can never ever give up and must continuously raise the bar for more meaningful results.

A mentee of mine, Dr. Rochelle Ford, a dean at Elon University in North Carolina, describes today's efforts for diversity and inclusion in the public relations field as the tortoise from the children's story, "The Tortoise and the Hare." She says, "We have not won the race, but we are still in it. I believe we are making solid strides and are ahead in some meaningful ways."

In my opinion, it is absolutely mandatory that diversity and inclusion programs be part of any organization — corporate, nonprofit, educational, government ... and supported with reasonable budgets for success and a set of realistic to-dos for all managers.

Just to have a D&I program, however, for window dressing and image building doesn't fool anyone or accomplish anything sustainable among a company's constituents.

I believe that diversity and inclusion activities are about "doing the right thing." And doing it again, again and again.

Diving deeper into the D&I subject, it should be noted that diversity is not just about issues between black and white people and the retention and advancement of blacks in predominantly white institutions. Nor is it just about gender. It's much, much more.

Some companies have excellent D&I programs. Hewlett Packard, Accenture and Merck have solid and continuous ones. The Jackie Robinson Foundation is a diversity and inclusion organization all by itself.

Others need to stop hiding behind their communications and diversity chiefs and build an organization that mirrors the population of America.

Merck's philosophy about diversity is one to copy if you're in the market for recommending a D&I program for someone to check out. Chairman and CEO Kenneth C. Frazier says: "At Merck we believe there is strength in differences. Our ability to continue delivering on our mission of saving and improving lives around the world relies on having globally and locally diverse teams of talented employees at all levels. Every day we strive to create an inclusive workplace, where diversity perspectives are respected and all opinions matter."

As any human resource professional or CEO should know, diversity within the workplace encompasses providing a supportive environment for everybody — people of color, women, those in lesbian, gay, bisexual, transgender (LGBT) and disability communities.

From a number of recent conversations with diversity and crisis communications experts I have had, I know there are plenty of corrective actions companies can take to turn around their diversity and inclusion programs or even start one. Here are three from my friend Mike Paul, president of The Reputation Doctor® LLC of New York City:

- Build diversity into every aspect of your organization's talent management.
- Make diversity a pivotal plan of the internal and external global brand with proper marketing and communications.
- Incorporate diversity goals and objectives in performance and compensation processes.

Fortunately, for those of us here at Hitchcock Presbyterian, we are indeed a diverse and inclusive group that visibly shows outward support for one another. That attitude is in all of our DNA. We get it, and that is simply wonderful. We have a safe religious environment for all of us.

You and I know that God doesn't see races or skin color or nationalities like some people in the United States and around the globe unfortunately sometimes do. Pure and simple, they are bigots and racists.

The white supremacy march in Charlottesville a year ago was the antithesis of any positive D&I thinking and should never, ever be tolerated. It was a black mark on America.

Today is the first anniversary of that tragedy when a counter-protester was murdered. Another white nationalist rally is scheduled for 5 p.m. this evening in Washington, D.C., and counter-protesters plan to show up again. Please pray for everyone's safety and hope there won't be any contentious tweets from the White House about it tomorrow morning.

Diversity is part of being human. God delights in the plethora of differences His human creatures possess. The book of Revelation, chapter 7: verse 9, describes the final gathering of God's people from "every nation, tribe and tongue."

Our very own Rudy White, a ruling elder, Mr. Midnight Run, and an attorney with the Cochran's Firm's New York City office, told me for my book, "In the last 15 to 20 years, things have gotten worse instead of better regarding diversity and discrimination. What we are seeing now is window dressing when it comes to diversity programs being developed and implemented by companies and service organizations.

"Early on in their careers, young black lawyers are visible in the courtrooms and at meetings with clients. But they never seem to make it to the top at the prestigious law firms and disappear in about five years. They don't survive in the big, white shoe law firms.

"Diversity and inclusion programs in the public and private sectors are what will save America," Rudy says. "Let's go for it."

Another insightful comment comes from my friend Michelle Gadsden-Williams. She is a fellow board member of the Jackie Robinson Foundation and the managing director of North-American diversity and inclusion at Accenture. Speaking about African-American women in particular, Michelle says in her new book, CLIMB, "Sitting at the intersection of biases around race and gender, African-American women must labor to overcome both. While white women speak of shattering the glass ceiling, women of color describe their barriers of advancement differently. Many women of color who have made it to the executive suite describe the process as breaking through a concrete ceiling."

As Oprah Winfrey says, "Real integrity is doing the right thing, knowing that nobody's going to know whether you did it or not."

Even if she doesn't run for president someday, I know her, like her, and like what she says.

Stay strong in your beliefs.

Believe in diversity and inclusion. It's the Christian thing to do.

We need as many of those programs as possible to ensure equal footing for one and all.

Go in peace.

God loves you.

Amen.

13.
GROWING UP AT COLGATE

"In a single year, my priorities and responsibilities as a college student have forced me to grow faster than I did in four years of high school."

— Sabrina Sequeira, Princeton University Freshman in the April 26, 2018 issue of the *Daily Princetonian*

I graduated from Utica Free Academy (UFA) in June of 1955 with a better than satisfactory grade point average, and I was prepared to take on the world. I had been accepted to Colgate University, and I was ready for the challenge.

Or was I?

At least, I thought I was prepared. I had followed all of the suggestions of Roger N. Murphy, my high school counselor, and I had taken all the required college preparatory courses during my four years of high school. This meant I could safely advance to the next chapter of my life. Before leaving for college, I even re-read Murphy's advice from the 1955 *Academician* yearbook: "This is your life. Your opportunity. Don't be content to let it come to you. Reach, extend yourself. Your 'luck' will be much of your own making."

As it turned out, I needed a lot of luck early on at Colgate because I was lost in its Chenango Valley campus and needed guidance at every turn just to make it through the first year. As smart as I thought I was, Colgate's core curriculum courses, a major in a new subject called economics, college Spanish and whatever else I took that first year were challenging. I was "reaching," as Murphy had advised, but sometimes it felt more like I was clawing my way to survival.

As a freshman requirement, I had memorized the Colgate Alma Mater and knew Colgate was founded by 13 men, with 13 prayers, 13 dollars, and 13 articles. I got it — the number 13 is considered lucky for Colgate. How about me? Luck or no luck, I wondered to myself why I was there because it sometimes seemed like I didn't belong. I was only 17, among the youngest in my class, and the whole situation was overwhelming.

Certain questions kept coming to mind: "Why were these core courses so difficult? Why did these other courses seem totally foreign to me? Should it matter whether I knew why I was taking them or not? What about 'just do your job and learn?'" My conclusion was that the people in charge must have had a reason why. So, I reckoned, I should just study hard, pay attention and learn all the unfamiliar information. Even if my friends back home in Utica didn't care, I knew I must.

After all, it's called a liberal arts education, and the end goal is a Bachelor of Arts degree.

I didn't fully realize it until I had settled in during the first few months of college, but I had never totally learned how to study properly or, for that matter, write a satisfactory term paper in high school. My early writing training under the tutelage of Ellen Hanford, English teacher and advisor to the *Academic Observer* magazine and *Academician* yearbook at UFA, wasn't enough to curb my nervousness and apprehension when I was assigned my first college papers. I wondered if other freshmen might be struggling, too.

My high school, where only 24 percent of the graduating class went onto college, either had not well prepared me, or I simply hadn't taken advantage of its opportunities to prep students to handle college's increased workloads. As I was struggling to keep up, I kept wondering if Aunt Elsie, my mentor, was right. She had urged me many times to attend a private prep school after my junior year in high school. I would have attended for two years total — to either Mt. Hermon, in Massachusetts, or Taft, in Connecticut — which would have increased my stay in high school to five years. Not wanting to be in school longer than necessary, I rejected her offer to pay for the prep school, stayed home and graduated from a public high school in four years.

In those first few months of college, I only talked about my academic situation with Chuck Berky from Lansdale, Pennsylvania, my freshman roommate in West Hall. He was kind and consoling. As a future political science major, he was also learning to cope with the newness of college, albeit much better than I. Chuck was balancing his studies, freshman football and the glee club. I was just worrying about the academics.

Sometimes I roamed the floors of West Hall and checked in with other classmates, Mert Hersh, Harrison Dolan, Dick Driscoll, Alan Williams and others. I was looking for clues about getting through the semester at Colgate but soon realized I was on my own. My classmates seemed to be managing, so I knew I had to had to develop my own plan to stay in college and graduate in four years. I decided that whatever storm clouds might have been on the horizon for me, I had to bring academic sunshine and some new scholarly thinking into my life. And I had to do it immediately.

Not wanting to disappoint my father Fred, Colgate class of 1926, or my brother Robert, then a senior at the college, or Aunt Elsie, who had offered to pay for my prep school education, I mapped out a strategy for success. At the recommendation of my advisor, I enrolled in a tutorial class provided by the university. Although I didn't want to admit to myself or anybody else that I needed this extra course, it taught me much needed study habits, including reading skills and excellent tips on writing term papers.

Another strategy to improve my performance at Colgate was to spend more time in the library and to limit weekend trips to my hometown of Utica, only 30 miles away, or to any other place. This way, I would better integrate myself in my new place of residence and engage in meaningful academic activity for the next four years. I was starting to grow up.

Another step in my freshman-year maturation was to take advantage of "the older student seminars" before each core curriculum course exam. This was especially helpful in my combined philosophy and religion class. The "sophomore teachers" made plenty of money on those pre-test seminars, and they deserved it, because at least two-thirds of the freshman class took advantage of the sessions and subsequently passed their exams.

I began to get the hang of it all in the second semester of my freshman year, and I saw improvement in my grades. However, I knew I had to continue to do better and keep my GPA at a satisfactory level. As part of my "get with it" plan, I enrolled in two summer courses, economics and history, at Utica College. I transferred those credits and grades to Colgate, which helped strengthen my GPA. What I had learned in Colgate's tutorial class added value to that summer program, and I felt satisfactorily prepared for class, exams and the term papers. I was even able to squeeze in a city playground supervisory job and umpire Little League baseball games that summer.

In order to continue this upward academic momentum and build my confidence about succeeding in college, I decided to live in a private home in Hamilton, New York, my second year. It was a decision intended to help improve my study habits in a quieter environment. My new living quarters were located at Mrs. Dickerson's house, a small green shingled abode on Kendrick Avenue, just down the street from the Delta Upsilon fraternity house, which I officially joined in the first semester of my sophomore year. Since the fraternity house bedrooms were usually crowded for sophomores, several fraternity brothers joined me in the move to Kendrick Avenue.

With less commotion than what the fraternity house or a dormitory would have provided, my grades steadily improved, so I asked Mrs. Dickerson if I could stay for my junior year. She was very particular about her tenants and watched us like a hawk. She acquiesced because she had housed my father there many years ago when he was a student at Colgate, and she liked our family.

By living in a private home, I could participate in fraternity life on my own terms. I ate all my meals there, including breakfast, which consisted of fresh eggs, bacon and the whole nine yards, prepared by our cook, Miss Ruby, every weekday morning at 7 a.m. Finally, in my senior year, I moved out of Mrs. Dickerson's house and lived in the DU house with Mert Hersh as my roommate. We had a suite with two adjoining bedrooms, so I was still able to study.

My years at Colgate were an experience like no other. Something new was happening every day, every week, every month, and it was exhilarating. I was growing up, exploring new ideas, learning new skills and experiencing what felt like "real life." Part of my exuberance could be attributed to the excellence and flexibility of the professors who challenged me to think differently. Another part of the challenge came from having to manage my own time and being grown up.

One of my favorite professors was Frank A. Farnsworth, Colgate '39, of the economics department, who once told me, "If I had one legacy to leave my son, I would make that enthusiasm — for with that all else is possible." It sounds like something a college football coach would say, but it could equally be applied to all life situations. I used Farnsworth's quote in an article I wrote about him for *D&B Reports Magazine* and which was reprinted in the *Colgate Scene* in September 1984.

The article also stated, "The affable, bearded professor is known by most of his former students (some of whom have become millionaires) and hundreds of entrepreneurs in the Northeast, especially the Central New York region, as a true champion of small business. A 'professor of small business,' if you will." Working with the little guys of the Northeast, Farnsworth was a guiding light in helping hundreds of people launch their own companies. He told entrepreneurs they didn't need to be "psychologically trapped" in somebody else's business. He encouraged them to set up their own businesses — and reminded them that the important element of enthusiasm must be present for a venture to be successful.

Farnsworth's own small business venture began in 1967. Called the Poolville Country Store, it was a community store that sold a potpourri of merchandise to local residents and some college students. Subsequently, the store involved junior and seniors in Farnsworth's advanced business organization class. I had taken the same class nine years earlier and, unfortunately, that was too early to be involved with the store, which was founded five miles from campus. Speaking of his dual role as teacher and small-business consultant, Farnsworth told me for the article, "There isn't anything more satisfying than this."

Farnsworth wasn't the only Colgate professor who got my attention. Ford B. Saunders, music and core curriculum professor who was also the organist in the Colgate Memorial Chapel, demanded I learn about operas and symphonies in order to appreciate their structure and artistry. Stan Kinney, an English professor, was my first public speaking coach. He encouraged me to take on unusual speaking topics, such as a dissection of multiple mafia arrests in the Binghamton area orchestrated by the New York State police, as well as a three-month review of the *New York Post* newspaper. English Professor H.L. Hackett was determined to make a first-class writer out of me and took it upon himself to edit my weekly "Press Box Chatter" sports columns in the *Colgate Maroon* after they had been printed. Wilson Farman, professor of accounting, hounded me until I fully understood all the accounting principles and could be awarded a B in his 4-credit class. Professor J.C. "Doc" Austin of the classical languages department always had a twinkle in his eye when trying to get an important point across.

I knew I was on my way to growing up when, as sports editor of the *Maroon* in my senior year, I was equipped with superb confidence while I interviewed both Everett N. Case, the college president, and Everett D. "Eppie" Barnes, the athletic director. Each time, I was able to ask all the right questions and get insightful answers needed for my columns. In order to keep my nerves in check for those assignments, I kept replaying the first two verses of the Colgate song, "1819," in my head:

> Long ago, in the valley of Chenango, gathered thirteen.
> Funds were low, but abundant was their pluck, in eighteen-nineteen.
> Thirteen prayers were said with rapt devotion,
> Thirteen dollars set the thing in motion,
> Thus began old Colgate University in eighteen-nineteen.
>
> Live true to the memory of those thirteen men of yore.
> Whose faith made tradition that shall live for evermore.
> Whose deeds give us courage to strive as they strove then.
> 'Tis the spirit that is Colgate, dear mother of men.

Now as Colgate marks its 200th anniversary in 2019, the university is still recognized as a highly esteemed liberal arts college. But unlike the lyrics stated in the "1819" song, today Colgate's population of over 2,800 students includes both men and women, who will undoubtedly grow up faster than they ever could have imagined. Go 'Gate!

DOESCHER LESSON: *When backed into a corner with seemingly few options to turn things around, don't panic. Patience, determination, guts and a strategic plan will provide the needed ingredients, over time, for success.*

14.
THE NEXT RED SMITH

"Today's game is always different from yesterday's game."

— Red Smith

We should be grateful for every opportunity that comes our way. And in return, we should create new opportunities for others.

I never really intended to be a full-time sportswriter, but there I was anyway. In June 1959, with a Colgate University diploma in hand and only a smattering of journalism experience, I became the fifth man in a five-man sports department headed by John W. Fox, at *The Evening Press* in Binghamton, New York.

It was one of only two job offers I had after graduation. The other was as a sportswriter with Arnie Burdick, sports editor of the *Syracuse Herald-Journal.* About three months into the *Press* job, I received a third job offer. Charley Loftus, director of sports information at Yale University, offered me a position as his assistant. I declined because I wanted to show loyalty to Fox for giving me a break, and I did not want to be known as a job hopper early in my career. Also, Charley's reputation for three-martini lunches scared me.

Back then, I used to wonder what qualified me to be a sportswriter. I had some experience, but my college major — economics — was totally unrelated to sports writing. So how exactly did I get this job? I reasoned that my liberal arts education must have helped, particularly my experience with the core courses that were reputed to broaden and stretch Colgate students' minds.

But maybe that wasn't entirely it. No doubt my deep interest in sports and the fact that I had been following the Utica Blue Sox Eastern League baseball team since the late 1940s certainly didn't hurt. The Blue Sox team played its home games at McConnell Field in North Utica, and my father Fred, older brother Robert and I went to many games. The team featured some of the "Whiz Kids" of the 1950 National League Champion Philadelphia Phillies, such as Hall-of-Famer Richie Ashburn, Stan Lopata, Granny Hammer and Putsey Caballero. Eddie Sawyer, the manager, also made it to the Phillies.

On the job at the *Press*, my Colgate connection paid off when I was at ease interviewing former Colgate football star, successful Triple Cities area high school football coach and tennis champion, Fran Angeline, in 1959. The Colgate connection also helped when discussing athletics and the future football schedule with the new Colgate football coach Alva Kelly, who came from Brown University to rescue the Raiders' football program.

So, what really was the pathway to my first job out of college?

In the end, it came down to a recommendation. When Walter D. Splain, an alum who was the longtime sports information director at Colgate University, was asked by Fox if he knew anybody who could fill a position within his department in Binghamton, Splain said, "There's this guy Doescher, who has been Colgate's sports correspondent for the Utica newspapers while going to school. He might be interested. He was also sports editor of the *Colgate Maroon*, and you can teach him the rest." My competition for the *Press* job probably would have been Bradley N. Tufts, a Delta Upsilon fraternity brother, who worked for Splain in the sports information department while going to school. Although we graduated at the same time, Brad had already taken a job with Bucknell University as sports information director, where he stayed for more than 30 years. It proved to be a good choice for him, since he eventually became the university's public relations director and interim athletics director, while also coaching the men's and women's golf teams.

Since Brad had already lined up a job, I became the recommendation. Fox took a chance and offered me the position for $75 per week, which was $15 more than Arnie Burdick was offering at the *Syracuse Herald-Journal*. In addition to the higher pay, I figured Fox, with his journalism degree from Syracuse University, could teach me more about being a sportswriter. As it turned out, I was right.

In addition to Fox's guidance, the four other sportswriters at the Binghamton *Press* job provided sound advice about covering local sports and editing a sports section. They often let me know I was a rookie among some very serious newspapermen. I had a lot to learn, and they didn't let me forget it. It was sort of like the "special conditioning" that rookies receive today from veterans in Major League Baseball.

On my first day on the job, I showed up in the newsroom wearing a dressy sport coat and a hat. It was more formal attire than usual in that environment, and from that day onward, I was known as "Hat."

My newsroom teachers included everyone on our small team: Russ Worman, makeup man who supervised wire copy, wrote catchy headlines and was a no-nonsense type who protected his space better than anybody I have met since; Charley Peet, an affable writer with 23 years of experience who covered bowling and the Binghamton Triplets, which was the Eastern League farm team of the New York Yankees; John Lake, last man in before me, who also had a Syracuse University journalism degree, covered the Triplets and high school sports and would go on to become a sportswriter for the *New York Herald Tribune* and a sports editor at *Newsweek;* and, of course, Fox, a prolific writer and columnist who coordinated the entire national and local coverage as well as reported on the choicest college football games across the upstate New York landscape.

Lake, who was closest to my age, was the most patient and relaxed member of the sportswriting team. One night after work, during my first month on the job, he took me aside and gave me some tips. I filled a yellow pad with notes. The most critical advice involved headline writing and editing, as it was the newsroom's practice to edit and write headlines for each other's stories.

During our first of many training sessions, I asked Lake about his career goals. He said he wanted to become the next Red Smith. Smith, one of the most famous American sportswriters, was a Pulitzer Prize-winning columnist who wrote for the *New York Herald Tribune* from 1945 to 1966 and then for *The New York Times* from 1971 until his death in 1982 at age 75. Spanning a remarkable 55 years, Smith often characterized his career with his famous quote: "Writing is easy. You just open a vein and bleed."

Lake's goal of emulating Red Smith sounded good to me, so I adopted it too and made the legend my role model. Neither Lake nor I ever succeeded at achieving such notoriety, but Lake got the closest. He even worked with Smith at the *Tribune* for some time before moving to *Newsweek* where he really started making a name for himself.

Lake tragically and mysteriously disappeared in New York City in 1967. He was never found and was declared legally dead in 1975. Thirty years later, Dan Barry, in a *New York Times* article in 2005, hypothesized that money trouble, drinking trouble and marriage trouble may have contributed to Lake's disappearance and presumed death. At one point, Lake's son Eric made a concerted effort to find out what happened to his father and contacted many of Lake's former associates, including me. But Eric's research did not prevail, and Lake's fate has remained a mystery.

After working as a sportswriter for a short period of time in 1959 and 1960, I finally realized it wasn't a lifelong career for me. I switched direction, went to graduate school and then entered the world of public relations. I knew, long-term, that the pay would be better in a corporate setting. Also, while I certainly liked watching and playing some sports, I did not like the environment of living all sports 24/7.

At the *Press*, I had been assigned to cover high-school football and basketball. Sometimes, I also got to share coverage of the local Binghamton Triplets Eastern League baseball team and the region's robust world of amateur golf. I was also often assigned to report on sporting events and personalities that no one else felt like covering in the area of Binghamton, Endicott and Johnson City.

I did have the opportunity to write some important and interesting pieces too. There were stories about PGA golfers Arnold Palmer and Ken Venturi; National Basketball Association stars Bill Sharman of the Boston Celtics, and Red Kerr of the Syracuse Nationals; Major League Baseball players Mickey Mantle of the New York Yankees, Bill Virdon and Elroy Face of the Pittsburgh Pirates, and Johnny Logan of the Milwaukee Braves; and the well-known boxer Carmen Basilio.

I specifically recall one assignment covering high-school football in October 1959. It began with an 11 a.m. downpour that drenched me through my clothes while I was walking to the stadium press box. Without a change of shirt and pants, I shivered in the unheated press box for the entire game and couldn't wait to go home and change into dry clothes. But before I was able to do that, I dictated my story over the phone to Worman, back in the newsroom, in order to meet the deadline for the paper's 3-star edition that Saturday afternoon. Those were the days before computers and the internet. So, I told Worman all the details that I had observed — about how Elmira Southside defeated Union-Endicott, 7–6, on a missed extra point and about how that missed point stemmed from a bad pass from center that caused the placekicker, normally a tackle, to run for it before being pummeled at the 2-yard line. After making the immediate Saturday edition deadline over the phone, I returned to the newsroom, with dry clothes, to help prepare the sports pages for the next day's Sunday's edition. We all left the office at 2 a.m., just enough time to get the pages submitted for printing and delivery. Readers of the paper, of course, took all the news for granted and had no idea about the incredible effort it took to keep on top of current events and produce the paper every day.

Another assignment I well remember involved the Mickey Mantle All-Stars versus the Willie Mays All-Stars in a barnstorming tour game at MacArthur Stadium in Syracuse. At that time, Major League Baseball players were able to pick up some extra postseason cash in such events because the World Series ended earlier than it does now.

After covering the event, I had collected two stories for the Binghamton *Press*; however, only one was printed.

This is what happened ... Mantle, who had a noticeable liquor breath on him, told me in an interview that he would quit baseball and retire unless George Weiss, the Yankees General Manager, gave him a raise for the 1960 season. I proceeded to ask him some other questions, but as Mantle was annoyed that he had to talk to a reporter, he picked me up and threw me into the stands. I landed on my feet and moved across the diamond to the Mays dugout, where I could look for another story.

There, I asked Pittsburgh Pirates pitcher Elroy Face if he would be willing to tell me how he pitched to his All-Star teammates when he opposed them in the National League. He obliged, and I had my second story. It was a great read as Face passed along pitching tips related to the batting styles of Gil Hodges, Willie McCovey and Hobie Landrith. The story's headline read, "Face Reveals NL Book," and it was the story my editor chose to run.

I also wrote the Mantle scoop, but it never ran. The next morning, on my day off and after I submitted the story to the newsroom, the phone rang in the house where I was renting a room. I answered the call, and it was Worman on the line. He wanted to know if Mantle had actually said what I reported in the story. My answer was, of course, yes. I was upset that my integrity as a reporter had been questioned. Yet, I also understood the reason for his call, as I was still an inexperienced "rookie" in his mind. I had to prove myself, particularly since I had no previous journalism training.

Mantle absolutely did tell me what I wrote, but the *Press* elected not to run my story. I guess Fox feared his reputation as an editor and possible controversy if my story had misquoted or misinterpreted Mantle. The accuracy of my reporting, however, was confirmed two days later when the Associated Press ran a nationwide story very similar to "my Mantle story." So the *Press* didn't get its scoop, and I never got an apology.

After I gave up sportswriting to build a successful professional career in public relations, I continued to dabble in the genre. Several pieces have appeared in local weeklies under my own byline or the pseudonym William Fredericks. These have included stories in the *Hickory News* and the *Scarsdale Inquirer*, representing hometown newspaper coverage in two places where I have lived, in North Carolina and New York. I have enjoyed keeping active, pro bono, with local sports coverage because I recognize that sportswriting gave me the start I needed in the communications world.

I have never forgotten about Red Smith and the power of his simple and direct style. After I had abandoned professional sportswriting and obtained a master's degree in public relations, I arrived in New York City for my first PR job at The Chase Manhattan Bank in 1961. Smith was still writing his column at *The New York Times* three or four times a week. Over my lunch hour, I pored over Smith's words every time the column was published.

It has been proven many times that sportswriters are indeed good writers. Red was one of the best in the field, and at one time, his columns were syndicated in 275 newspapers in the United States and in an additional 225 papers across 30 foreign countries.

After decades of experience in communications, I came to understand that Red Smith, like Ernest Hemingway, commanded power through his clean and direct approach. Nobody has been able to replace Smith in the field of sportswriting. He never used flowery language, never used unnecessary words and always got his point across with honesty and flair. I have tried to copy that style over the years, maintaining a philosophy that simple is better than complicated. The "Gutenberg Bible" style of writing wasn't and isn't for me.

DOESCHER LESSON: *Learn from every job and grow with every experience. Always reach for the highest goals. Never be afraid to change jobs or careers, especially if you think you won't be able to provide a high degree of excellence to your company or, more important, to yourself.*

15.
ALMOST THE COMMISSIONER OF THE ABA

"I can accept failure; everyone fails at something. But I can't accept not trying."

— Michael Jordan

Sometimes, the best story is one that doesn't make the headline. I know this firsthand from my own experience. You'd never read about it in a paper, but I almost became the commissioner of the American Basketball Association. It was unbelievable, exhilarating, and of course disappointing when I did not get the job. But my father, Fred Doescher, gave me good advice when he heard the news, "Just remember, when you get as close as that — they are not all misses. It gave you a rich experience you cannot buy."

My dad was right.

It was October 29, 1969, and the official news in professional basketball was that Jack Dolph, director of sports for CBS Television, had been named commissioner of the American Basketball Association. In being named to take the job, he replaced George Mikan, a former National Basketball Association great with the Minneapolis Lakers. This, of course, was the story that made headlines.

The more interesting — yet unreported — story was that former sportswriter Bill Doescher, who was then a 31-year-old advertising manager with U.S. Plywood-Champion Papers, Inc. in New York City, was among four finalists for the job. These finalists had been selected from an original list of 1,000 applicants and nominees.

So how did this opportunity come about? It began with a letter of recommendation written by my friend Lee Koppelman, who worked for Ivy Hill Lithograph Corporation. In the 1950s, Lee had played basketball for Bobby Davies, the former Rochester Royals great, at Gettysburg College, in Pennsylvania. Using his connections, Lee decided to reach out to Jim Gardner, acting ABA Commissioner and president and owner of the Carolina Cougars. Lee's letter recommended me for the job without initially giving my name. His strategy was a kind of marketing intrigue, implemented to create interest and suspense.

Not expecting to hear from Gardner, I was surprised when he asked Lee to have me identify myself. I complied and showed up for an interview session directed, individually, at the four finalists. It took place at the Yale Club on Vanderbilt Avenue in New York City. I was the first finalist to meet with the committee, which is never a good sign for success, even though the odds had increased from 1,000-to-1 to 4-to-1.

The search committee was comprised of Earl Foreman of the Washington Caps, Roy Boe of the New York Nets and Richard Tinkham of the Indiana Pacers. The 55-minute interview went well, and I still think I nailed every question they threw at me. My preparation included carefully studying both the ABA and NBA organizations' management structures, as well as memorizing every team's roster. I wanted to be ready for any possible question, and I was. Later, of course, I realized I did not need to know such information.

At the conclusion of the interview, Boe said it was the most interesting interview he had ever participated in. He also said three of the four finalists were alums of Colgate, my alma mater. Dolph, who ended up getting the job, was the only non-Colgate finalist. Since the committee never revealed the other two candidates, I could only speculate. My best guesses at the time were Carl Braun, a former New York Knicks great and Wall Street banker, and Garry Valk, publisher of *Sports Illustrated*.

Dolph did not experience much success in the position. Television advertising sales proved to be low, and as a result, disappointed ABA owners eased Dolph out of the position in 1972. He became an independent sports producer and died of a heart attack in 1981 at the age of 53.

According to a March 1974 *Sports Illustrated* article by Peter Carry, a New York corporate lawyer named Bob Carlson was named as Dolph's temporary replacement. He was mainly chosen to handle the ABA's complex legal affairs. In September 1974, Mike Storen was then named Commissioner of the ABA. Storen had been involved with the ABA since its beginning, as vice president and general manager of the Indiana Pacers. He was also someone I met in the lobby of the Yale Club on that interview day in 1969.

On August 5, 1976, the NBA and its rival, the ABA, officially merged. The new NBA absorbed the ABA's four most successful franchises — the Denver Nuggets, the Indiana Pacers, the New York Nets (which later became the New Jersey Nets) and the San Antonio Spurs. Three of the seven original ABA franchises were dismantled, and their players were incorporated into the NBA. Larry O'Brien, then commissioner of the NBA (1975–1984), directed the merger. He was followed as commissioner by David J. Stern, a lawyer with excellent marketing and negotiating skills, who held the position of NBA Commissioner for 30 years until his retirement in 2014. I admire Stern for a lot of reasons and because he took the game of professional basketball to heights not commonly seen in professional sports.

I have known Stern for a long time. He and I are fellow residents of the Village of Scarsdale. We run into one another at local events and dine at the same area restaurants. I never told him about my ABA experience because I didn't think it was necessary. Even when he unexpectedly called me one day to handle an executive recruiting assignment, I didn't say a word. Instead, I just fulfilled the executive recruiting role to the best of my ability, and Stern was satisfied.

So, while I didn't get the ABA position in 1969, I did have a wonderful experience working with Stern's lieutenants during the executive job search. They were business people worrying about basketball. Not basketball people worrying about business. Stern ran a tight ship, and his continued success with the NBA proved his approach was right. It was exciting to be part of Stern's NBA operation for the time he needed my services. And it's still exciting to think that I, remarkably, once came close to be the Commissioner of the ABA.

DOESCHER LESSON: *Allow your dreams to be big, even bigger than you think is possible. There's no victory like the underdog's win. And as my father said, "Just remember, when you get close but do not succeed — they are not all misses. Rich experiences have value you cannot buy."*

16.
Why Newhouse?

"You just can't beat the person who won't give up."

— Babe Ruth

As soon as I knew I did not want a life dedicated to sportswriting, I switched direction and pursued a new path. It started with my resolve to attend graduate school and subsequently led to a full and rewarding career in public relations.

The year was 1960. I was 22 years old and working at *The Evening Press* in Binghamton, New York. I had just finished a six-month tour of duty as a U.S. Army reservist, which was part of a total commitment of almost six years. I had joined the Reserves as an alternative to being drafted for a two-year stint of active duty in the regular U.S. Army, as my number was rising to the top at my local draft board. The newspaper had kept my job open for me while I had put in my obligated time with the Army, and I was truly grateful for my editor's flexibility. I enjoyed my role as a sportswriter, but as soon as I got back into the newsroom's routine, I could not stop wondering if I really wanted to do that job for the rest of my life.

I played sports, and I liked sports. But I realized early on that my professional duties would rarely include exciting opportunities such as interviewing professional athletes like New York Yankees star Mickey Mantle, Boston Celtics stalwart Bill Sharman, golf's Arnold Palmer or boxing's Carmen Basilio — although I did actually interview each of these legends at least once for individual stories. Instead, the workaday sports world for a regional reporter would more likely revolve around interviews with local sports' personalities — amateur golf sensations, high school basketball and football coaches and minor league baseball players who would, most likely, never make it to the "bigs."

The need to develop a long-term career plan, and my father's strong suggestion of working for one company that would provide a suitable retirement package, were also in the back of my mind. Since my dad was a traveling salesman, he had to fund his own pension from his earnings. Although I was far from thinking about retiring from anywhere, I listened to his advice.

One day, I came across a paid announcement in *Newsweek* magazine. Although I did not realize it then, that New York Life ad for its career advancement program would change my life. In the ad, New York Life presented a simple formula for achievement. It stated that any successful public relations applicant should be able to state the following items on his or her curriculum vitae:

- A bachelor's degree with a major in economics from a reputable college.
- Writing experience in a full-time position either at a newspaper or magazine or in radio or television.

- A master's degree in public relations from a communications school.

I looked at the ad and noted I already had two out of the three. I immediately felt a successful PR career was in sight. I just needed to complete the third leg of the journey and get a master's degree. Then, I would be ready. It all sounded easy enough, so I made the decision to proceed.

I began to consider my options, taking my undergraduate experience at Colgate into account. I surmised that any esteemed graduate program might be a reach since my college grade point average would not make me a stellar applicant. But then again, that was just on paper. I reflected on all that I had learned at Colgate and on all the ways that I had grown. Colgate's breadth of study had inspired deep critical thinking, a thorough investigation of core curriculum courses and opportunities to immerse myself in new subjects. It was there that I learned how to study, albeit a little late, and there that I became immersed in economics, operas, symphonies and literature for the first time. I waded my way through oceans of books, including Leo Tolstoy's *War and Peace,* with its complex themes, daunting list of characters and hard-to-pronounce names. By the end of my undergraduate career at Colgate, I had learned to master whatever material could be thrown at me. So, regardless of what my transcript might suggest, I felt prepared to pursue a master's degree — and absolutely confident I would succeed.

I now needed a plan. I focused my attention on the School of Journalism at Syracuse University and decided it would be the only school to which I would apply. The School of Journalism was the name of the communications school at Syracuse University before it changed to the S.I. Newhouse School of Public Communications, at SU, due to generous funding by the Newhouse family in 1964. I kept working my day job at the *Press* and didn't tell anyone what I was doing, not even the two fellow *Press* sportswriters who had obtained their undergraduate degrees in journalism there. I didn't even tell Aunt Elsie, who had always supported my ambitions and counseled me to pursue additional education at the graduate level. Nevertheless, while she was not directly involved, I knew I had her backing.

Part of my strategy to get accepted to the School of Journalism was to get noticed by its dean, Wesley C. Clark. It was July, and I started by writing letters and making phone calls, but these didn't seem to be working. I knew I needed face-to-face time. So, on my day off from the *Press*, which happened to be a Tuesday, I drove my 1961 Pontiac, a gift from Aunt Elsie, to the SU campus. I sat outside Clark's office and waited. Even though my visit was unannounced, Clark eventually agreed to see me. What else could he do? My visit was after six phone calls and four letters — so he already had an idea of my persistence.

Once inside Clark's office, I decided to be direct and get to the point. I told Clark I was there because I had to attend graduate school at the School of Journalism. I phrased it as more of a statement, than as a request. I'm not sure what Clark thought of my unconventional approach, but, as a kind man, he sympathetically listened to me, as he probably did to all the students and applicants.

At the end of that first meeting, Clark politely dismissed me from his office. He was probably not expecting to see me again — but he did. Two more times. On my third unannounced visit to plead my case, Clark stood up from behind his desk, took me by the hand and led me to the graduate school administration building. There, he introduced me to the admissions chief and instructed him to accept me to the School of Journalism on a one-semester provisional basis. Clark then looked me in the eyes and told me, "Young man, if you're going to make it here, you've got to show it in the first semester. If you don't, you're out."

His words didn't scare me. I was in, and I had my marching orders. The rest was up to me. In less than one month, I would be starting graduate school.

I went back to Binghamton and promptly resigned from the *Press* job. I did not yet know how I would pay for graduate school, but since my persistence and determination had opened the door for me, I knew I would find the money somehow. If you believe there is always a way, there is.

Just like that — the tuition money soon materialized. I borrowed $800 from the Oneida National Bank, in Utica, in a loan countersigned by my father. Through Syracuse University, I also obtained a federal student loan of approximately $600, financed through the National Defense Education Act of 1958. The rest of the money was borrowed from Aunt Elsie. Initially, Aunt Elsie's loan consisted of $1,500 and was later supplemented by a few hundred dollars more for books and gasoline. After graduation, all of the loans were to be paid back as soon as reasonably possible — and they were.

To save money, I took my meals at the Phi Gamma Delta fraternity house on Comstock Avenue where Dick Scala, my childhood Utica friend, was a member. I boarded in a private home on Ostrom Avenue, where I rented one room from a widow with two college-age kids. I was given the daughter's room while she was away at college; however, part of the deal was that I agreed to give the room back to her during Thanksgiving and Christmas breaks. So, during those periods, I had to return to my parents' house. The widow's son, on the other hand, attended college locally and lived at home. He played the trombone in the Syracuse University band, and his practice noise used to keep me awake at night. On the other hand, I always tried to keep quiet to not disturb anyone. I even devised a way to silence the noise of my portable Royal typewriter by placing a pillow under it as I banged out papers late at night.

The living arrangements in the widow's house were somewhat confining, so I decided to move out in March of my second semester. I joined a group of three acquaintances — a full-time student, a part-time student and a high-school English teacher who was the cousin of the part-time student

— to share a three-bedroom apartment on South Beech Street that included a kitchen, dining room and living room. Fortunately, as the most serious of the three students, I negotiated my own room and used the dining room table as my study hall.

With my tuition taken care of and without the burden of having to work part-time, I was able to concentrate on my coursework. I even gave up basketball and other activities that I had enjoyed as an undergraduate. Dating was also off the table for a while.

Graduate school had made me a serious student, and I was finding myself in the library a lot, handing in well-proofed essays, reading all the assignments carefully and preparing myself to make major contributions in all my courses. I periodically checked in with Dean Clark and always carefully listened to his wisdom and advice. I came to think of him as one of my first mentors on the Syracuse campus and still value his role in shaping my experience there.

As a result, I completed my first year in graduate school with all A's and two B's. In order to expedite the degree, I completed nine hours of summer coursework, wrote a major thesis and passed a comprehensive exam — between Memorial Day and Labor Day in the summer of 1961. The intensity paid off. Before I had to take out further tuition loans, I graduated with my master's degree in public relations in 1961. I finished the degree in 14 months, instead of the typical two-year period taken by most students.

Now having obtained all three ingredients noted in that original New York Life ad, I quickly learned that the strategy had been correct. I had five job offers upon graduation. The first was for a public relations junior position with BBDO, an advertising agency in New York City. The second was for an associate position in a small PR firm that handled the Foster Grant sunglasses line, also in New York City. The third was for an associate position in the public relations department of Lehigh University, in Bethlehem, Pennsylvania. The fourth was for a marketing and communications job in the nutritional division of Mead Johnson, in Evansville, Indiana. All good possibilities but I accepted the fifth job offer instead — a position in the public relations department at The Chase Manhattan Bank, at 1 Chase Manhattan Plaza, located in Manhattan's Wall Street district. By accepting the offer, I was able to boost my credentials from the beginning with a blue-chip name that has remained on my CV ever since.

But that's not the only reason I took the job. The chance to work with David Rockefeller, who, over the years, came to serve various positions with the bank, including president, chairman and CEO, made the opportunity especially intriguing. As a 24-year-old newbie employee, I was thrilled to be trusted with the task of handling some of Mr. David's PR projects. Mr. David, as he was called, proved to be a delightful boss, a true gentleman and an extremely intelligent leader.

There's no question that Newhouse changed my life's course, and I am especially grateful to Dean Clark for taking a chance on my potential and letting me in. I emphasized this sentiment in a major lecture, "Embracing Change: 50 Years in Public Relations," which I delivered to 400 PR students in Newhouse's Joyce B. Hergenhan Auditorium in 2011.

By way of giving back, I have served on the institution's advisory board for more than 20 years and have funded the Doescher Campaigns Lab for Advertising and Public Relations. This facility reflects the environment of a Madison Avenue agency where students can conduct research and create campaigns for real clients. I have also provided a special annual prize for the top PR graduate student, as determined by a faculty committee, and I interview prospective students throughout Westchester County and southern Connecticut. When students talk to me about their earnest aspirations to attend Newhouse, I often remember Dean Clark's patience, attentive ear and generosity in giving me a chance to work toward my master's degree at Syracuse.

As I have said many times, to many different audiences, Newhouse changed my life forever.

DOESCHER LESSON: *When you want something badly enough, find a way to make it happen. Be steadfast even if it involves making sacrifices or changing your lifestyle and mindset along the way. Your determination could change your life forever.*

17.
THE FIRST AMENDMENT AT NEWHOUSE

"Congress shall make no law respecting an establishment of religion or prohibiting the free exercise thereof; or abridging the freedom of speech, or of the press; or the right of the people peaceably to assemble, and to petition the government for a redress of grievances."

— The First Amendment — which, along with the rest of the Bill of Rights, was submitted to the States for ratification on September 25, 1789, and adopted on December 15, 1791.

Whenever I look back on my education, I am proud to recall that it was the Syracuse University School of Journalism, later called the S.I. Newhouse School of Public Communications, that started me out, well prepared, for a career in public relations. Newhouse is not just a school. It is an institution at the forefront of the communications industry. It provides a solid foundation, informed by traditional communications practices and historical philosophies, while also fostering innovation in a rapidly changing landscape of new media. My ongoing association with the school has fostered wonderful and invigorating relationships over the years.

Within the last 15 years I had a chance of a lifetime to play a small but active role in the decision to have the words of the First Amendment adorn the outside structure of Newhouse-3, a building designed to house classrooms, offices, a collaborative media room and the Joyce B. Hergenhan Auditorium on the campus of Syracuse University.

It was a magnificent idea, and it was thrilling to experience the project of the Amendment's "Liberty Wrap" come to life. My role on the advisory board, at the time, positioned me as an involved overseer, and I enthusiastically endorsed the project. The real decision makers were former Newhouse Dean David Rubin; Susan K. Nash, who was director of administration at Newhouse; and architect Tomas Rossant of Polshek Partnership (now Ennead Architects). Rubin was the brain behind the project. It was his initial idea, and he first presented the concept to Chancellor Nancy Canter and Donald Newhouse, of the Newhouse family. Once they gave their official support in 2005, the project was off and running.

While I had certainly studied the First Amendment and Constitution, starting with my grammar school social studies classes and concluding with my master's degree coursework, Rubin's proposed project caused me to pause. His passion to post the First Amendment on an important campus building prompted all of us to reflect on the meaning and importance of this critical right. It was at Newhouse's advisory board meeting in New York City, in

2005, that Rubin first announced his recommendation. His vision was to spell out the words of the First Amendment in letters six feet high, etched in glass, and wrapping the edifice of the soon-to-be-built Newhouse-3 building.

Rubin's vision was bold. The design called for a striking message. It was modeled after Times Square's famous "zipper," the iconic five-foot-high and 880-foot-long electric display, wrapped around a building to provide crowds with breaking news. But Rubin's intended message for Newhouse was even more important — he wanted all Americans to never forget what the First Amendment means to our democracy.

The First Amendment is the cornerstone of a free press and a safeguard to our right to know the truth. As such, free speech protects much more than one's personal choice of words. It enables one's ability to challenge ideas, criticize people in power, present new solutions and demand change in tired institutions.

As communicators, we must be vigilant in not forgetting the purpose of the First Amendment. At Newhouse-3's dedication ceremony, Rubin said, "This is who we are, and this is what we do. Without the First Amendment, most of what we do in the Newhouse School would not be possible or would be done in a vastly different way."

Our country's history and identity depend on an informed public and on open, public debate. Founding Father Thomas Jefferson once said, "Our liberty cannot be guarded but by the freedom of the press." His sentiment especially rings true today.

The democratic function of the First Amendment positions journalists as necessary watch dogs. Referring to the founding fathers' drafting of the First Amendment, Jay Wright, an expert in communications law, known for decades as "Mr. Comm Law at Newhouse," and co-author of *The First Amendment and the Fourth Estate*, once said: "There was a suspicion of a government that was too strong, a suspicion about letting government control what got printed and what got said. The assumption would be that in a democracy, if you have power resting in the press to expose wrongdoing by the government, you're less likely to have wrongdoing."

According to Charlotte Grimes, Newhouse's former Knight Chair in Political Reporting: "History tells us that the First Amendment is constantly under threat, and that it always will be. We have to keep fighting for it. Anybody who believes that we're ever going to be able to stop fighting for the First Amendment is deluded."

The words circling the outer walls of Newhouse-3 stand as an ever-present reminder for students to keep vigilant in this fight. Likewise, the words demonstrate the school's fierce commitment to the First Amendment.

"The Newhouse School must be a place that challenges government to respect the value of free speech and open debate, and its graduates must accept the responsibility of advancing this cause in their own work," Rubin believes.

"We are charged with promoting the free speech and press that the founding fathers knew were necessary to a functioning democracy."

As a marketing and PR guy, I have also thought about how putting the First Amendment on the building was also like an act of branding. Rubin reminded me of that recently.

He said, "I wanted people to know that this building was the Newhouse School, *not* because they read a sign outside that said so, but because First Amendment was written on the skin of the building.

"I knew it was working that way, when, shortly after the building opened in 2007, I was visiting admissions across the street from Newhouse-3. A man and his high-school-age daughter were there to tour SU, not Newhouse. The man didn't know who I was. He asked me, 'Is that the Newhouse School across the street?' I said, yes, and asked him how he knew. He said, 'What else could it be with the First Amendment written on the glass?' Bingo. The branding was working. No one who visits SU will ever forget this brand. I am very proud of that."

Today, within the present contemporary culture, I feel it is more important than ever before in my lifetime to recognize and promote the critical value of the First Amendment. In an era of Trump's presidency and his tendency to call members of the media "dishonest," "purveyors of fake news," and "the enemy of the American people," I believe we should all take action to safeguard free press and free speech. Without it, our democracy, our freedoms and our very way of life might not stand a chance.

DOESCHER LESSON: *The First Amendment and the Constitution of the United States protect our fundamental democratic rights and enable the press, importantly, to act as an impartial watch dog. Citizens of many other countries in the world do not benefit from this freedom. We should never take this right for granted, as it is the basis of our democratic way of life.*

18.
HEY, LARRY, WANNA ROB THE CHASE MANHATTAN BANK?

"I rob banks because that's where the money is."

— Attributed to the famous bank robber Willie Sutton

One day during my first PR job at The Chase Manhattan Bank in the early 1960s, Joseph T. Nolan, who was then the bank's senior vice president of public relations and advertising, stopped by my desk. He said, "We need to get coverage in both the morning and evening papers announcing the bank has completed the installation of protection cameras in all 155 branches in the city."

He followed his statement by asking me, a young, 26-year-old at a big blue-chip bank, "What's your idea for placement in the afternoon papers?"

He actually wanted to hear my opinion, and I was thrilled.

The afternoon papers in the Big Apple back then were the *Journal-American* and the *World-Telegram & Sun*. For the morning papers, which included *The New York Times, New York Daily News, New York Daily Mirror* and *The Wall Street Journal,* we would supply information with a straightforward news approach and accompanying photos.

Being creative, and excited to be asked about how to approach the afternoon papers' coverage, I exclaimed, "We could get one of the local reporters to rob the bank on camera and give him or her the film to go with the story."

The idea didn't seem like a risk to me, and Nolan must not have thought so either, because he gave me an enthusiastic thumbs up. It was a brilliant plan as far as we both were concerned.

The first step was to obtain proper clearance from Gerry Van Doren, Chase's vice president of security and a former FBI man. I then called Lawrence Van Gelder of the *New York Journal-American,* whom I had met at a New York Fire Department charity event, and I asked him if he'd like to rob The Chase Manhattan Bank on camera.

Like any enterprising reporter, Larry jumped at the opportunity and said yes.

We planned a day and decided the "robbery" would take place at the bank's Union Square branch near 14th Street in Manhattan, when the bank was empty of customers but not employees. The staged robbery went as beautifully as we had orchestrated it — except for one problem. Our Holmes Protection people, who were responsible for monitoring all of our cameras and alarms, forgot to remind their staff that the dramatic robbery was only a test.

So guess what happened next? Five carloads of New York's finest arrived on scene with blaring sirens, flashing lights, adrenaline pumping and guns drawn.

Hearing the sirens grow louder as the patrol cars approached, Van Doren positioned himself at the front door and displayed his security credentials. His plan was to meet the police officers and tell them the "robbery" was only a test. In the meantime, I pushed Van Gelder, our "robber," into a chair at the assistant branch manager's desk, and we began play-acting a conversation about a banking matter. I asked him not to say a word, and he complied. The cops did not seem too happy about our alarm and camera test, and they left talking to themselves.

Now, what to do with Van Gelder? Because of the brouhaha, he suddenly had a much bigger story than he ever could have imagined. I made a deal with him that he could have the film from the protection camera and run the story only if he didn't mention which bank branch he had "robbed." He agreed, and the story ran on the front page of the next afternoon's paper. Above the name of the paper was an oversized 8-column headline stating: "I Robbed The Chase Manhattan Bank."

But that's not the end of the story.

The next morning, Francis Scully of the Associated Press called and wanted to know if he, too, could rob the Chase Manhattan Bank. Still gun-shy from the last "robbery," I wondered if I should take a chance and try again?

I deliberated briefly and silently thought to myself, "Why not?" After all, I hadn't been fired from the last caper, and it would be good publicity for the bank. So, again with proper clearance from Van Doren, we orchestrated a second staged robbery. This time, it was scheduled for the branch at 42nd Street and Second Avenue, and we made sure the Holmes Protection people were well informed about our test. Needless to say, the cops didn't show up for an encore performance.

Scully's AP story, complete with photos captured by the protection camera, appeared in newspapers and magazines all over the world.

I was invigorated by the success of the mission. It was a crazy, brilliant idea that turned out to be one of my most successful press relations stories ever. And I was just getting started. As the years progressed, there would be more to come.

In retrospect, I am grateful to Nolan for believing in me and giving me the opportunity to work so creatively. He was one of my first professional mentors and a true role model. Coincidentally, I later learned he graduated from Crosby High School, just like my father, in Waterbury, Connecticut. Although they didn't know each other personally because they attended at different times, this connection created a feeling of camaraderie that went beyond our work roles.

Everyone who encountered Nolan could see what made him a PR legend. He has been honored by a number of organizations, including the Public Relations Society of America, and he has shared accolades with fellow PR superstars Dan Edelman and Chester Burger. I was fortunate to know all three of these gentlemen as trusted "go-to mentors." Impressively, each of their creative and determined styles have pioneered the kind of forward-thinking momentum that continues to move the industry into the future.

Prior to his PR career, Nolan was a successful journalist. He worked for United Press International and *The New York Times*, where he contributed to the "News of the Week in Review" section when it won a 1953 Pulitzer Prize. In the early years of television, he wrote for programs hosted by John Daly and Walter Cronkite. In 1956, Nolan moved into PR, working for RCA's chairman and television pioneer David Sarnoff. Six years later, Nolan moved to The Chase Manhattan Bank to oversee PR and advertising. He also wrote many speeches for David Rockefeller, who was then chairman and CEO of the bank.

What people usually didn't know about Nolan contributed to his strength as a leader. Although he rarely talked about it, one summer during college, Nolan contracted polio. He spent time in an iron lung to protect his breathing, and he had to relearn the ability to speak. You would have never known it, hearing his booming, newscaster-type voice. His recovery was so successful because he did not allow himself to give up. Later, in his professional career, this attitude helped shape Nolan. He never shied away from challenge, nor was he reluctant to take chances. Instead, he always forged ahead with steady determination and committed resolve.

I respected Nolan's way of thinking and acting. Early in my career, I modeled my own professionalism after portions of his repertoire. In particular, I credited Nolan with teaching me to embrace calculated risk and to never give up. Many accomplishments in my career started from this perspective.

DOESCHER LESSON: *If you're in the communications or business world, don't be afraid to be creative. Just be smart about it. Always get proper approvals to avoid putting yourself in a compromising position. Then, within that framework of support and backing, march on boldly.*

19.
A WHITE PAPER EQUALS OPPORTUNITY

John DeGarmo, chairman of DeGarmo, Inc. advertising agency in New York City, Bill and Howard Haworth, president of Drexel Heritage Furnishings (pictured left to right) at PGA's Heritage Golf Classic tournament in Hilton Head Island, South Carolina, 1975

"A time comes when you need to stop waiting for the man you want to become and start being the man you want to be."

— Bruce Springsteen

Sometimes taking a chance on the unexpected achieves an amazing result. Because you will rarely know when a business or personal opportunity is about to come out of left field, you should always be poised and ready. Expect to be a little scared, especially if you're the kind of person who likes to plan. Allow yourself a moment of hesitation, then get over it. Always be aware. Always be open to whatever may happen. And never brush any opportunity aside. This is a mistake I almost made, and I'm lucky I didn't.

Early in my career, at age 34, I almost did not accept a bona fide job offer even though I correctly perceived it to be a solid stepping stone in my career — and, worst of all, my overall reasoning was flawed. At the time, I had moved on from my PR position at The Chase Manhattan Bank, completed a short stint at Interchemical Corporation and was working as director of corporate advertising at Champion International in New York City. Champion had purchased Drexel Heritage Furnishings, based in Drexel, North Carolina, and my boss, Allen Mackenzie, asked me to write a white paper about the newly acquired company. As part of the assignment, I also wrote a profile for what I thought would be an upcoming open position, that of vice president–advertising and public relations.

Although I was perfectly suited for the job, I had taken myself out of the competition. Why did I do this? I thought my reason was simple. I didn't want to relocate. That would have meant putting geographical distance between my young family and nearby relatives who acted as a support system for my first wife and our children, who were approximately seven and three at the time. It also would have meant disrupting the kids' security in an above-average New York school district, for an unfamiliar Southern-style community in North Carolina. I was not petrified to make the move, but I was truly a little scared. On the other hand, my first wife, the former Carol Wetmore, thought we should go.

While my rationale was straightforward, it wasn't exactly smart in the corporate world. Then, like now, it was not uncommon for people to move around, sometimes a lot, in the hope of moving up the ladder. One business associate told me he had moved 13 times in order to get to the top of the heap, where he could stay put at corporate headquarters.

What I didn't realize then was that not wanting to relocate is not a good enough reason to refuse a promotion, a bigger job title or more money. Worse yet, it just might lead to getting fired without any recourse.

So what happened in my case? The short version of the story is that I did not get fired. Instead, I reconsidered my aversion to relocating and moved to North Carolina where I took the job. Of course, the transition wasn't as direct as my retrospective summary might sound. Here is how the long version of the story unfolded. Champion International, then known as U.S. Plywood-Champion Papers Inc., had purchased Drexel for stock valued at $100 million in 1968 while I was an employee of the firm. A joint statement by the two companies noted complementary markets and a vision to broaden their distinct product bases through a combined commitment to provide furnishings and building materials for homes, institutional and educational facilities, hotels and commercial buildings.

Karl R. Bendetsen, the newly-elected CEO of the corporation, explained the rationale for the acquisition like this: "Our building materials create the space, and Drexel will help fill it."

Since I knew something about the furniture business because my father had been involved as a manufacturer's sales rep since 1929, Mackenzie asked me to visit Drexel, view its plants and talk with Drexel's executives, communications folks and U.S. customers. After conducting that research, I prepared a white paper and made recommendations about the furniture manufacturer's public relations and advertising functions.

I recommended many changes, including the hiring of a new vice president of advertising and public relations. I suggested bringing in a professional from the outside to fill the new role. In my opinion, nobody within the company had any formal training in the communications field; nor did anyone have enough on-the-job training to handle the role.

I knew what was needed to be successful in the position, but since I did not want to move to North Carolina at the time, I emphasized I was definitely not a candidate for the job. My boss said the company would do a nationwide search. Six weeks later, the search committee said they had found the perfect person for the job. It was Bill Doescher.

I hadn't expected that, but after thinking about it for a day or two, I accepted the offer and moved to North Carolina.

Even with some trepidation about uprooting my family and moving from an East Coast environment to a Southern U.S. lifestyle, taking the job turned out to be a rewarding decision. I learned new management and communication skills, and I became part of the local community. Using the pseudonym William Fredericks, I even wrote opinion pieces and special features, including one titled "The Wedding of the Decade" about a socialite's nuptials, for the local *Hickory News* weekly. I stayed on in my position at Drexel Heritage for more than seven years before moving back east to join Dun & Bradstreet, in New York City, in 1978.

During my time in North Carolina, some unexpected good things happened. I matured as a manager and had the opportunity to work on creative communications materials I developed for the first time in that position. For example, between 1976 and 1977, I managed the process of producing a nearly 200-page, four-color consumer book, *Lifestyles by Drexel Heritage,* which we sold to furniture dealers to provide to their retail customers. Many dealers wanted to be gifted the books for nothing, but I wouldn't budge. I took the position that somebody had to pay for the production and use of this slick publication. And, it wasn't going to be Drexel Heritage.

The introductory copy immediately invited the reader: "You are at the beginning of a new adventure — creating a home that is like no other — a home that reflects your very individual, very different way of life ... a home that expresses your interests and your taste, your memories of the past and your dreams for the future. Drexel Heritage hopes the scores of rooms on these pages will show you how to make your dreams come true." Photos of elegant rooms featuring furniture scenes were enhanced by decorating tips and contemporary comments written by leading U.S. interior designers.

In addition to the *Lifestyles* book, I also had the opportunity to develop branding through a new corporate identification system. This included a new logo and revamped national and retail advertising programs, product brochures, public relations campaigns and product publicity efforts. I was learning on the job, and my commitment enabled me to give the company the best communications programs and materials it had ever received.

But the greatest highlight of the job, for me, was being able to recommend and manage Drexel Heritage's involvement with the Heritage Golf Classic, held annually on Hilton Head Island, South Carolina. It was 1974, and as a former sportswriter and ongoing fan, I stayed current about many aspects of all sports. One day, I read the announcement in a local paper, that Chrysler was pulling out as a sponsor of the Heritage. I knew this would leave only Sea Pines Plantation and Delta Airlines as sponsors, and I had an idea. I immediately called Dean Berman, the PGA Commissioner, and asked if Drexel Heritage could make a presentation to replace Chrysler and become the tournament's third sponsor. Berman's answer was a conditional "yes" — he would listen to our pitch, but we had to make the presentation the next day, several states away. I went to the office of my boss, Howard Haworth, president of Drexel Heritage. Fortunately, he was excited about my spontaneous plan and agreed to fly to Florida. The next day, we made the presentation together. Soon thereafter, it was confirmed that our efforts had paid off. We got the sponsorship.

Back in North Carolina, I immediately got to work devising a total marketing and communications program to promote maximum exposure for the company through its new role as a Heritage Golf Classic sponsor. This included messages for the customers, employees, members of the furniture trades and the editorial departments of any publications near all Drexel Heritage facilities. One of my most successful promotional ideas was to award Drexel Heritage merchandise, valued at $10,000, to the pro who shot closest to the pin on the par 3, 17th hole during the final round.

For the 1975 Heritage Golf Classic — Drexel Heritage's first year of sponsorship — Jack Nicklaus, one of America's all-time great professional golfers, won the tournament and the furniture. Later, Jack called me to assist him in selecting furniture for a clubhouse that would be part of a tournament he was starting in Ohio. It would be my only furniture sale ever. Soon thereafter, arrangements were made for Jack's interior designer, from New York City, to fly to North Carolina and meet with me. As the designer proceeded to pick out everything for the order, I asked how he was able to so confidently select fabric colors without Jack's approval. The designer responded, "It won't matter; Jack is colorblind."

Throughout my involvement with the Heritage Golf Classic, something else happened. I was able to not only meet the golfers, but also interact with some of them in casual, informal ways that resulted in lasting friendships. Hale Irwin, three-time winner of the Heritage Classic, three-time U.S. Open Champion and 45-time winner on the PGA Champions Tour, was one of those golfers. We became friends and continued to stay in touch after I eventually left Drexel.

Later, in my new position at Dun & Bradstreet, Hale graciously accepted my invitation to become the D&B golfer for all customer golf events in the U.S. and Japan. That arrangement lasted eight years, and the company, Hale and I were better off because of it.

Thinking back on my hesitation to uproot my life for a new job in North Carolina, I am glad I ultimately accepted the position with Drexel Heritage. It rewarded me with many unexpected benefits and provided numerous opportunities for growth. Of course, without knowing it at the time, that Drexel Heritage job also positioned me to move to a top role at D&B, my most important corporate job ever.

DOESCHER LESSON: *The unknown may be scary, but it is not necessarily negative. Consider all the facts and all the potential opportunities before making a career decision. Saying "no" to requests by higher-ups, such as to expand responsibilities or move to a new office, could be disastrous for your career. Otherwise, be open to change — and embrace, with positivity, all of the possibilities inherent in the unknown.*

20.
REINVENTING A MAGAZINE

"A graphic designer, you know, who understands ideas and understands that ideas are what makes the world go around, could change the world with a magazine. If one talent could do it right now, everybody would stop saying it's the death of magazines."

— George Lois

While I enjoyed my work with Drexel and had built a successful career there, I always knew I would somehow find my way back to New York. Nevertheless, interviewing for a possible new job in the Big Apple, while living and working for a furniture company in North Carolina, is nearly impossible. But, somehow, I was able to pull it off.

It started with a dinner in Philadelphia. For a long time, my second wife of less than a year, Linda Blair, wanted me to meet Barbara and Howard Crane, good friends from another life. Early in 1978, our schedules aligned, and we finally made it happen in a popular restaurant in the "City of Brotherly Love." When the conversation turned to business, Howard confided that he was thinking about changing jobs and was deliberating over two senior communications positions in New York City. One was with MCI, the telephone company, and the other was with the diverse, multi-billion-dollar Dun & Bradstreet Corporation. Since he was favoring the MCI job, he wondered if I would like to take a shot at the D&B position. On the surface it made sense, since our backgrounds were very similar. Among other parallels, we had each been the sports editor of our college newspapers (Colgate and University of Miami), and we had each worked for a blue-chip company — IBM for Howard and The Chase Manhattan Bank for me. Interested, I took down the contact information for the person in charge of hiring at D&B — and the rest is history. Howard, by the way, also got the job at MCI.

When I accepted my new position — vice president–communications for D&B, Inc. — part of the job entailed publishing a less-than-sophisticated magazine called *Dun & Bradstreet Reports*.

Nobody in authority seemed concerned about the magazine's lack of quality, and I was sure no one was spending sleepless nights worrying about it. As in most multi-billion-dollar companies in the 1970s and 1980s, increases in revenue, profit and quarterly earnings per share were the top priorities — and what Wall Street and investors were interested in. Since the magazine wasn't a big part of those balance sheet items, it had largely been forgotten.

Even though I was told in the job interviews that the magazine wasn't meant to be a major part of my new job, I still had the task of fixing it. And since I would be assuming the role of the incoming publisher, I saw it as an excellent opportunity for the magazine and me to stand out in the crowd. I had read many past issues of *Dun & Bradstreet Reports* before my arrival, and I was already devising changes that would improve graphics, editorial content, advertising possibilities and readership.

I surmised I would never have the chance of becoming a top publisher with the stature of such industry legends as Arthur Ochs Sulzberger, Jr., of *The New York Times*, Katharine Graham of the *The Washington Post,* DeWitt Wallace of *Reader's Digest,* Steve Forbes of *Forbes*, or Earl (Butch) Graves of *Black Enterprise*. I also reasoned that the magazine's circulation would probably never be large enough to merit the attention of *Ad Age* or a similar publication, so competing with *Fortune* and *Businessweek* was out of the question. But I asked myself: Could I give *Inc.* and *Entrepreneur* magazines a run for their money? Yes, I thought, embracing the challenge; maybe I could.

To add to the challenge and the complexities involved with revamping this magazine, I had to deal with the reality that D&B Corporation owned Technical Publishing Company, which had more revenue and was responsible for publishing a slew of other industry-specific magazines. In addition, the more visible *Dun's Review* magazine, which was targeted toward big business leaders and advertisers, was also under D&B's umbrella. In most publishing categories, *Dun's Review* ranked fourth when stacked against *Forbes, Fortune*, and *Businessweek*, so it was already considered successful.

At some point, there was a brief internal conversation about combining *Dun's Review* and a much-improved *D&B Reports* magazine under my leadership as publisher, but that idea never went anywhere. I recommended against such a merger reasoning that *Dun's Review* readers were in the big business category and the readers of *D&B Reports* came from the small business arena. The magazines were totally different, and the combined publication would have been difficult to market and promote. I correctly sensed my reasoning was enough to end the conversation before it even got off the ground.

As the new publisher, I knew I needed to radically revamp my own D&B magazine. Staying with a format that wasn't working was not an option. I developed a plan and outlined my vision. I told anyone who would listen, including newcomers who joined our staff, that I wanted to make the publication "a real magazine." That meant it should be relevant in the readers' marketplace, whatever that ended up being.

One early decision I made was to accept advertising for the revamped magazine — but not for cigarettes or liquor. My staff wondered why. I told them I wanted the magazine to be clean and pristine. It was a choice that just felt right, and it was not motivated by any particular social stance or religious belief. While such advertising might have greatly increased revenue, I felt we had to commit to a higher standard.

As the new publisher, I assigned myself the task of reading back issues cover to cover. I familiarized myself with all aspects of the magazine to research its editorial voice. To my surprise, I discovered an alarming trend. In story after story, I found numerous typos in the back of each magazine. The editor at the time said he never bothered editing pieces placed at the back of the publication "because no one read that far." Determined to no longer tolerate such sloppiness with the new magazine, I promptly found another job for that editor.

Commitment to quality became my priority. At my first meeting with existing staff members, I wrote the following objectives on a transparency placed on an overhead projector: "Quality," "No typos" and "First Class." I said if anyone had a problem fulfilling those objectives, I would provide that person with an exit package or have the person transferred. Three people subsequently came to my office asking to be reassigned. One person was on roller skates.

I then set out to search for a talented group to join my team. I was building a lineup for success and felt confident in moving forward with the magazine. Mark Maxwell came over from *Redbook* to be our first head of advertising sales. Later, Theodore V. Herrmann, a seasoned marketing executive, joined as manager of marketing. He sold ads and supervised the magazine's staff of seven U.S. advertising representatives. Ford, Jeep and Manufacturers Hanover Trust were among our first advertisers.

Getting to work myself, I started to rebuild the magazine with a simple name change. I decided to shorten the magazine's title, while keeping the well-known D&B moniker out front. From the original magazine's launch in 1976 until when I took over as publisher, the publication had been known as *Dun & Bradstreet Reports*. However, my redesign and repositioning allowed it to be elegantly reborn in 1980 as *D&B Reports*.

In keeping with the sleek new name, the magazine's visual form also underwent a transformation. What had previously looked like a holdover from the 1950s suddenly lost its stilted look. The new *D&B Reports*, instead, epitomized a clean, branded look, focused by the optimism of the current times.

Equally important to these formal changes, I continued to work on creating a new team. This was essential, not only to clean up the magazine, but also to invest the project with fresh energy and unconventional ideas. Following a nationwide search, I eventually hired Patricia W. Hamilton as the new editor. I immediately liked her writing, editing and proofreading acumen, as well as her smart thoughts about how to revive a tired magazine. With a master's degree and teaching certificate from Columbia University, Pat was a former English teacher who spoke her mind and knew her craft better than most anyone I knew. It didn't matter that she had never worked in a corporate setting or had a fancy job title. The important thing was that she knew her stuff and she could approach the magazine, not only from the inside out, but also, from the outside in. She could approach the magazine as both an editor and a reader, and I was convinced she could do the job.

Certainly, there were other candidates who looked better on paper than Pat. They had impressive career histories involving big-name organizations. But when I observed and listened to them in the one-on-one interviews, something was missing in their personalities. So I did what I have always done: I followed my instinct and hired the person, not the resume. And it turned out to be a very wise decision because Pat never disappointed me. Pat also had a gift of being able to identify talent to meet our needs, and she recruited a renowned proofreader — Mary Grace, of *Fortune* — to join us.

At the same time I brought Pat on board, I reached out to Ken Resen, a graphic designer whom I knew through successful collaborations at two different companies. I was confident with Ken's work and asked him to become the magazine's art director. His first task was to totally revamp the magazine's design. As a Yale School of Design grad and a principal of the design firm, Page, Arbitro & Resen, Ken was excellent. His graphic work was creative and distinct, yet it always felt cohesive with the magazine's textual components. Ken always read the entire copy before doing the design, which was not always the case with other professional graphic designers. But more than that, Ken actually read the copy carefully enough to be able to make comments about it. He was one of the only graphic designers I knew at the time who worked this way.

Ken was the right person for the job because he blended a corporate style with imagination in ways that I liked and could believe in. Since I had known him and worked with him since 1965, we had achieved a level of trust that's hard to find and almost impossible to buy. I always gave him the freedom to do the designs "the Doescher way," which was really his way. However, this was not a problem because Ken always knew the look I wanted to achieve, even when I couldn't describe it. As our professional relationship at D&B continued, Ken's role grew to include being the designer of the more than 35 annual reports I produced over the years.

There were other professionals involved with the magazine's publication. To keep our budgets, finances and personnel responsibilities in proper order, we relied on John Pemrick, a D&B veteran with many years of dedicated service, and Virginia Simone. Virginia wore the additional hat of circulation manager. Their administrative titles never seemed to match up with the work they actually did because I usually involved them in all aspects of the magazine's process. Listening to their advice and counsel was the easiest part of my job as publisher. They were honest, forthright, downright terrific and always available.

That first full year, 1980, was tentative but exciting for *D&B Reports*. The magazine was my baby, but it certainly had a lot of very involved aunts and uncles. Because I had hired a great editorial team, I was able to step back and let my professionals do their jobs. I never played boss. Together, we all knew what had to be done, and we each knew how to accomplish it.

The first edition of the new magazine, which came out in the spring of 1979 after I joined the company in December 1978, had already succeeded in improving the magazine's look and in eliminating typos and errors. I knew we were definitely headed in the right direction.

However, to really make the magazine take off, I knew it had to be more relevant to readers. The first step in achieving this was to observe and listen. I was confident our subscribers and the world would provide the answers we needed to develop our niche.

We started our research by sending out a subscriber survey at the start of 1980. The importance of the small business market became abundantly clear to us when we received feedback from that mailing. The survey identified our typical reader as a principal in a company with $8.9 million in sales and 85 employees.

With this information in hand, we knew we were on to something. If we tailored content to small business management, we could uniquely service this market in ways that larger publications were not able to do. As Pat contemporaneously told Phil Dougherty, advertising columnist for *The New York Times,* we decided to become "a service magazine for small business management." It proved to be the right decision as it allowed us to align our editorial direction with the biggest thing to happen in the U.S. economy since the end of World War II: the entrepreneurial explosion.

To further improve on our early success and cultivate continued momentum, I hired Stephen J. Witt, a fellow Colgate alum and former chairman of Albert Frank-Guenther Law agency. The firm was the oldest combined advertising and public relations firm in the country at the time, and Steve was brought on board to provide his creative thoughts four times a month, as well as to help with advertising. We agreed on that arrangement with a handshake at a Colgate University President's Club gala at the Waldorf Astoria in Manhattan. Steve had just completed a turnaround of the AFGL firm where he had worked for eight years. Most importantly, for both of us, he believed in my vision for the magazine.

My staff and I always had fun putting out the magazine, and circulation eventually reached 75,000 subscribers. It never seemed like work. None of us hesitated to come in early, stay late or work weekends when the magazine was involved. We felt like entrepreneurs ourselves, writing about other entrepreneurs.

For all of us at *D&B Reports*, what made the small business sector so fascinating was the way that it mirrored changes in the economic and social life of the country. Those changes included extraordinary growth in businesses formed by women, the internationalization of local economies and the ascendance of the personal computer and digital technology.

The owners of small companies were a pleasure to write about. We enjoyed learning about their opportunities and problems in the small business marketplace, and we brought in an outstanding stable of writers to craft meaningful stories about them.

A chance meeting with Jim Howard, a communications professional from the Nixon administration, was one of the first additions to our lineup of writers. I encountered Jim at a business conference in Tarrytown, New York, led by a long-time friend, Dale Everett from Utica. Bob Steck, a Washington speechwriter who often penned prose for sitting U.S. presidents, was next. Soon we added Steve Rothman, with his Master of Science degree from the Columbia Journalism School and witty writing style, to the masthead. Then we found Kevin McDermott, a tireless and capable writer, who eventually became the magazine's managing editor in the early 1990s. Joe Duncan, D&B's vice president, corporate economist and chief statistician, checked in regularly with a report on the economy, which he wrote himself.

Carol Riggs, a holdover from the original magazine and an unabashed New York Yankees fan, was our own "utility infielder." She handled any assignment we gave her and pitched one interesting idea after another. Reid Gearhart, who handled PR assignments at D&B and edited the internal magazine *D&B News*, frequently contributed stories for us as well. His pieces were especially passionate because they often covered his favorite subjects. One memorable story was about a tugboat company located in New York City that he engaged for an extended trip.

Pat and I also did our share of writing for the magazine. Pat capably balanced her own reporting with editing and handing out assignments. My favorite stories from her were insightful pieces about doing business in Russia, written after Pat's participation in a learning trip there, with 18 fellow journalists and small business owners. The group was assembled by the Alliance of American and Russian Women, and the participants stayed in touch for a number of years after the trip.

One of the highlights of the annual editorial calendar was working closely with Jim Howard on the magazine's coverage of the "Small Business of the Year" winners, as chosen by the Small Business Administration, in Washington, D.C. My favorite winner was an early one — the Vermont Teddy Bear Company of Shelburne, Vermont. Founded in 1981 by John Sortino, this business grew to become one of the largest sellers of teddy bears by mail and online. It now produces almost 500,000 teddy bears each year, and I have purchased many for my family.

In exploring the world of the small business owner, I was delighted to discover that some of my boyhood friends had become successful in unique and entrepreneurial ways. Don and Sharon Oberriter were knocking it out of the park with their Cooperstown Bat Company. John Ligas had overcome his battle with the Guillain-Barre Syndrome to become the CEO of a burgeoning building supply company in Utica. Dick Scala left a senior marketing job at Xerox Corporation to become president and CEO of a small business that manufactured home products. Dick salvaged the business, which was based in New Jersey and eventually sold it with a sizeable profit for investors.

I have many fond memories as publisher of the magazine and of researching the stories I personally wrote, including a piece about the personal computer explosion. In large measure, the story focused on Dan Fylstra, the founder of a small company called VisiCorp, which made the PC a useful tool for small business owners. His $200 software program, VisiCalc, harnessed the power of an Apple computer to perform a task that even mainframes couldn't handle: spreadsheets. Soon even the smallest offices were finding a place for at least one PC, where typewriters had previously been.

In 1994, Dun & Bradstreet decided to exit the magazine publishing business for good and refocus energy on its core businesses. In my column as publisher for that final issue, I reflected: "Publishing *D&B Reports* was a wonderful opportunity for all of us to acquire a continuing education in economics and society. We received a kind of MBA by osmosis, and we had the country's small business owners to teach us."

DOESCHER LESSON: *Having the right knowledge and making good decisions depends on being able to ask questions, observe and listen. Being relevant in business is not only about "what I can do for you." It is also about recognizing "what you need from me."*

21.
Hire Jack; He's Your Man

"A CCO must have an in-depth grasp of the business, good critical thinking skills and the ability to use communications to help further the organization's success. Judgment and ethics remain the keystone."

— Bill Heyman, President and CEO, Heyman Associates, from the August 2012 edition of *PRWeek*

There are many ways to find the perfect person for a specific senior-level PR job, such as chief communications officer. One straightforward approach is to consult a professional executive search firm, such as Bill Heyman's Heyman Associates, that is well versed in the business and the people in it.

However, you don't always need such a formal process to find the right candidate. Sometimes, as happened with my own introduction to D&B, it is the result of a personal approach.

A secret weapon that I have used many times is the old trick of asking my friends. It's simple, but effective. This method has worked for me, no matter which side of the equation I've been on.

In 1966 I was employed for a short time at Interchemical Corporation following my 3 ½-year stint in the public relations department at The Chase Manhattan

Bank. But that would soon change. I was fortunate enough to be the focus of a friend's recommendation which resulted in an invitation to join the public relations department of the U.S. Plywood Corporation.

U.S. Plywood's Wynn Moseley, soon to be my boss, asked his cousin, Terry Robards, a business writer for the *New York Herald Tribune*, if he knew anyone who might qualify for the position of manager of editorial services. Terry's answer was Bill Doescher, and I got the job. I had originally met Terry through my PR position at The Chase Manhattan Bank, when I was assigned to speak with him and supply information for the business stories he was writing.

Fast forward to almost 20 years later, to the days following the 1984 acquisition of AC Nielsen by Dun & Bradstreet. I was a corporate vice president with an emphasis on communications, as well as the publisher of *D&B Reports* magazine. Suddenly I was also put in charge of handling much of the public relations matters for Nielsen Media Research. My plate was already full, and as one person I could not reasonably handle all the work for several jobs at the same time — at least not effectively and successfully.

Constant calls about Nielsen Media Research from *The New York Times* and *The Wall Street Journal,* plus inquiries related to features in trade publications such as *Broadcasting Magazine* and *Television/Radio Age,* told me the new Nielsen responsibilities were most likely a full-time position. I quickly decided I needed to hire a real pro, savvy with television and communications experience, for Nielsen Media Research. And I needed to do it fast!

Before engaging an executive search firm, I took a shot at the old school method. I surveyed friends in the industry, and I asked my golfing buddies if they knew anyone with the kind of talent I was seeking.

One of my friends claimed to know someone, and he was convinced that candidate would be perfect for the job. Scott Robb, a lawyer and a regular golfing partner at the Scarsdale Golf Club, in Westchester County, New York, was not shy about his recommendation.

"Hire Jack Loftus, he's your man," Scott said.

I remember I had casually met Jack, but I neither knew him well nor was familiar with his background — which turned out to be considerable. By way of introduction, I learned that Jack had been vice president–communications at Madison Square Garden and was the editor of a major television magazine. The magazine role provided him with valuable behind-the-scenes information and insight into what was right and wrong with the industry. I scheduled an interview, and Jack convinced me he knew as much, if not more, about the TV industry than anyone whom I had previously met.

His future bosses agreed, and Jack was hired. As soon as Jack took over Nielsen's communications, and throughout his career, he was often praised by the executives in charge. These included John Dimling, the broadcasting- and media-savvy president and CEO of Nielsen Media Research; Bill Jacobi, executive VP of D&B and Chairman of Nielsen Media Research; and Jack Holt, executive VP of D&B responsible for all of Nielsen. On more than one occasion, each of these men thanked me for finding Jack for the company.

Almost from his first day on the job, Jack, the forever optimist, imbued the place with a sense of calm and a professionalism that heretofore had been missing. He knew those tantalizing TV media folks as well, if not better, than his new bosses and was capable of "talking the talk" with them. Over a brief period of time, Jack was able to successfully convince the reporters that Nielsen TV ratings were fair, honest and backed with quality data, as they reported on stories involving Nielsen.

In addition to the press relations function of his new communications job, Jack counseled management on issues related to the industry, prepared press releases and wrote press comments and speeches for his bosses. He even brought members of the press to the data gathering facility in Dunedin, Florida, for tours and observation visits. This transparency furthered Loftus's reasoning about Nielsen Media's data quality. He was a consummate pro, and seemingly every top Nielsen manager relied on him for communications and marketing advice at one time or another.

After I got to know Jack better, I learned he was an outstanding women's soccer coach for an amateur

Westchester County team. Players in the league knew him as a tough, but fair, coach — just like his modus operandi at Nielsen. There's no question that Jack Loftus was a prize. From the moment of his arrival, the powers-that-be knew the strength of his capabilities and encouraged him to develop a long career there. Jack was promoted to handle communications for all of Nielsen, including Nielsen Marketing Research. He eventually retired as senior VP and chief communications officer for The Nielsen Company.

I remember feeling tremendous relief as soon as Jack came on board. Without hesitation, I could go back to my primary jobs and leave Nielsen Media Research in Jack's capable hands. As executive recruitment goes, and using baseball terminology, it was an 18-year-long grand slam for everyone.

DOESCHER LESSON: *Finding an important person for a professional team is strategic and clever — and should benefit the whole team. Without such a move, stress, disorder and inefficiency could erupt. So, don't wait; hiring the right person to save your sanity or your job is the smart thing to do.*

22.
A CANDID LEADER

"Truth-and-trust leadership is one of those things in life that is greater than the sum of its parts."

— from *The Real-Life MBA: Your No-BS Guide to Winning the Game, Building a Team, and Growing Your Career*, by Jack and Suzy Welch

The leader of Champion International from 1974–1996, Andy Sigler was a good-guy CEO with strong opinions and a management style that didn't always please Wall Street or the politicians in Washington, D.C. But his leadership as one of corporate America's nonconformists must have pleased the board of directors of Champion International as he held the position of chief from 1974 to 1996.

Moreover, astute investors like Warren Buffett, Laurence Tisch and John Templeton invested in Champion when Sigler was the CEO. According to an article in the May 11, 1992, issue of *Forbes* magazine, "In 1989 Buffett bought $300 million worth of 9.25 percent preferred, convertible into common at $38 a share. Starting in 1990 Tisch's Loews Corporation accumulated 16 percent of Champion common, and Templeton owns 1.4 percent."

I liked Andy from our very first meeting and admired his management style. He was pleasant and casual, except when it came to making decisions, criticizing corporate raiders, challenging institutional investors or speaking to Congress. He was an outspoken proponent of long-term planning, and he never veered from that path.

In an article in *The New York Times* on August 12, 1984, he said, "To think you can run a company by concentrating on the next quarter's results is lunacy." Most CEOs at that time stayed away from that controversy. In the same article, he said, "I think any policy that puts the welfare of employees below a bunch of institutional investors is crazy."

Andy and I first met when U.S. Plywood Corporation of New York City and Champion Papers Inc. of Hamilton, Ohio, merged in 1967, and some of the executives and corporate communications folks from both sides got together at 777 Third Avenue in New York City to strategize for the future. Other such meetings were later held at Champion's headquarters in Hamilton, Ohio.

I had the title of director of corporate advertising, which meant many things like writing, producing the annual report and advertising. I was mostly a listener in those early introductory conversations. Nothing of substance was agreed upon at those meetings, but as the saying goes, "It's better to know the enemy than to not know the enemy."

Sigler, a Champion guy, and I, a Plywood guy, established a solid business relationship and easy way of communicating with one another that lasted until I left Drexel Heritage Furnishings, which was then part of Champion International, for Dun & Bradstreet in 1978.

Earlier, Andy was my point of contact when I had to pull the company's annual report off the press, for the second year in a row, because of defects in the Champion paper at Young & Klein printers in Cincinnati, Ohio. He said, "If you and the Champion tech consultant say the paper is bad, pull it. I'm not coming over there to inspect it."

In 1967, the two CEOs from the merged companies, Karl R. Bendetsen of Champion and Gene C. Brewer of U.S. Plywood, vowed to work together and share the leadership of the new company at least in the merger press release, but it didn't work out — not even on the surface. Bendetsen soon became the Chairman & CEO of U.S. Plywood-Champion Papers Inc., and Brewer, who was president of the merged company, resigned.

Bob Hart of Champion and Allen Mackenzie of Plywood, the public affairs and communications heads of their respective companies before the merger, were among a few of the new company's executives who managed to get along and successfully led the communications function jointly. Others seemed to be vying for key positions on the executive committee. Mackenzie eventually became the president of the Furnishings Group, which included Drexel Heritage Furnishings, Birmingham Ornamental Iron and Trend carpets.

Edward Russell, Jr., vice president-marketing services for Champion for over 20 years, didn't become involved with the corporate affairs efforts as had been suspected, and he continued to promote Champion's products among art directors and graphic designers while providing merchants with an effective marketing tool. His successful "Imagination Series" books, which targeted the design community to stunningly showcase creative uses of paper, was legendary.

The name of the company was changed to Champion International in 1972, and that same year Thomas F. Willers, a former top executive of Hooker Chemical and Occidental Petroleum, was brought in to be president and possible successor to Bendetsen as chairman.

Willers did indeed become chairman and chief executive, but in 1974, citing policy disagreements with the board, he resigned. Although Bendetsen was no longer on the board, he didn't like the changes Willers was making and recommended Sigler, then 42, for the position of CEO.

Sigler's career at Champion was long. He started with the company after graduating from the Dartmouth College Amos Tuck Business School in 1956. From then on, he assumed increasingly important positions until his retirement in 1996.

As chairman and CEO of Champion and as chairman of The Business Roundtable's Task Force on Corporate Responsibility, he always let his thoughts be known. He testified before the Senate Committee on Banking, Housing, and Urban Affairs in the U.S. Senate, as well as to the House Energy and Commerce Committee of the 99th Congress, and other places where he felt people needed to listen. He never sugarcoated his remarks, and sometimes they weren't well received.

According to a relatively recent *Fortune* magazine, in a "Where are they now?" article, he was labeled "a critic of hostile takeovers and institutional shareholders and a target for his relatively high compensation." Quoted in the article, he said, "When I retired, I did not want to be around old guys who tell you how important they used to be."

True to his word, Sigler headed to Vermont with his wife Margaret (Peg) Romefelt. They met in high school, in Ridgewood, New Jersey, when he was captain of the football team and she was a cheerleader. In 2000, after settling into Vermont, the Siglers started a small dairy farm there. They also bought land in New Hampshire to build a private golf course called Montcalm. In 2016, the couple donated a portion of the dairy farm, leading an effort to expand agricultural education and dairy-production training in Vermont.

DOESCHER LESSON: *Being a leader, in part, means having the determination to speak out and take action.*

23.
WHAT THE CEO WANTS

Bill with the "Live at Five," WNBC-TV, New York, anchors Jack Cafferty and Sue Simmons, being interviewed about the economy, 1986

"The senior executive of a company charged with overall strategy and responsible to the board of directors for business performance."

— Definition of a chief executive officer, from Financial Times Lexicon

No matter the leadership or size of the company, any reputable chief communications officer will have to determine what the chief executive officer wants. What I learned from my own career is that the relationship between the CCO and the CEO begins and ends with trust. Of course, the CEO will expect the CCO to be an astute manager of people, an excellent writer across various media, a savvy editor and an expert in current technologies. Additionally, the CCO should be able to anticipate and react to the ever-changing dynamics influencing business, society and the company's established business model.

But getting back to core values — if you start with trust, you are off to a good start with any CEO.

In my career, I have paid attention to the observations and experiences of others, which has helped shape my perspectives. Dick Martin, who spent 32 years at AT&T and eventually became the corporation's top communicator, provides some of the best advice. His astute observation was this: "If your chemistry with the CEO is bad, you can be a combination of Peter Drucker, Mother Teresa and Jack Welch, but you'll be passed over."

He's right.

During my 22 years at Dun & Bradstreet I worked for seven CEOs, corporate and divisional. Although they represented different personalities and leaderships styles, one priority remained consistent — I made sure to develop a good relationship with each of them. I saw this as indisputable and necessary to achieve effectiveness in my job and success in my career.

Martin's wisdom informs his advice. Delving into specifics, he said: "Assuming the personal chemistry is right,

CEOs look for three things in a PR counselor: judgment based on deep business knowledge rather than political correctness; creativity applied to solving business problems rather than crafting nifty slogans or dreaming up cheap publicity stunts; and the integrity to stand for what is right even at a high personal cost."

Particularly useful, Martin reminds any CCO of two tenets of success. First, always strive to make your boss look good. Second, surround yourself with good people who compensate for your weaknesses. I have found both to be excellent statements of guidance, which I have followed and shared with colleagues and mentees, throughout my career. Likewise, the straightforward perspective of Bob Dilenschneider, president of The Dilenschneider Group, is equally instructive. According to Dilenschneider, a good CCO brings integrity to his or her position: "Honesty and candor are the top two expectations. The CEO also wants a sense of what is happening in the marketplace. After this, the CEO looks for a strategy that is consistent with the company's business strategy."

To consider the opinions of another industry great, we can look to Harold Burson, the founder of Burson-Marsteller and a PR legend. Going further to characterize the relationship between the CEO and the CCO, Burson describes a sensitive collaboration in which the CCO can act as a thermometer for decision-making. Burson said: "CEOs increasingly are looking to their senior PR officers for advice and counsel. They expect them to be sensors of social change, to be prepared for changes in societal expectations and for programs that fulfill the company's obligation to society. Communications and media relations are one part of the mix; the other is providing input for policy and management decisions."

In providing such input, I have learned it is never smart to play politics. Usually, such games will bring heartache and may sometimes cause dismissal. In order to stay informed about trends, happenings and energies operating within the larger playing field, a CCO must become familiar with opposing groups' theories, ideas, successes and failures. When bringing this knowledge to the CEO, I recommend asking for a private meeting to state your researched case and strategize appropriate ideas. Be polite and straightforward. Never raise your voice. It's never a good idea to openly attack a CEO's policies or management decisions, unless you are absolutely convinced it would be extremely detrimental to the company if you did not speak up. Even then, find a way to respectfully argue your position and back up everything you say with solid evidence or data.

The critical role that communications executives play in delivering informed reality checks has been recognized by modern PR leaders. Gary Grates, principal of W2O Group, addressed this important function of the CCO with regard to complex business decisions. "The CEO must be able to rely on truthful, proactive, strategic and sophisticated PR counsel; there is no room for selective storytelling or reactivity. Nor can PR practitioners operate in a vacuum, sending messages and materials without regard to the corporate strategy, direction or situation.

"PR executives must provide a constant reality check. PR counsel must be present at the leadership table as critical decisions are made so that the impact of such agreements on a company's constituents can be factored in. Communications executives can factor in how best to communicate decisions. Given the complexities of the global business environment, today's CEO should expect nothing less."

I learned early on that you are not doing the CEO any favors by not speaking up, by not stating your opinions and by not providing a battle plan for success. Actually, it's all part of your job.

Bill Heyman, president & CEO of Heyman Associates, agrees. He described how a CCO's multi-faceted viewpoint can inform strategies for direction, as well as create messaging to best support the CEO and his or her goals. Heyman said: "CEOs are ultimately the chief spokespersons for their organizations. ... PR leaders can help those executives and their organizations achieve their goals and do the right things."

This may be easier said than done during critical transitions or episodes of negative feedback from the marketplace. However, it is precisely in those times of stress that a CCO will show his or her true value.

Ron Culp, program director of public relations and advertising at DePaul University's College of

Communication, knows this, and remarked: "CEOs sometimes expect the impossible when it comes to communications although they are more realistic than they outwardly appear. They desire positive media and analyst coverage. When news is not good, they expect investor relations and public relations staffs to help present the company's side of the story — buying time as the organization sorts through the issues. CEOs will not long work with IR and PR executives who are not media and analyst savvy."

Reflecting on my corporate roles, I always knew it was important to use honesty and candor when talking to my CEOs. "You're always the CEO, but you're not always right," I would often say. "So please listen to my ideas, and if you disagree with them, we'll obviously go with your direction."

My batting average with that approach was pretty good. More importantly, I never got fired.

Sometimes, my CEOs would take the time to show their appreciation. Other times, my dedication and achievements were expected with the job. One event stands out as the best response I have ever received from a CEO. It occurred after a special week of carefully orchestrated activities centered around The Dun & Bradstreet Corporation's 150th Anniversary Celebration in Tokyo, Japan, in March 1991. The week of festivities included events for the press, investors, customers, employees, as well as a special reception featuring dignitaries like Helmut Schmidt, former chancellor of The Federal Republic of Germany;

Yukiharu Kodama, administrative vice minister of Japan's Ministry of International Trade and Industry (MITI); and Charles W. Moritz, chairman and chief executive officer of The Dun & Bradstreet Corporation.

After the anniversary gala had concluded and Moritz and I were preparing to return to the U.S., he turned to me at the Narita airport and said, "Bill, I just want you to know that all the events this week, down to the last table setting, were flawless. Congratulations!"

I wish I had that comment on tape.

DOESCHER LESSON: *By definition, the CEO is always right.... It's your job to make sure that he or she actually is.*

24.
ADMIRATION BY THE DOZEN

Meeting guests at the Jackie Robinson Foundation charity golf event in Montclair, New Jersey. Pictured left to right: David Nolan, of JPMorgan Chase; Rachel Robinson, founder of JRF and widow of Jackie Robinson; and Bill, 2004

"I have always admired men and women who used their talents to serve the community, and who were highly respected and admired for their efforts and sacrifices, even though they held no office whatsoever in government or society."

— Nelson Mandela

Throughout my life, I've been an observer of people. Curious and interested, I've never had a problem striking up a spirited conversation with a friend or a stranger. I appreciate the variety of people I've met and have always believed everyone's story is worthwhile.

I believe it's important to learn from others and emulate good examples. It motivates me to explore beyond my comfort zone, inspire goal-oriented self-improvement, break free from perceived limitations and achieve more.

As an exercise, I recommend reflecting on people you respect and admire to create a blueprint of traits and behaviors you wish to develop within yourself. With the exception of close friends and relatives, here is my list of 12 people whom I have personally met along the way and whom I most admire. They come from interactions experienced in my long business career, my volunteer work in the non-profit and collegiate worlds, my activity in religious groups and my personal outreach to people.

My slate of "12 Most Admired" consists of unique individuals who stand out because of distinct characteristics — such as striking skills and accomplishments, exceptional creativity and drive, courageous personal qualities or resounding leadership. Having had the distinct pleasure of personally meeting each of these individuals, I would be pleased for at least one more opportunity to sit down with any of them to discuss a plethora of subjects over lunch.

They appear in alphabetical order:

1. Jeff Bezos (b. 1964)
Founder, chairman and CEO of Amazon

I personally met Jeff Bezos at a 2013 event at the Westchester Country Club, when Jeff's brother Mark Bezos was being honored with the "Open Door Award for Community Service," presented by Scarsdale Edgemont Family Counseling Service. Recognized as the world's richest man, with a purported net worth of $158 billion, Jeff was joyfully videotaping his brother's award ceremony — just like a regular guy. The Princeton graduate is a former Wall Street computer engineer who created Amazon in 1994. Originally started to sell books online, Amazon now sells an unbeatable volume of diverse products, millions of which are purveyed by third-party vendors. But more than just achieving such unbelievable growth, Amazon has succeeded in a total overhaul of the consumer marketplace and the consumer experience. In 2018, *Forbes* magazine described Jeff as "America's most innovative and feared business leader." In that same story, Jeff described how he leveraged new technology to promote his company's success yet remained true to tradition: "We're in the midst of a gigantic transition, where customers have incredible power as a result of transparency and word of mouth. It used to be that if you made a customer happy, they would tell five friends. Now with the megaphone of the internet, whether online customer reviews or social media, they can tell 5,000 friends." I admire Jeff Bezos for a lot of reasons but mainly because he is an absolute genius. He has turned consumers' behaviors upside down simply by changing their purchasing experiences on a grand scale. Leaders in commerce today feel threatened by Jeff's brilliance and are afraid of what he might do next. One of those startling surprises was Jeff's decision to buy *The Washington Post.* I am envious of that purchase because I wish I had his money and bought the paper myself. I am sure the late former publisher Katharine Graham, with whom I had a number of stimulating and intelligent conversations, would be pleased with Jeff's purchase.

2. Harold Burson (b. 1921)
   Co-founder of Burson-Marsteller, one of the world's largest public relations firms

I admire Harold Burson for the major role he played in transforming the practice of public relations from a cottage industry into a global enterprise. His book, *The Business of Persuasion*, has become a virtual bible for the industry. As a result of his accomplishments and influence, Harold has been recognized by legions of PR leaders, corporate executives and even some former U.S. presidents. I, too, have been a huge fan for as long as I can remember, and I proudly claim Harold as one of my important mentors. One of his lessons, repeated in his book, is classic Harold: "You have two eyes, two ears, and only one mouth for a reason. If you look and listen twice as much as you speak, you will learn more than you would otherwise." A few years ago, City College in New York City invited Harold to be a featured guest at one of its "Lunch with Leaders" events, and I was invited to listen in. Sitting with Lynn Appelbaum, professor of advertising and public relations at CCNY, and John L. Paluszek, senior counselor at Ketchum Public Relations, I had the distinct opportunity to once again listen to Harold's personal wisdom. For approximately 90 minutes, he talked non-stop about his career, the PR industry and life. He spoke extemporaneously without notes and offered many meaningful takeaways for the students and everyone else who was listening. I admire Harold because ... well ... he's Harold — a legend in the PR field, unassuming, straightforward in his talk, honest and proud of the alumni who have, over the years, worked at Burson-Marsteller. If you can believe it, he counts them all as his friends and vice versa. His biggest admiration, however, is saved for his late wife, Bette. They were married for 63 years, and appropriately for him she's still No. 1 in his life.

3. Rebecca Chopp (b. 1952)
   Chancellor of the University of Denver, past president of Swarthmore College and Colgate University, former dean and Titus Street Professor of Theology at the Yale Divinity School and a religion scholar

Simply put, Dr. Rebecca Chopp is, in my opinion, the best president Colgate University has had in my lifetime. I base my assessment on looking at the office from both the inside and from afar. Rebecca broke a gender barrier to become Colgate's first female president, and she has been the only woman to hold that position at Colgate to date. More than that, Rebecca has expanded her achievement by the quality of her work. She has consistently demonstrated the vision, management skills, intelligence, personality, wherewithal and guts to lead and manage periods of change at various educational institutions. Rebecca's work has left a lasting impact wherever she has been, and all of the institutions she has served have become better as a result of her leadership. In particular, I admire Rebecca's commitment to sustainable progress as a way of safeguarding academic and creative success for generations of student experiences. I say all of this as a Colgate graduate, scholarship donor, former alumni corporation trustee and a Maroon Citation award winner.

4. Ernie Davis (1939–1963)
   A football player at Syracuse University and the 1961 Heisman Trophy winner

Ernie Davis was the first African-American to win football's Heisman Trophy in 1961. I met him when he played college football for Syracuse University at the same time I attended graduate school there. In 1962, Ernie was the first pick of the NFL draft and the first black athlete to be chosen overall by the NFL. A promising career appeared to be ahead of him, but tragically Ernie never played a game. He became sick with leukemia and died at the age of 23. Not forgotten, a statue on campus honors him, No. 44, and the football field in the Carrier Dome has been appropriately named the "Ernie Davis Legends Field." Ernie's legacy continues to inspire young athletes today. In addition to his achievements with the Heisman and NFL draft, Ernie was first a three-time All-American halfback who, as a sophomore, led Syracuse to the national football championship. In 1979, he was posthumously inducted into the College Hall of Fame. However, to me, Ernie was more than just a star athlete. He was a pal and a consummate role model. He did not allow prejudice to stop him from pursuing his dreams. Before he succeeded in challenging racial bias on the football field, he boldly became the first African-American man to join Sigma Alpha Mu, a nationally-recognized fraternity that was initially comprised of Jews. I first became aware of the star player named Ernie Davis when I was a sportswriter for Binghamton's *The Evening Press*. At that time, Ernie was earning All-American honors in high school basketball and football in his nearby hometown of Elmira, New York. Later, Ernie and I became further acquainted in the journalism library at Syracuse. Most weekday mornings we, the M.S. candidate in public relations and the college football star, would share a copy of *The New York Times* and engage in conversations that followed the news.

5. Harrington (Duke) Drake (1919–2016)
   Former chairman and CEO of The Dun & Bradstreet Corporation (1975–85) and former chairman of the board of trustees at Colgate University (1979–85)

Always adhering to high moral standards, Duke Drake liked to be thought of as a "man's man." He cultivated the image of a "boy scout" with strong and resourceful leadership skills. Because I had the pleasure of working with him, I benefitted from his commitment to high goals and his incomparable ability to commandeer team spirit. Duke's "pep cheers" were legendary and never failed to stir energy. His successful initiatives garnered him numerous accolades and awards, including "One of the Great American Business Leaders of the 20th Century" by Harvard Business School, in 1984, and The Ernest T. Stewart Award, presented by the U.S. Secretary of Education, as the highest award granted by Council for Advancement and Support of Education, in 1983. Duke was passionate about giving back. He encouraged by example, such as championing D&B's forward-thinking adoption of a 4-to-1 matching gifts program to support and reward generosity. I admire Duke as an exemplary leader.

6. Jon C. Iwata (b. 1962)
Retired senior vice president and chief brand officer of IBM Corporation; IBM senior advisor and executive fellow at Yale School of Management

After nine years of overseeing marketing and communications for IBM, Jon Iwata shifted his focus to the stewardship of the IBM brand and to the positioning of IBM as a global-agenda-setter. This succeeded in shaping the company's dialogue with the world. Jon's tenure as marketing and communications SVP positioned him as one of the first communications executives to lead an integrated function, still something of a rarity. Jon was the architect of several of innovative IBM brands, including Smarter Planet and Watson. I first met Jon at "The Seminar" conference in California when he was an up-and-coming young man in the PR field. At first, he seemed laid back, and he listened. As time went on, however, he began to speak up, and the audience, including senior PR folks, paid attention. All of us knew then that Jon was a PR star in the making. Since that time, as Jon has become established as a leader in his field, many professional groups have honored him. The Arthur W. Page Society, of which I am a member, presented Jon with its lifetime achievement Hall of Fame Award. But no matter how distinguished the awards became or how busy Jon was, he always made time for the people who needed him — his staff, industry peers, students and me. Jon's generosity is real, and his willingness to share knowledge and encouragement have never faltered. This is part of the reason I selected him as one of my twelve most admired. One time, at my request, Jon gave me an impromptu "postgraduate course" on the subject of social media. Our 100-minute session was authoritative and enlightening, and despite taxing the patience of employees waiting for an audience with their boss, Jon never made me feel rushed. A true gentleman, Jon's manners are exemplary, and his respectful interaction with people stands out.

7. John McCain (1936–2018)
War Hero, American patriot, Arizona senator, two-time presidential candidate

Senator John McCain was a maverick Republican and a national hero. He loved family and country, and he could be outspoken in his staunch defense of the Constitution and Bill of Rights, including the First Amendment's protection of free speech. Senator McCain's death from terminal brain cancer at the age of 81 riddled the nation. I recall watching his emotional funeral on TV and being struck with an overwhelming sense of grief. Senator McCain served America with distinction, virtue and a firm commitment to bipartisanship. He was honorable and set an example of higher purpose. He was a fierce advocate for country over politics. I had the privilege of meeting Senator McCain and his wife, Cindy, in the mid-1990s. I was representing Dun & Bradstreet at a gathering of 16 Republican senators and a collection of corporate folks in Williamsburg, Virginia. The event had been organized by the government affairs offices of various companies and was intended to better the relationship between government and business. Suddenly, on the back porch of a Colonial-era house, I encountered Senator McCain. I introduced myself, and we shook hands. The senator graciously replied that he already knew much about me and my company, which he proceeded to explain. As always, he was well prepared, and I was very impressed.

8. Rachel Robinson (b. 1922)
Former registered nurse and professor; widow of baseball icon Jackie Robinson; and founder of the Jackie Robinson Foundation

In 1973, Rachel Robinson founded the Jackie Robinson Foundation, a nonprofit organization focused around the mission of providing college scholarships and leadership training to minority students. I have been proud to have served on the JRF board of directors for over 20 years. Throughout her life, Rachel has been a crusader for opportunity through education, and I admire her for this. She has engaged leaders in corporate America, and others, to support the Foundation's efforts to cultivate talented future leaders and to provide a path for young people to fulfill their dreams by obtaining a college education. When Rachel speaks, she inspires. Scholars, executives and bystanders all listen intently. Everyone knows from history that Rachel's husband, Jackie Robinson, broke the color barrier in Major League Baseball in 1947, when he became the first black man to play for an MLB team, the Brooklyn Dodgers. Rachel lived that moment with her husband — and many others. She was always by Jackie's side during the struggles and challenges that preceded Jackie's acceptance into the MLB and which continued, in more subtle ways, afterward. In addition to supporting her husband, Rachel is a star in her own right. Her work in education and civil rights has earned her numerous awards, including the Candace Award for Distinguished Service from the National Coalition of 100 Black Women, as well as honorary doctorates from eight colleges. Always commanding noticeable grace, intelligence and elegance, Rachel's demeanor stands out. At the wedding of my daughter Cinda, in 2003, a guest from England looked to Rachel and asked my wife Linda, "Is that lady over there royalty?" Without a second thought, Linda answered, "Yes."

9. David Rockefeller (1915–2017)
Chairman and CEO of The Chase Manhattan Bank and patriarch of the Rockefeller family (2004–2017)

When David Rockefeller died at the age of 101, his obituary in *The New York Times* described him as "a banker and philanthropist with the fabled family name who controlled The Chase Manhattan Bank for more than a decade and who wielded vast influence around the world, for even longer, as he spread the gospel of American capitalism." The obituary continued: "His stature was greater than any corporate title might convey. ... His influence was felt in Washington and foreign capitals, in the corridors of New York City government, in art museums, in great universities and in public schools." It was precisely that wide-reaching influence that attracted me to David Rockefeller, first as a figure, and then as a person. It was that same larger-than-life influence and personality that prompted me to take my first PR position with The Chase Manhattan Bank in 1961. I had hopes of one day of working on projects with "Mr. David," as he was known. I started the job without any guarantee that I would ever even meet "Mr. David," but I finally did. I was invited to work with him, specifically, on a few of his international activities, and I found him to be bright, delightful and considerate. Despite living in a privileged world, "Mr. David" was a very nice man who thoughtfully engaged all people with whom he came in contact. "Mr. David" possessed many admirable qualities, but the one that impressed me the most was his social responsibility. In that regard, his efforts reminded me of a guiding motto I had learned long ago at Camp Dudley: "The Other Fellow First."

10. David Rubin (b. 1946)
Former dean of the S.I. Newhouse School of Public Communications, Syracuse University

After 18 years at the helm, David Rubin stepped down from his position as Dean of the S.I. Newhouse School of Public Communications, at Syracuse University, in 2008 — only to return shortly thereafter to teach a course or two. David finally retired in 2016, concluding a career in education that spanned more than four decades. That kind of dedication to the advancement of one's profession is admirable. I know David personally through my previous work, of over 20 years, with the Newhouse advisory board. He is, first and foremost, a pleasant and capable man who quickly shows you that he is also a steady and effective leader. According to his former students, David was a brilliant communications professor who taught and guided many current leaders in the field. As a Newhouse advisory board member, I watched him lead a significant increase in annual giving to the school. As significant gifts and donations rolled in, David's work made it all seem effortless. Among the projects he got donors to finance was a $15 million gift from the Newhouse Foundation to construct Newhouse-3 and an additional development fund gift to guarantee the future health of the school. David's influence, along with that of PR Professor Maria Russell, persuaded me to fund the William F. Doescher Campaigns Lab for Advertising and Public Relations in Newhouse-1 in 1998. David is included in my list of most admired people because I, like many leaders in their respective fields, am convinced that David Rubin is the No. 1 reason that the Newhouse School is what it is today — the gold standard for communications schools.

11. Lisa Scala Maguire (b. 1966)
Daughter of Dick Scala, a boyhood friend from Utica

I had the honor of walking Lisa Scala down the aisle at her marriage to Kevin Maguire in 2015. The "Utica Boys" — Johnny Ligas, Tommy Zagaroli and I — were there in force to support her at this important moment. Our spouses and Lisa's mother were also there. Her father, Dick Scala, the fourth member of the "Utica Boys," had passed away years earlier. Prior to her wedding, I had had the privilege of being Lisa's mentor for many years. It was during a challenging time in her life, and I helped Lisa rediscover herself. I also supported her efforts to overcome some serious problems that were holding her back from succeeding in life, personal relationships and satisfactory career advancements. I marvel at Lisa's spirit and her hard-fought determination to overcome the personal demons that threatened to derail her life. Her late parents would be most proud of her turnaround. Linda and I are. I know it wasn't an easy path, and that's why I will always admire Lisa.

12. David Stern (b. 1942)
Former commissioner of the National Basketball Association

Over the years, I have had the pleasure of introducing David Stern as the featured speaker at certain venues, including engagements for the Weisman Group (of PR executives) at the Harvard Club in New York City, and a civic group at the local Scarsdale Public Library in Westchester County, New York. The introductions were always easy because I noted — and still believe — that David was the best commissioner of any sports league at that time. With a solid background in law, David brought sound business sensibility to the job, which allowed the sport to thrive. When David retired in September 2014, he had been in charge of the NBA for 30 years. It was certainly a different league when he first took the reins in 1984, but when he left, the NBA was delivering $12 billion in value to its owners. Of course, David was blessed to have players like Michael Jordan, Larry Bird, Magic Johnson, Shaquille O'Neal, Kobe Bryant and LeBron James playing in the NBA during his tenure; but his success was not just dependent on those superstars. David's 30-year run as the commissioner should become a case study at the Harvard Business School. At his retirement celebration, Stern told the crowd, "I'd like to think I did an adequate job." In my opinion, he did more than that. David deserves his position on my list of "12 Most Admired" because, in my opinion, there may never be another commissioner of a major sports organization quite like him. Who else could possess the kind of masterful leadership qualities, unbelievable negotiating powers and crisis communications skills that David consistently exhibited in his position as NBA Commissioner?

DOESCHER LESSON: *Always seek out people to admire and respect. If you do, valuable lessons will materialize before you. To become the person you want to be, follow worthwhile examples and model yourself accordingly.*

25.
WHERE IS PR HEADED?

"It takes 20 years to build a reputation and five minutes to ruin it. If you think about that, you'll do things differently."

— Warren Buffett, Chief Executive Officer, Berkshire Hathaway

WHERE IS PUBLIC RELATIONS HEADED?

The short answer is that public relations is headed in many different directions as it responds to the changing contexts of the contemporary world. Some industry experts even predict that the descriptor "public relations" will eventually evolve into another categorical title, more reflective of the industry's active and versatile roles. We may perhaps see this change in the next three to five years or possibly even sooner.

WHAT WILL THIS NEW LANDSCAPE LOOK LIKE?

Expect to see the distinctions that have long separated the professions of public relations, communications, advertising and marketing to become more fluid. Also expect that rapid technological advances and a robust need for information management will require professional communicators to become adaptive through versatility.

Also, as we are seeing today, artificial intelligence will continue to find its way into the PR storytelling function, and we must develop new strategies to be prepared for it.

In a tribute to Jack O'Dwyer and his 50 years of publishing, the July 19th (2018) edition of *O'Dwyer's Newsletter* included a forward-thinking article about the future of public relations, "Public Relations: The Next 50 Years." In writing his article, Henry Feintuch, president of Feintuch Communications and a former president of the New York chapter of the Public Relations Society of America, turned to some industry friends and colleagues, including me, to weigh in. Based on our collective responses, Feintuch found "technology" and "societal changes" were two common issues shaping his colleagues' predictions for the future of PR.

Natan Edelsburg, chief operating officer of Muck Rack and the Shorty Awards and a fellow Board Member of PRSA-NY, was one of the experts consulted for the Feintuch article. Edelsburg, whose grandfather was the first president of PRSA-NY, said, "PR is going to significantly move away from any kind of mass distribution since it is no longer going to be necessary. Journalism's fragility and evolution is going to force more customization than ever before. Because of advancements in technology and social platforms, it will be easier to target the right journalists and get a brand's message across in a sincere way. As a result, the PR industry is going to help boost a renaissance within a journalism industry that has been plagued by outdated business models and mass layoffs. The future is bright for those who take their time to build relationships and use technology to scale."

Feintuch summed up his article with the following advice: "Regardless of the tools, it's the people who use the tools and advocate for their firms and clients that are the constant. The technology allows us to be more thoughtful, to target better, interpret and free up our creativity. Tech will not replace the practitioner; it will empower us in ways previously unimaginable."

I believe he's right, and I advise all PR folks to pay careful attention to the next steps in their careers. Whether you're an 18- to 22-year-old, a millennial, a Gen-Xer, a baby boomer or one of the more senior folks, keep current by taking refresher courses in the changing field or by having meaningful conversations with savvy mentors. Such proactive development is one of the best ways to maintain the upward curve of any successful communications career. It may even lead to a promotion, increased income, a more prestigious title or a safe retirement nest egg down the road.

The communications revolution is indeed underway, and it will reflect changes demanded by the culture at large. Diversity, in particular, is one of the areas by which change will be measured. Meaningful D&I programs will result in real and sustainable gains for companies that embrace them — in part because clients and consumers will demand and support such changes. Increased diversity and inclusion in hiring and decision-making is really the only way to generate systemic and lasting change. More than just a window-dressing of diversity statistics, a commitment to diversity and inclusion at the leadership level will succeed multifold. Not only will diversity and inclusion at leadership levels modify the industry's culture from the inside out; it will also create a revised system of reference in which success will be measured by a "new (diverse) normal."

Going forward, trust will continue to be another important factor in the industry. Building and cultivating relationships of trust between senders and receivers of messages has always been paramount to PR success, but it is even more crucial in today's world of information and misinformation. The principle of telling the truth in all communications should be demonstrated with commitment, for once trust is broken, it can rarely be regained.

STARTED PR CAREER IN 1961

Much has changed since I started my career. The mechanisms of public relations now operate in a different context, and I am fortunate to have been able to embrace industry changes with an open sense of development and an appreciation for growth. When I made my debut in public relations at The Chase Manhattan Bank in 1961, my job felt like basic blocking and tackling. In those days I served as the internal newspaper editor and was responsible for press releases and imaginative media placements. I wrote speech and brochure prose, and I worked on letters for top executives. I orchestrated some events for branch openings and made preparations for dozens of David Rockefeller's international trips. The only thing I did not do was write the company's annual report. That task was allocated to Joseph T. Nolan, the senior vice president for PR and advertising. He represented our department extremely well and was more than capable of doing the heavy lifting to write and produce that important document.

Over time, Nolan, who had initially worked as a journalist for United Press International and *The New York Times*, did whatever he could to support David Rockefeller's efforts towards social responsibility. This stance positioned The Chase Manhattan Bank at the forefront of its industry and contributed to a viewpoint of success that always looked forward.

In the 1960s, Chase resembled most other banks and industrial corporations with its all-male, all-white board of directors. Nolan recognized the limitations of this homogeneity and began building a diverse dossier of potential candidates. Eventually, he succeeded in bringing a black businessman and a female lawyer onto the Chase board. While such inclusions may be a *sine qua non* among Fortune 500 companies today, they were virtually unheard of at the time.

Nolan's groundbreaking perspectives and leadership did not go unnoticed. In 2001, he was honored as a "living legend" by the Public Relations Society of America, and I was proud to be in attendance at the Society's annual conference in Atlanta when Nolan received that award. At the honorary luncheon, I remember taking special note of Nolan's words, as he said, "Over the next decade, we will be getting an influx of young people who are already persuaded of the need to maintain high ethical standards." More than 15 years later, his words have proven themselves to be correct.

As an industry pioneer, Nolan lived his philosophy and became a legend in the field. He was the kind of executive who went out of his way to do the right thing. I appreciated his commitment to ethical standards and relied on him as a mentor, even after I stopped working for him directly. No matter where he was or what he was doing, Nolan always took time to answer my phone calls whenever I sought his advice during various phases of my career. That meant a lot to me and demonstrated Nolan's fierce conviction to invest in people.

Recalling my early days in PR at The Chase Manhattan Bank, I remember working within a system of professional compartmentalization that was, then, the norm. Although we were all located on the same floor at 1 Chase Manhattan Plaza in lower Manhattan, individual players in the separate advertising and public relations departments did not interact much with each other. Of course, we would say hello as we passed in the halls, and we'd share a "good evening" nod upon leaving the building at the close of the business day — but that was about all. We were in our own worlds without much overlap — functioning independently, in a way that could be compared to the separation of church and state.

Today, that kind of insularity is no longer the case. Today, collaborative strategies and brand messaging touch on all aspects of a company from its corporate culture to its imaging to its products and services. As such, the departments of public relations, press relations, advertising, executive communications, social media, paid media, digital data miners, and others must operate in conjunction with one another. There must be communication to ensure the consistency of a unified vision and philosophy, with the shared goal of achieving the best results with the furthest reach. With today's information-rich internet and the expansive potential of platforms such as Google, Twitter, Instagram and Facebook, the old standards, which govern communication and connection, must evolve in tandem with the fast-moving digital culture. On one hand, digital strategies present tremendous opportunities to innovatively connect with and engage new groups of consumers. However, this same digital culture also presents challenges related to uncertainty. In particular, consumers' confidence in social media sites and digital messaging will have to be addressed in order for digital communications to succeed. This means communications professionals must look beyond their own output and develop strategies to effectively manage the impact of peer commentators, public reviews and social media influencers — not to mention potential misinformation distributed by hackers and propaganda machines.

Richard Edelman, chief executive officer of Edelman, the world's largest independent public relations firm, suggests that communications professionals might even take a role in shaping the dynamics of digital culture. He was quoted in a June 19, 2018, *Wall Street Journal* article by Suzanne Vranica, as saying, "'People want the platforms to change,' and it is in the best interest of 'brands to demand that change.'"

MARKETING COMMUNICATIONS GAINING ACCEPTANCE

Current and past PR leaders suggest that public relations has been developing into an industry that some have already started to call "marketing communications." The concept of marketing communications expands the definition of public relations to include a focus on creating specific brand awareness among potential customers. Marketing communications addresses the way companies send and manage messages about their products and services, either directly or indirectly. Indirect methods include word-of-mouth messages or messaging placed on digital platforms. Today, the umbrella of marketing communications includes advertising, sales promotion, events and experiences, public relations and publicity, direct marketing, interactive marketing and personal selling.

In a June 2018 blog post, Edelman outlined some ways that his own company is staying current and adapting for the future. While saying that "public relations continues to be the essence of our business," Edelman also talks about being committed to helping clients "solve their problems in new ways, collaborating with them and supporting them as they act with certainty." To achieve this ambition, Edelman has brought in new staff to fill different professional roles. An 800-person social digital firm is in place, and 600 professionals were also added to fill roles in the areas of creative content, planning and paid media.

REMEMBERING HISTORICAL PRECEDENTS

No matter if the industry continues to be identified as public relations, or if it accepts a new title such as marketing communications, some proponents hold that the industry's fundamental tenets remain the same, even while strategies may be adapting. During my 57-year career in the field, there have been plenty of discussions, books and articles on the subject of public relations. In collegiate settings, most introductory courses still begin with an explanation of the differences between public relations and the functions of marketing and advertising. Having been involved with these practices — sometimes simultaneously directing all three in a global environment — it is useful to remember that marketing and advertising promote products or services, while public relations beats the drums for the entire organization. The main goal for all three, however, is actually the same — to create unique brand identity.

In 1985, Art Stevens, former president of the Lobsenz-Stevens PR agency, past president of PRSA-NY, and a merger and acquisition guru specializing in PR agencies, published a relevant book for the times, *The Persuasion Explosion*. In this book, Stevens credited Scott Cutlip and Allen H. Center, co-authors of *Effective Public Relations*, with saying, "PR is often confused with its functional parts — for example, publicity, institutional advertising, product promotion and lobbying. The field with which public relations is most often confused by the public is advertising." Stevens then set forth a definition of public relations that he stands by today: "Public relations is the shaping of perception, through communication, for the achievement of positive goals." Although Stevens's book was written more than 30 years ago, his comments sound very contemporary and could aptly be applied to the current industry culture. Other historical precedents are similarly relevant.

Fraser P. Seitel, managing partner of Emerald Partners, an adjunct professor at New York University and author of a quintessential textbook on PR, *The Practice of Public Relations*, identified one of the founders of public relations and recounted a philosophy that holds true today. In the 13th edition of his textbook, Seitel stated, "Ivy Lee helped to open the gates for modern public relations. After he helped establish the idea that high-powered companies and individuals have a responsibility to inform their publics, the practice began to grow in every sector of American society." Lee was known as "the real father of modern public relations."

Lee's perspective brought him into the world of John D. Rockefeller, Jr., who hired Lee as the first, modern-day public relations counselor. John D. Rockefeller, Jr., was an American financier, philanthropist and a prominent member of the Rockefeller family. He was also the father of David Rockefeller, for whom I worked in the early days of my public relations career at The Chase Manhattan Bank. Seitel served as David Rockefeller's personal consultant for 51 years until his boss's death at the age of 101. According to Seitel's book, Lee's advice to John D. Rockefeller, Jr. was simple: "Tell the truth, because sooner or later the public will find it out anyway. And if the public doesn't like what you are doing, change your policies, and bring them into line with what the people want."

INVESTOR RELATIONS ALSO IMPORTANT

Keeping the public informed is not only smart. Sometimes, it's the law. In the corporate realm, the function of investor relations is a necessary legal consideration and an important factor in any communications landscape. While teaching a class on investor relations to PR undergraduates and graduate students at S.I. Newhouse School of Public Communications at Syracuse University for four years, I emphasized that investor relations, more often than not, operates out of a company's finance department headed by the chief financial officer, rather than being overseen by the public relations leader.

According to the history books, the modern profession of investor relations originated with Ralph Cordiner, a chairman of General Electric, who in 1953 created a function with authority over all shareholder communications. Fifty years later, the National Investor Relations Institute Board of Directors adopted an official definition of investor relations as "a strategic management responsibility that integrates finance, communication, marketing and securities law compliance to enable the most effective two-way communication between a company, the financial community and other constituencies, which ultimately contributes to a company's securities achieving fair valuation."

A successful investor relations team must equally rely on communications and financial skill sets. In order to keep shareholders and investors properly informed and legally up-to-date, there must be cooperation and transparency among the departments of public relations, marketing, finance and securities law compliance. In 2000, the Securities & Exchange Commission adopted Regulation FD, commonly called "fair disclosure," that requires companies to widely disseminate any "material information" to all interested parties at the same time. That regulation now allows the dissemination of such information through social media platforms, including Twitter and Facebook.

There is no question that PR is difficult to define. It always has been and probably always will be. The first time I seriously considered the question was in 1961, while still a graduate student working to obtain a master's degree at Newhouse. For an essay in an advanced PR theory class, I considered public relations through the lens of functional communication, thus defining it as an instrument in building common knowledge and collective community. In my paper, I wrote: "All individuals depend upon cooperation and pooling of information for knowledge. Therefore, a human being is never dependent upon his own experience, alone, for his information. Language is the indispensable mechanism of human life."

Seitel's textbook states, "The term public relations is really a misnomer," and I concur. He goes on to say that "public relations, or relations with the publics, would be more to the point. Practitioners must communicate with many different publics — not just the general public — each having its own special needs and requiring different types of communication."

Today, Seitel's observations seem more accurate than ever before. Contemporary PR practitioners must wear many hats to reach and connect with various audiences and to best serve diverse groups and constituents. Thus, public relations practitioners must be adept at speaking the distinct languages of media relations, internal communications, executive communications, crisis communications, government relations, public affairs, community relations, special events, website management, graphics and photography, qualitative and quantitative research and investor relations. The all-important function of writing remains essential throughout all of these channels and is pivotal in producing targeted and successful campaigns, as well as day-to-day materials such as press releases, speeches, annual reports, company brochures and other documents.

MUST BE A GOOD WRITER

In order to be successful in public relations, one must be a good writer. This means producing copy that is clear, clean, concise and engaging — and able to deliver the desired message and outcome. I have emphasized the importance of this skill to colleagues and students from the beginning of my career and throughout the eight colleges and universities where I taught and lectured. When teaching a graduate course on internal communications at an Ivy League university, I downgraded students' papers for poor writing, inadequate proofreading and — believe it or not — grammatical errors. It was an attempt to not only encourage them to hone their writing skills, but also to improve their performance for future professional positions.

At another reputable university where I taught, one graduate student had the audacity to spell "tenets" both correctly and incorrectly in the same paper. Clearly, although his word choice suggested otherwise, he was not referring to people who rent apartments. When he received a lower grade than expected, he argued that both versions of the word "spell-checked" correctly and therefore his grade should not have been lowered. I informed him that he should always re-read any document and check for errors before submitting — no matter what his computer indicates. A good writer is also a good editor.

EXPERT OPINIONS

Roger Bolton, president of the Arthur W. Page Society, who previously served as senior vice president of communications at Aetna and held top public affairs positions under two U.S. presidents — George H. W. Bush and Ronald Reagan— discussed the role of the chief communications officer. "Some practitioners may still be stuck at the tactical level," he said, "but the profession has changed radically in recent years, and many CCOs now hold strategic roles at the center of the enterprise's senior policymaking group. A Page survey of CEOs in 2017 found that they see the strategic advisory role as 'a core competency of the high-performing CCO.'"

Cheryl Procter-Rogers, a 38-year veteran public relations/business strategist and executive coach, with whom I worked when she was in charge of PR at Nielsen, agrees. Procter-Rogers, who now runs the global consulting practice, A Step Ahead, and is a former national president of PRSA, said, "Today and in the years ahead, the PR professional is uniquely positioned to become a trusted advisor to the senior leadership team. This role presents us with both exciting challenges and unique opportunities to impact the growth of organizations. To be successful in the role of advisor, the chief communications officer must expand his or her knowledge and expertise beyond public relations and communications to include an understanding of business and organizational strategy, economics and leadership coaching."

The Page model, which was introduced in 2012, argues that the first job of the CCO is to help the enterprise "define, activate, and align its mission, vision, values, culture, business model, strategy and brand." According to Bolton, "This is a significant departure from the old model, where the CCO waited for others to make decisions and then sought to explain them to stakeholders. Now the CCO takes an active role in encouraging and sometimes leading the enterprise's definition of its essential identity.'"

Bolton cited five different Page publications about "the new era of the CCO" supporting his claim that "building corporate character and authentic advocacy are important in today's business environment in which most enterprises are experiencing profound disruption — from powerful digital platforms, shifting global markets and new consumer, citizen and employee expectations."

"If CCOs can help enterprises cope with their challenges by playing the senior strategic role and helping them define and activate their unique differentiating identities, while earning stakeholder trust and advocacy, the future of both their enterprises and their profession will be secure," Bolton added.

Likewise, Richard Edelman, president and CEO of Edelman, a leading communications marketing firm, also addresses the topic of trust. In a speech delivered at Sacred Heart University in Fairfield, Connecticut, on May 12, 2018, he told the audience, "The biggest challenge of all — for you, the graduates — is an epic downfall of trust in situations that began decades ago. For 18 years, the Edelman Trust Barometer has measured people's trust in government, business, media and NGOs around the world. Here's a shocking finding. In this country, the informed population — the college-educated and higher-income audience — now has the world's lowest levels of trust in these four institutions, lower than Brazil or Argentina or Russia. Our trust in our country plunged 23 points in a single year."

He called on the graduates to "make your work a force for change" and dubbed them "The Significant Generation." Edelman's view positions public relations professionals as change agents.

In another speech delivered at the Annenberg School, at the University of Southern California, in April 2018, Edelman said, "The real job of the communications firm must be to bring ideas to clients that are consistent with the new aspirations of business. We should be the ones with the creative spark that starts movements, to bring purpose to each brand and to solve big problems in society."

Mark Weiner, former CEO of PRIME Research, LP, an international research-based communications consultancy, which was acquired by Cision on January 24,

2018, defines public relations in a more practical way. In an online post for the Institute for Public Relations, in September 2017, he wrote: "Public relations is more than media and more than brand-building. In times of growing skepticism, public relations defends against corporate mistrust by engaging and promoting dialogue in a consistent, visible and genuine manner. Ideally, authentic and transparent communication reinforces a constructive predisposition during good times as well draws on an organization's positive reputation during times of scrutiny or crises. To do so, communicators need accurate research, actionable insights and the forethought to act."

Other industry leaders anticipate the future of PR by addressing the shift from traditional communications platforms to digital culture. It is a fact that most people in the Western world now consume news digitally and rely on information promoted by social platforms. Traditional print outlets, such as newspapers and magazines, are aggressively turning to digital models to maintain engagement, increase profits and stay relevant. More and more, PR agencies and corporations are adopting an interdisciplinary approach to communications to remain effective and ready in a rapidly changing world.

Anthony D'Angelo, professor and director of the executive master's program in communications management at Newhouse, has held PR leadership roles in the corporate and agency sectors for more than 25 years. From his perspective, he sees PR and other disciplines aligning along a number of critical axes. According to D'Angelo, the walls separating public relations, communications, advertising, marketing and content management are "coming down rapidly, as paid, earned, shared and owned media are destroying what were once silos into a convergence of skills and methods that are increasingly required of a versatile professional communicator." D'Angelo notes that the rules guiding how news information was published, shared and consumed have been "permanently altered." He predicts that "as physical and virtual realities come together, face-to-face conversations will remain the most effective communication method but will be altered because the other face may well be virtual."

People working in public relations today are already demonstrating the kind of forward-thinking flexibility that D'Angelo represents. Professionals are defining their roles through creative titles, such as "storyteller specialist," "fearless digital marketing expert," "full-time perfectionist" and "nurturer of world-class diverse teams." Through their newly defined roles, the current crop of PR professionals is invested in changing the world for their clients and bosses, using disruptive strategies and combining digital strategy and software development in order to successfully service the client or company. Their recommendations are innovative, yet backed up with research, strategy and trend analysis.

If this is the picture of public relations today, what does it all mean?

BACK TO BASICS

Marcia Horowitz, managing director of Rubenstein and a senior crisis communications specialist for more than three decades, sees a blurring between the contemporary worlds of public relations and paid advertising. As a result, she believes, “Advertising is finding new platforms for promotion, but public relations in the true sense of the words seems to be a dying breed.

“Now if you want to get listed in the ‘executive moves’ section in *Crain’s New York Business* you have to pay to get listed. If you want to have your name highlighted in the *Best Lawyers* list you need to pay for that. But I think the pendulum will swing back at some point. There will be calls for transparency and true reporting of the facts. There is a void now but someone will step up to the plate. It is a fundamental mandate of the Fourth Estate [the press] and our democracy.”

Horowitz predicts that “public relations will get back to the basics, and the profession will revert back to those professionals who can tell their client’s story in the *New York Times* rather than just to an influencer on Twitter. It will prove out Lincoln’s quote that you can fool some of the people all of the time, and all of the people some of the time, but you can’t fool all of the people all of the time.”

Dean Lorraine E. Branham, of Newhouse, has observed: “Traditional media are struggling with major changes in business models; media are growing rapidly from fledgling experiments to powerful communication tools; even new media is no longer new."

Branham's assessment is accurate. New kinds of storytelling and engagement, new delivery and distribution channels and new technologies are upon us and changing faster than most people can keep up. Facebook, LinkedIn, Twitter and Pinterest are old news. Really old news. For those willing to stay relevant and up-to-date, it will be necessary to pay close attention to what the next group of digital generation geniuses are saying and predicting.

Certainly, the need for public relations is not dead, although its contemporary machinations and functional name may be changing. Public relations, at its best, is an art — and it should remain that way.

Harold Burson, the 97-year-old founder of the PR giant Burson-Marsteller, and one of my key mentors, offered a definition that I think will never go out of style. In his book, *The Business of Persuasion*, published in October 2017, Burson asserts, "Public relations is doing good and getting credit for it."

What more can you say? Let's just get on with business.

DOESCHER LESSONS: *Here are 12 to consider, all of which have positively influenced my career:*

1. *You must be a good writer to be successful in PR — or any career.*
2. *Never give up on your dreams.*
3. *Always make yourself stand out to achieve your goal; self-promotion is your other job.*
4. *Always adhere to a personal ethics policy.*
5. *Never be afraid to be creative — just be smart about it.*
6. *Never burn your bridges.*
7. *Understand what the CEO wants.*
8. *Take advantage of opportunities when they arise.*
9. *Be sure to network with friends, industry associates, and find a mentor — or two or three.*
10. *Follow a plan to give back to society — it's extremely important and can definitely help your career.*
11. *Have an unwavering commitment to learning.*
12. *Always strive for excellence.*

26.
LOST AT MADISON SQUARE GARDEN

"Parents rarely let go of their children, so children let go of them."

— Paul Coelho, author

As demanding as your professional work might be, you will often find that your kids can trump any stress, any time. If you don't believe me, read on....

It was an ideal day for an outing, the perfect day to take my kids, Doug and Cinda, to a circus at Madison Square Garden. Excited by the spectacle of "The Greatest Show on Earth," Doug ran ahead of Cinda and me. He was following the joyful clowns and the parade elephants that preceded the opening acts of the Ringling Brothers and Barnum & Bailey Circus.

I kept my eye on him, or so I thought.

At the time, Doug was nine, and Cinda was five. We were visiting the Big Apple from Hickory, North Carolina, and I was trying my best to entertain them with special activities. In the midst of the Garden, I suddenly felt like we were country bumpkins.

Even though I had been to Madison Square Garden many times in the past, this was different. This was a big-time circus with lots of energetic kids, plenty of noise and large animals that, alone, would make any father with two little children nervous.

While I was concentrating on keeping hold of Cinda's hand, Doug suddenly vanished from my eyesight. I concentrated my gaze and scanned the crowd. Doug was nowhere to be seen. He was gone.

The realization immediately set in. My son was lost in Madison Square Garden, alone in busy New York City.

And this was all before the circus started, even before we had taken our seats. I thought of everything I had envisioned when I decided that the circus would be a wonderful treat for the kids — their anticipation in listening to the spirited ringmaster, their fun in seeing the tigers' tricks, and their suspense in watching the daring young men on the flying trapeze. But all of that was not to be. Instead, my son was lost. It was a detail I had certainly not envisioned.

In fact, it was a parent's nightmare. My heart was beating fast, and my hands were sweating as I ran ahead of the elephants. He wasn't there. I ran back the other way, and I still didn't see him. I did not know what to do. I was in a state of panic, and in that moment, I believed I might never find him. I wondered, too, if I could possibly have a heart attack as a result of my panicked feeling (but that wouldn't happen for another 42 years).

To make matters worse, I was separated from my children's mother, Carol, and in the early stages of divorce.

How would I be able to tell her I had lost Doug? Being a former journalist, I imagined a front-page headline in the *New York Daily News*: "Father loses son in Madison Square Garden." Or worse.

Gripping Cinda's hand even tighter than before — because I didn't want to lose two children — I retreated to the last place I thought Doug had seen us. I was hoping he would remember my warning: "If you ever get lost, go back to the last place you saw me." Thank God, he did.

Down two escalators to an open area, I heard Doug before I saw him. He was bawling, louder than I thought possible, and standing next to a young, muscular New York City policeman. Cinda and I rushed over to him, and even the policeman seemed relieved. I don't think he otherwise knew how to stop Doug from crying.

Those 20 minutes of high drama seemed like a lifetime.

At that point, I decided to forgo the animal parade and other circus preliminaries. Whether my kids liked it or not, for the sake of safety and my own mental relief, we went to our seats and waited for the show to start.

Shortly thereafter, Cinda had to go to the bathroom. Not wanting to lose Doug again or leave him alone in his seat, we all went to the restroom together. Hesitant to take my five-year-old daughter into a public men's room, we instead entered the ladies' room. My son was embarrassed to be there, but I wasn't. We were all safe and together — and that was important to me.

At my 80th birthday celebration, Doug, who was then 54, took the floor and shared the story about getting lost in Madison Square Garden while visiting the circus with his dad and sister, way back when. The birthday crowd was amused, but I couldn't quite share the humor. I still remembered that horrible feeling of losing my son in a massive crowd 45 years ago. Such a scare is something a parent does not forget.

After Doug spoke at the party, his wife of 21 years, Marie Menna Doescher, led everyone in the "Happy Birthday" song. Marie is a professional singer, and she directed the crowd beautifully. I thanked her for the song and for taking care of Doug all these years.

With a smile, she looked at me and replied, "I haven't lost him yet."

DOESCHER LESSON: *Never forget that parents are human. This means we will sometimes make mistakes, and we won't always be right in dealing with our children. The best a parent can do is to always be aware of acting in accordance with his or her children's best interests and to always teach them to approach life with independence, resilience and positive thinking. And, while you're at it, never forget to enjoy the adventure!*

27.
STARTING A NEW LIFE

"You can't start the next chapter of your life if you keep re-reading the last one."

— Unknown

A friend once told me, "If you think you might be lost, it's probably time to change direction." She was referring to her own decision to change careers, but her attitude can equally apply to personal matters — such as the decision to end a marriage.

Divorce is never easy. I know this, because I went through one. And despite all the reasons that justified the decision, my divorce was still a terrible experience — mainly because I did not hate my first wife, Carol. Quite the contrary. We liked one another, but we just weren't compatible. We probably knew it early on in the marriage, but we did nothing to overcome our differences or compensate for them. Our life goals never meshed the way a couple's should. We sometimes even disagreed on what was best for our children. We were too different to stay married. When major issues arose between us, we tried to brush them aside as if they weren't important. We soldiered on for 15 years and naively thought it might work just by being together, but in the end, we realized our differences had created a void between us that was just too hard to overcome. Things were not going to change.

So it was up to us to change direction.

Carol and I agreed that our two great children were the best part of our marriage. Doug was born in 1964, and Cinda followed four years later, in 1968. They, alone, have made that difficult marriage worth it. In adulthood, Doug and Cinda have each remarked, individually, "You probably shouldn't have gotten married in the first place." My response has always been, "Then, we wouldn't have the two of you, joys of my life, and all that followed."

When I took Doug and Cinda to New York City during the week of Easter, 1973, and proceeded to lose Doug at Madison Square Garden, Carol and I were in the first of two trial marital separations.

I had met Carol at Syracuse University when she was an undergraduate art education major and member of the Delta Delta Delta sorority. I was there as a graduate student, working toward a master's degree in public relations. After graduation, in 1961, she got a job as an art editor at Harcourt Brace Jovanovich, the book publishers, in New York City. She was originally from Tarrytown, New York in Westchester County, and was happy to move back to southern New York, closer to her family.

Carol was an artist and illustrated a children's book — *A Horse for Claudia and Dennis*, by Duell, Sloan and Pearce publishers — in 1958, while still a student. The book was enjoyed by many young people interested in horses, and used copies remain available today.

We married on December 9, 1961, the date of my 24th birthday. Our wedding took place at the Second Reformed Church in Tarrytown. Carol had just turned 22. Together, we lived in the New York communities of Tarrytown, Briarcliff Manor and Jackson Heights, Queens. We also relocated, as a family, to Hickory, North Carolina, when I started working with Drexel Heritage.

After years of separation, Carol and I officially divorced in 1976. We each went on with our respective lives.

I met a wonderful woman, Linda Blair, whom I married in Darien, Connecticut, in 1977. We blended our families of two children each into one large and happy "Brady Bunch" group. Our combined four children — Doug and Cinda and Michelle and Marc — moved with us to Scarsdale, New York, in 1978. That was when I took a job with Dun & Bradstreet in New York City and Linda continued to work as an interior designer in the greater metropolitan area. Our children, in turn, settled into a warm family life and embraced the community together.

Carol also got remarried — to Charles "Chuck" McKinley. The wedding took place in her parents' home in Tarrytown in 1982, and the couple moved to Ogden, Utah. Four years later, in 1986, Carol died an untimely death, at the age of 46. She was being treated at St. Luke's Roosevelt Hospital in New York City after a long battle with cancer and related illnesses. Doug, Cinda and I were at her side.

Carol's memorial service was held at the church where we had been first married and where Doug and Cinda had been baptized. It was a touching service, and Cinda shared beautiful poems she had written about her mother.

DOESCHER LESSON: *If you have exhausted all options to save a marriage, sometimes divorce is necessary for everyone in the family — children included.*

28.
SCARSDALE: WE FOUND A HOME

"But a room is not a house ... And a house is not a home ... When the two of us are far apart."

— Lyrics from "A House is not a Home," written by Burt Bacharach and Hal David in 1964 and popularly sung by Dionne Warwick

In the fall of 1978, Linda Blair, my wife of nearly a year, and I were in the midst of diligently searching for an affordable house in the New York City suburbs. One day, we got lucky and found our home.

After we ruled out Manhattan due to the high cost of private school education for our four kids, we started looking to settle in one of the surrounding bedroom communities. We visited towns in New Jersey and Connecticut but ruled those out after not being able to find anything we liked. Turning our attention to the New York suburbs, I used my Colgate connections and found alumnus Joel Parker working at the Houlihan Lawrence real estate office in Bronxville, New York. I introduced myself, and Joel and I could not resist belting out the first verse of the Colgate alma mater in unison. After that little song, he was more than happy to set us up with associates who could provide a wide range of showings. With Joel's colleagues, we were to visit houses in Bronxville, Dobbs Ferry, Tarrytown, Irvington, Scarsdale and other Westchester County towns.

To assist, Linda and I were asked to write our wish list for a house. First, we needed at least five bedrooms for our newly blended family — one for each of the four kids, ages eight to 13, and one for us. Second, we were looking for a good school system and, third, a reasonable commute to my new job at Dun & Bradstreet in Manhattan's financial district. We also shared with Joel that we needed someone to help with the down payment, as both Linda and I had each recently gotten divorced and our respective settlements did not allow for much financial flexibility. An easy task, right? Wrong.

Since I had formerly lived in Tarrytown, in a house in the woods, and then in Briarcliff Manor, I was familiar with some of the communities in Westchester — but not all. We needed a pro to navigate our wish list and show us around.

One of Joel's Houlihan Lawrence associates was Pat Dumke. She also happened to be the wife of a Colgate alum. Pat understood our needs, and we immediately hit it off. One of the first properties she showed us was a charming, Tudor-style house in Bronxville within walking distance of the train station. While it caught our eye and was tempting, it was too small for our large family. So, we continued looking.

With Pat, we explored listings in a variety of towns and eventually decided to pinpoint our search in Scarsdale. In part, our decision was motivated by Scarsdale's religious diversity and its reputation of welcoming, equally, both Jewish and Christian families. As I am Protestant and Linda is Jewish, it was important for us to find a community where everyone — particularly each of our children — felt comfortable.

One Saturday, we decided to get serious. With Linda's mother and my father in tow, we set out to tour several houses in Scarsdale. Magda Bierman and Fred Doescher, our respective parents, did not get out of the car for the first three houses that Pat presented. In their wisdom, our parents knew those first houses would not be contenders.

A change of attitude occurred, however, when Pat pulled up in front of a colonial on Fox Meadow Road. With both of our parents getting out of the car and heading toward the front door, Linda and I knew we better take a good look at this house. We not only respected our parents' opinions, we also desired their approval since we would need at least one of them to help us with the down payment.

As it turned out, all of us immediately fell in love with that house. It had been built in 1915 and occupied a stately position on the picturesque, tree-lined street of Fox Meadow Road. Its generous size afforded six bedrooms, instead of five, which meant there would be enough room for whichever in-law happened to be visiting.

At first sight, we were struck by the house's warmth, beauty and curb appeal. It had a romantic porch running the entire length of the front, and it was situated against a vibrant backdrop of fall foliage in an ample yard. From the outside view, it looked like a postcard image of home-sweet-home.

Once we went inside and began to look around, graceful rooms unfolded. Details perfectly balanced old-world charm with modern amenities. Plus, with six bedrooms and three and a half baths, we knew it would be comfortable and private for everyone.

The location of Fox Meadow Road was ideal, too. Situated minutes away from the village center and train station, the house could well serve the entire family. I would be afforded an easy commute to my office in New York City. Linda could easily access her interior design clients in both the city and the suburbs. And the kids could ride their bikes to school and into town to meet with friends. The location of the house also suited Linda's mother Magda, who appreciatively noted that the house was only "a quick train ride away" from her apartment on East 72nd Street in Manhattan, the same place that Linda grew up.

My father, who had recently become a widower, also liked the house. He pointed out a flip-top table in the foyer that was almost identical to a table in his own home in Utica. He said his table would become ours if we purchased the house, reasoning that such a table perfectly complemented the house's turn-of-the-century architecture.

Could it be that the lookalike tables were a signal that this house should become our home?

Magda was decisive and did not hesitate to give her opinion first. She told Linda and me that we should definitely take the house. Soon thereafter, we followed her advice and made an offer. It was accepted, and my father helped us with the small down payment required at the time. A mortgage with Citibank provided the rest. And just like that, we were off and running in a new life.

The house proved to be a great investment over time. It started with so many features from our wish list, and, with Linda's interior design imagination, we knew we could make changes and improvements. As the years progressed, we patiently upgraded various rooms. Eventually, we added a dynamic kitchen with marble countertops and ample storage, a large modern family room and a three-car garage. We also renovated the master bedroom and bathroom to include lots of built-in storage and closets.

We lived in that house on Fox Meadow Road for 39 years, playing out the details of everyday family life, hosting decades of traditional Thanksgiving dinners and celebrating joyful holidays, Jewish and Christian. Using our house as a home base, we also involved ourselves in the community and formed close relationships with neighbors and friends.

All six of us in the family certainly benefited from living in Scarsdale and have come to think of the village as a most special place.

As Diana Reische said in her book, *Of Colonists and Commuters, a History of Scarsdale*, published in 1976, "The Scarsdale of noted schools and tree-lined streets is the work of 20th century activists. Getting organized has proved to be a Scarsdale specialty." The same sentiment remains true today.

However, for us, Scarsdale was more than just "tree-lined streets" and "good schools." While our four kids — Michelle Blair, Doug Doescher, Marc Blair and Cinda Doescher — certainly did get an excellent education at Scarsdale High School, their lives were also rich with community activity and involvement. In Scarsdale, the kids were encouraged to be individuals. They were afforded opportunities to play sports, sing, act in plays and pursue diverse interests — including playing the flute and being a devoted fan of Batman comics. The small village was a big world for them, as they could ride their bikes into the village, to friends' houses and up Mamaroneck Road to the Scarsdale public swimming pool. They socialized with more kids than we could have ever possibly fit into our large house at the same time. They eventually took driver's education at Regina Maria High School in Hartsdale, and then were allowed to drive our cars. We made sure they had opportunities to honor their religious beliefs — Jewish and Christian — in meaningful ways. In my mind, Scarsdale was a perfect setting for our kids, as they grew up and became prepared for life's challenges ahead.

Coming from Utica, it was important to me that our family values remained down-to-earth. Sometimes, this meant we had to break through the supposed sophistication of Scarsdale. To support an authentic and balanced view of life, our children got involved in service organizations and worked part-time jobs in town. Cinda was a checker at DeCicco's Marketplace grocery store after school, and Michelle worked for the recreation department in the summers. Doug toiled on afternoons and Saturdays at the Scarsdale Hardware Store, and Marc found a position he loved with a local ophthalmologist.

All of our kids were involved with the Senior Youth Fellowship at the Scarsdale Congregational Church. It turned out to be an important place for them to mature. The ecumenical youth group — which included members from the church, other churches or no church at all — met Sunday evenings and at organized social events. These included blindfolded, team-building "trust walks," dramatic plays and musicals.

These life-learning activities kept the kids occupied, off the streets, and, as all the parents hoped, "out of trouble." They learned about sharing, especially through songs and play acting. Marc even scored the lead in *Jesus Christ Superstar*, and his Mom cried at every performance when he died in the play. The kids also learned about democracy when the group's elections came around. Three of the four kids were officers, and Marc was elected president. The fact that Marc, being Jewish, could preside over this organization sent me a signal that this group supported wellbeing, inclusion and integration, which is a great philosophy for being part of the community.

What about the grown-ups?

Upon arrival, Linda and I immediately embraced the village's spirit of volunteerism, and we participated to the extent that our time allowed. We joined the Scarsdale Golf Club in Hartsdale, and quickly formed new friendships over Friday night buffets and weekend golf games.

If Linda and I had to select one volunteer project of which we are most proud, it would be the "Scarsdale Show House 2005," held at the Rowsley Estate of the Scarsdale Woman's Club on Drake Road. Linda was the lead decorator for the project, and she orchestrated the happening flawlessly. I was the chair of marketing and public relations.

The Show House was a major undertaking and a roaring success. It involved expert designers from the New York Chapter of the American Society of Interior Designers (ASID), event guru Ann Tucker, co-chairs Maureen Lambert, Gay McCreery, Georgene Mongarella, Michael Wiener, Karen Reuter and Belle Smith, and many volunteers. Linda Leavitt, the longtime editor of the *Scarsdale Inquirer*, reviewed it in her weekly editorial and called it the "Wow House."

Linda, who was in her second term as president of the New York Metropolitan Chapter of ASID, and Gay McCreery, president of the Scarsdale Woman's Club, successfully managed an amazing cooperation between the two organizations to produce 20 magnificently refurbished rooms.

Each room was refreshingly distinct, as sought-after interior designers created genuine atmospheres of their own, with magical moods and styles. The rooms were spectacular and drew large crowds that took in the event from May 7–22, 2005.

The overall value of the Woman's Club makeover was estimated at $1.5 million, and the designers left part or all of what they designed for their rooms. Linda designed the "Grand Salon," and she left a 19th century Chippendale mirror from her mother's collection on the salon's main wall after the event. Many weddings have been held in that room.

Whispers in the halls during the event centered around how the house had been saved from extinction. The financially strapped Woman's Club, otherwise, would not have been able to perform the multiple repairs needed by the 147-year-old house. From a design standpoint, the event succeeded in bringing an old manor house into the 21st Century, through thoughtful renovations. It was a win-win for everybody.

As a mother, wife and entrepreneur, Linda managed our own turn-of-the-century house on Fox Meadow Road and grew her interior design business. Early on in our residency in Scarsdale, she opened an office in the village and eventually moved to 1 Chase Road in the village center. From that base, she used her design talent to improve the lives of numerous clients in Scarsdale, Westchester County and New York City. She also contributed her expertise to several pro-bono designs, including the Scarsdale Public

Library, other parts of the Scarsdale Woman's Club, projects for clients of the Easter Seals Society and Rachel Robinson's office at the Jackie Robinson Foundation in Lower Manhattan.

Our involvement with Scarsdale has led Linda and me into positions with various civic organizations, where we could donate our professional experience and talents. Linda's knowledge was put to use as the chair and a member of the village's board of architectural review for 10 years and the committee for historic preservation. In addition, she was a member of the citizens nominating committee and served on the board of the Scarsdale Forum. Outside of Scarsdale, in addition to serving as president of the New York Chapter of ASID, she was also an officer of and donor for ELF, a design group that provides college scholarships for local design students. Linda has also taught classes on design and building codes at several colleges.

I have also been active in the community. I served as president of the Scarsdale Historical Society for more than seven years. I was chairman of the village's Ethics Committee, and a member of the Cable Commission. I put in time with the Forum and the Concours d'Elegance event. I regularly sing in the Chancel Choir and serve as an elder on the Session at Hitchcock Presbyterian Church. Outside of Scarsdale I have taught or lectured at eight colleges, been involved as a board member for the Jackie Robinson Foundation, the Newhouse School of Public Communications at Syracuse University, the Colgate

University Alumni Corporation, the American Cancer Society and Easter Seals Society.

Over the last 40 years, the community of Scarsdale has allowed us to live very connected, rich lives. Would we recommend Scarsdale — with its good schools, non-partisan political system, quaint village center, good restaurants, numerous recreational facilities, a variety of churches and synagogues and a reasonable commute to Manhattan — to a family looking for a new home today? You bet! We have thoroughly enjoyed our time in Scarsdale. Almost every day seemed like it was better than the last.

DOESCHER LESSON: *When looking to relocate, find a home — not just a house.*

29.
WE DID OUR BEST

Family picture of (pictured in back row, left to right) Linda, Bill, Doug, Michelle, and (pictured in front row, left to right) Cinda and Marc, taken at a post-wedding reception at Rolling Hills Country Club, in Wilton, Connecticut, 1977

"Stepparents are so much more than just parents; they made the choice to love when they didn't have to."

— Unknown

When you least expect it, a chance meeting may change your life forever. It happens all the time, and it even happened to me. Backing up the clock, I remember how my life as I know it today — happily married to Linda Blair — began.

It was New York City in the 1970s, and I was then the PR and advertising vice president for Drexel Heritage Furnishings in Drexel, North Carolina. On one of my regular trips to visit advertising agencies with whom I regularly worked, I scheduled a meeting with Linda Blair, the renowned interior designer from the Big Apple, to discuss a marketing and public relations strategy requested by one of her clients, Waring & Gillow, from London.

After introductions and pleasantries, I showed Linda my cache of marketing communications materials for a new Drexel Heritage store program, as well as a "double-exposure" photo of my two young children, Doug and Cinda, who were 10 and six at the time.

I wasn't sure if Linda was totally impressed with the professionalism of my 45-minute presentation, but I do know she liked the photo of my kids. Much later, she admitted she had immediately fallen in love with them. You could say the rest is history. But, like life itself, it wasn't that simple.

At the time of our first meeting, we were both in unsatisfactory marriages and close to divorce. Linda had been married for 17 years, and my marriage of 15 years was nearing its end. Of course, Linda and I did not share that news at our first meeting in New York.

Instead, we spoke about marketing and communications and kept our appointment on the professional level. The English furniture firm, which had 50 stores throughout Great Britain, had engaged Linda to be in charge of marketing and communications for its entrance into the American furniture industry. To assist with her proposal, I was brought in as a consultant. I offered to share the model of a total communications program I had developed for a newly developed store program in the U.S.

As it turned out, the English company changed its mind. It decided to neither use Linda for marketing and communications, nor adopt my total program. Nevertheless, the company purchased Drexel Heritage case goods and upholstery, and Linda and I stayed in touch by telephone, hoping to change her client's decision. That didn't happen. But something more important did.

After a period of being "just friends," Linda and I found ourselves purposely staying in touch and finding reasons to connect almost daily. Eventually, although we were hundreds of miles apart, we were relying on each to discuss our children's exploits, our business opportunities and news of the day. Every day, we called each other at 11 p.m. and never went to sleep until we said "goodnight." It was great to know we could be falling in love — and, this time, each with the right person.

Linda and I were married on November 25, 1977, in Darien, Connecticut. Our wedding took place in the home of my boyhood friend Dick Scala and his wife Pat. Another friend, Justice of the Peace Bob Fearon, performed the ceremony. Bob worked as a New York City advertising executive in his day job.

Forty-one years later, Linda and I are still going strong. Our blended family of four children has grown to include spouses and seven grandchildren.

Our marriage officially made us more than partners. It also made us stepparents.

Did we succeed all the time as stepparents? Although we naturally made mistakes along the way, we always tried to do our best for our four kids. We tried to put them first — no matter what.

Stepparenting, or being a stepsibling, presents exciting opportunities and some awkward moments. When families break up and reform, there may be less order, less certainty and a bit of trauma. But kids should also be reminded that they can end up with many loving parent figures.

In our case, in our blended family, we have always respected one another's religious beliefs. This means we celebrate all the Jewish and Christian holidays with equal enthusiasm and mark the milestones of each faith. Most recently, in November 2016, the entire extended family was in attendance as Sam Blair, our only grandson, celebrated his bar mitzvah in Washington Depot, Connecticut, and his six grandparents participated in the service. Sam's parents, Kimberly and Marc Blair, had organized a spectacular, daylong event that extended into the evening hours. Relatives came from everywhere, including Hong Kong, London, San Francisco, Los Angeles and Baton Rouge for the festivities. Sam's party welcomed friends of various generations, faiths and backgrounds. It was superb, and we all felt like family.

Another significant occasion for our "Brady Bunch" clan occurred when our son Doug Doescher, celebrated his 50th birthday on June 5, 2014. His stepsister, Michelle, called from San Francisco to congratulate him with this greeting: "Doug, I never thought of you as a stepbrother, but rather as a bonus brother."

I immediately responded with: "I guess that makes me a bonus father."

Complementing my role, Linda deserves the "bonus mother" title even more. From the beginning, she was there for all the meals, doctors' appointments, chauffeuring, outfitting, curfew checking, counseling and discipline if needed. Together, as Linda and I managed through all the tough decisions and messy situations, we remained committed to treating each of the children equally and with the same amount of attention and love. No matter what happened, we always tried to do our best.

As a result, we have been richly rewarded. It brought us great pleasure and pride to watch each of our children graduate from high school, go off to college, participate in each other's weddings, manage their careers, build families and achieve personal goals. Perhaps Cinda, our youngest daughter, best sums up our success. Now married and with three daughters of her own, Cinda presented us with a congratulatory poem on the occasion of our wedding anniversary in 1998. Her words summarized what she thought Linda and I had accomplished as stepparents, 21 years into our marriage.

Cinda wrote: "Take this moment of time to look back through the years. Realize all that you have both achieved. Starting with just a vow of love between two, grew to be much more. Joined two families, made them into one. Accepted each other's dreams. Helped each other succeed. You made a house into a home of love. Holidays into traditions. Birthdays and graduations into celebrations. Gave us siblings to pick on and lean on. Acceptance of things we might not have known. Awareness of things we might never have seen. Remember back to the beginning when it was just a vow of love between two. Look around you and see just what you two have achieved — a family of love."

DOESCHER LESSON: *A family is not only defined by flesh and blood. A family can be just as strong when created by attention and love.*

30.
Cooper

Bill and great-nephew Cooper Wertman after lunch in Bronxville, New York, 2013

"A life is not important except the impact it has on other people's lives."

—Jackie Robinson

"He was a nice boy."

That's what Fred Doescher, Cooper Wertman's great-grandfather, would have said about his great-grandson had they ever had the opportunity to meet and spend time together.

No doubt they would have loved one another. They both had a gift of gab and great enthusiasm for life. They each enjoyed sports — mostly from a spectator's point of view — and you could never turn them away from a game, no matter how hard you tried.

Cooper wanted to be a star football player, and while he did play some games for the Emmaus High School football team in Pennsylvania, he never became a starter. Early on, Cooper also tried his hand at baseball, and with usual optimism, envisioned future fame on the baseball diamond too.

Fred, Cooper's great-grandfather, was a lifeguard and swimmer in the 1920s, at Crosby High School, in Waterbury, Connecticut, but he wasn't particularly athletic. In midlife, he tried curling, a baffling game on a sheet of ice. Fred obviously had a knack for the unusual sport because he became proficient enough to join a curling team in Utica that traveled to Canada for tournaments called "bonspiels."

In addition, both Cooper and Fred loved cars. It was an automotive passion that came naturally.

Cooper inherited a love of cars from his father, Scott, who was knowledgeable about antique roadsters. Growing up, Cooper filled an outer room on the first floor of his Zionsville, Pennsylvania, home, with toy cars of all sizes. He spent hours playing there, pretending it was the Indianapolis 500 Speedway.

Fred, who never saw a Buick he didn't like, spent many hours at the McRorie Sauter Buick Dealership in Utica,

New York, chewing the fat with Lefty Stein, his favorite car salesman, and anybody else who wandered into the showroom. Hanging out with the guys in the Buick dealership was like reliving fraternity house camaraderie for Fred.

Fred's outgoing personality invigorated those showroom talks — and I'm sure he and his Utica Buick buddies came up with good answers to many of the world's problems, at least in their own minds. So while none of them ended up in Washington, D.C., or the New York State Senate or even the Utica mayor's office, those heated debates were good enough for them.

In their own way, Cooper and Fred were born communicators. Both were writers of sorts with great imaginations. Cooper filled journal after journal with his writing, and he often recorded notes about his favorite TV shows and songs. Cooper and I talked about those journals a lot. Fred, too, had been a gifted writer. Later in life, he turned out weekly "Dear Folks" letters and distributed them among the family. We all looked forward to reading Fred's letters and were delighted to be mentioned whenever there was news to share.

Cooper's writing ability translated to his interest in rapping, a genre of musical expression that developed long after Fred's passing. Fred, in his own day, preferred more traditional music, such as a waltz or the Colgate University fight song.

Fred died at the age of 84, in 1989. Cooper was not born until nine years later, in 1998. Cooper died tragically at age 19, on February 9, 2016.

I knew Cooper as my great-nephew. He was a curious and trusting soul who believed in the good of people. He didn't always recognize danger, and being somewhat naive, this may have precipitated circumstances that led to his death in an Emmaus rooming house in 2016. Local newspapers reported that Cooper was murdered and died from knife wounds inflicted by a Steven Dreisbach, 25, in a dispute over drugs. Dreisbach had been treated for schizophrenia and other mental illnesses since childhood, according to those reports.

Dreisbach was sentenced to 30-to-60 years in a state prison.

Cooper's passing was horrible. It shocked not only his immediate family, but also the community surrounding Emmaus, Pennsylvania. His death and the circumstances surrounding it have forever marked the lives of his parents, Deborah and Scott Wertman, and his sister, Ashley Wertman. As Cooper's great-uncle, I wish I could have been more helpful to him and his struggles to understand who he was and where he was going. Even though we talked a lot, it felt as though I wasn't getting through to him. Toward the end of his life, our weekly phone calls weren't happening.

At one point, Linda and I thought, with his parents' permission, Cooper should move in with us. It never took place.

I remember Cooper at his best — as an enthusiastic and extremely handsome young man, interested in music production and looking forward to a career in writing. I remember him walking and smiling all 18 holes of the golf course at the Scarsdale Golf Club in 2015 with my golfing buddies, Fred Riccio, Dave Seal and Bob Czufin. That day on the golf course, Cooper enjoyed his conversation with Tony Cox, our caddie, who befriended him and instilled thoughts that Cooper might like to try working as a summertime caddie, too.

It never came to pass. Fate had written a different story for my great-nephew.

DOESCHER LESSON: *Never stop loving the people who have made an impact on your life.*

31.
A CALL TO ACTION: DO THE RIGHT THING

Bill (pictured center) with former New York Yankees star reliever Mariano Rivera (left) and Baseball Hall-of-Famer Hank Aaron (right) at the Jackie Robinson Foundation "Chairman's Awards" event in New York City, 2009

"The Time is Always Right to Do Right."

— The title of a speech by Dr. Martin Luther King, Jr., delivered at Syracuse University in July 1965

Sometimes, despite our best efforts, things do not go as expected. What seems to be a straightforward process may instead reveal itself to be an exercise wrought with complication. For me, writing this essay evolved into an example of this very predicament — and none of the frustration and delay was because of me.

Deciding to address the topic of diversity, in business and life, was an obvious choice. As a lifelong believer in the value of D&I (the corporate world's acronym for "diversity and inclusion"), I was intent on writing a definitive essay to prompt readers to think about their own experiences with diversity and inclusion. I knew I could share my own thoughts, personal observations, experiences and perspectives. However, to provide even more relevant insight into how diversity and inclusion pertains to business and other places, I decided to survey experts and leaders from various industries. I wanted to evoke a conversation of diverse voices discussing how — and why — diversity and inclusion can work to benefit business and other organizations. Easy enough? ... Not quite.

Early on, I felt blocked at every turn. I reached out to executives, one university president and his staff, plus company leaders. I advanced a list of questions for their review. However, to my surprise, a lot of folks were reluctant to answer my questions and talk about D&I with any specificity. Some individuals did not even return my emails or phone calls.

One attempt to get the real story ended up being a six-week merry-go-round that included an unsatisfactory conference call with three executive members of a president's staff who ultimately admitted they didn't have much to say on the subject. That did it for me. I decided then that I should only reach out to folks who were willing to discuss D&I in an honest way. Trying to break through an organization's palace guards would only be another waste of time.

The lack of real response was disappointing because my intentions were for the essay to be authoritative and full of valuable information. So I adopted the strategy used by D&I expert Verna Myers, who is an author and the vice president of inclusion strategy at Netflix. Following Myers, I decided to seek input from a variety of sources to cull advice about ways to "disrupt the status quo ... so all cultures, all people and all voices can thrive." Just as Myers recommends in her book *Moving Diversity Forward—How to Go from Well-Meaning to Well-Doing*, my approach sought to openly address the complex issues around race, ethnicity, gender and difference without blame.

Myers, a graduate of Harvard Law School, makes a critical distinction between "diversity," which can be passive, and its more active counterpart of "inclusion." In particular, she advocates for the creation of inclusive environments and the recruitment, retention and advancement of underrepresented groups. "Diversity is about quantity, and inclusion is about quality," she writes in her book. "Diversity is being invited to the party. Inclusion is being asked to dance."

So, when reaching out to my ad-hoc panel, I hoped they would share positive examples of how people have been "dancing" together in their institutions. But no — the silence I encountered meant there would be no talk of dancing. No corporate cha-cha-cha, no boardroom rhythm and blues, no executive suite swing. The only kind of dancing I encountered, if any at all, was an attenuated waltz around my questions.

Was I surprised? Yes, I was surprised. I thought people would welcome the opportunity to present themselves and their companies in a favorable light. I expected them to expound on the progress of their D&I programs and the success of their philosophies. But I quickly learned this would not be happening, as I observed the runaround and lack of feedback I was getting. After all, I knew the playbook of the game.

As someone who was once the only company executive allowed to speak with reporters from *The Wall Street Journal* and other business publications, I understood my contacts' purposeful lack of response. Without saying it, a refusal to talk about D&I was akin to not wanting to talk. I only avoided conversations when I didn't have all the facts, prepared for presentation, at that particular time. It was my job, after all, to craft answers that were accurate but also presented the company in the best light. This required me to be totally professional, ethical and cordial while protecting the company, including its reputation, brands, executives and employees, as well as its revenue, profits and earnings per share. Once, a *Wall Street Journal* reporter walked out on me, leaving behind a seafood lunch in New

York City's Rockefeller Center, because he didn't like the evasive answers I was giving him. He knew the game, and he even paid the restaurant bill.

Regarding the silence of the experts I had approached for my own D&I essay, it was obvious that it wasn't a priority for those people to discuss the subject with me. But I still wondered why.

Possibly, they were busy with other matters, deemed to be more important. Or perhaps they were scared. In the end, I believe the latter was true. I believe they were actually afraid to talk about the topic of diversity and inclusion — either because they didn't have anything worthwhile to say, or because they didn't want to go on record about their D&I programs. I immediately wondered if their programs were falling short with regard to personal or corporate standards. Perhaps these leaders felt their D&I programs were a sham — possibly nothing more than window dressing. Or, maybe they weren't able or allowed to walk the talk. In any case, I was getting the message, and it was discouraging. Without any real, meaty substance from the professional world, my essay was reaching a standstill.

Then something happened. On a beautiful spring Saturday, May 19, 2018, Prince Harry, 33, and Meghan Markle, 36, his biracial, divorced, American actress bride, got married. As the world looked on, the couple said their vows in a fairytale ceremony, with at least 600 people in attendance and tens of millions watching on TV. From the commoners to the commentators, everyone fell in love with

Harry and Meghan's inspiring love story. Like the many journalists moved by the royal wedding's 21st century twist, Harry and Meghan's union encouraged me too. It was the push I needed to finish my own stalled-out essay. The sweet connection between Harry and Meghan and their ceremony's 13-minute sermon on love and inclusion got me back to my writing with renewed focus and perspective.

"We must discover the power of love, the redemptive power of love," said Michael Curry, the Chicago-born, African-American Episcopal bishop who quoted Dr. Martin Luther King, Jr., when he delivered the wedding sermon: "'And then when we do that, we will make of this old world, a new world. I'm talking about some power, real power. Power to change the world.'"

The crescendo of the new attitude was demonstrated when the Kingdom Choir — a Christian Gospel choir made up of black Britons from southeast London — performed Ben E. King's "Stand by Me" in one of Great Britain's most historical settings and traditional ceremonies. Certainly, it demonstrated that times were changing through the establishment of a new order with new norms.

In Scarsdale, the sentiment of the wedding energized local conversations. In his Sunday sermon at Hitchcock Presbyterian Church, Rev. Pete Jones referenced Curry's sermon, mentioning "love mandated by Jesus Christ," and "a healing balm, something that can make things right."

I was convinced again that what I had witnessed on TV the day before — essentially a black church service planned by Harry and Meghan and approved by the Queen — was indeed a beautiful model of earnest and authentic diversity and inclusion. Or was it a model of earnest and authentic humanity? I was beginning to wonder if there was a difference.

I was glad I watched the wedding on TV — not once, but twice.

DIVERSITY AND INCLUSION MATTERS — EVERYWHERE

Getting back to the question of diversity and inclusion's relation to decency and humanity, I decided to reflect on what is considered "normal" and "different" in various social groups — and how those identifications exist to support power hierarchies. As long as people with privilege and power continue to feel separate from other groups, the problem of exclusion and the need for corrective D&I programs will not go away. Real change will only occur if the people with privilege and power finally see themselves as belonging, with others, to a singular, diverse, human group.

Growing up in Utica, New York, I really felt part of a larger whole; so differences of race, religion, gender and background were not an issue. Back then, the city's population of 100,000 represented many different ethnic groups, and this all seemed normal among my peers. In my close-knit high school, Utica Free Academy, there were Italian and Polish families, Catholics, Protestants and Jews, as well as kids who looked like me and kids whose skin was darker. We hitchhiked to school together or took a public bus; we played sports together on local playgrounds and at gyms; we snuck out to go to friends' families' pubs together, and we regularly had old-school Italian dinners at each other's houses or shared my mother's favorite vegetable soup at mine. It was through that group of friends that I — a clean cut, white, middle class, Presbyterian boy — was introduced to the traditions of other cultures. I learned about the importance of Friday night Shabbat when my Jewish friends left me on the field to return home to join their families at the dinner table before sundown. On several occasions, I witnessed the camaraderie among classmates at Minor's Grill, a popular African-American bar owned by a black classmate's parents. Although I was technically an outsider, I felt welcome and included. So, it was natural for me to treat others that way.

It was only after leaving that environment and my diverse group of friends that I realized all towns and cities were not like Utica. I learned that at Colgate when I found myself in an all-white male student body. I was expecting the lack of women, but I wasn't expecting a lack of diversity. I also learned this at my first job as a sportswriter with *The Evening Press,* while covering the Binghamton Triplets, the hometown minor league baseball team for the Triple Cities of Endicott, Johnson City and Binghamton. What surprised me was the fact that there weren't a lot of minorities on the team, even though Jackie Robinson had broken baseball's color barrier in 1947. It was 1959–1960, and such integration, I came to learn, was not yet widespread in the minor leagues.

In 1961, when I got a job at The Chase Manhattan Bank in lower Manhattan, things still hadn't changed much. Walking the halls in the corporate office, I mostly saw people who looked like me. If there was a woman, everyone assumed she was a secretary. If there was a black person, everyone assumed he was one of the young men who worked in the mailroom or in one of the services' departments and maybe even played on the company's basketball team in the Bankers League. Unfortunately, most of these assumptions were usually correct, as leadership and management positions were primarily occupied by white men. Even when I was one of those white men working as an advisory consultant, I recommended that a well-known American icon of a company change the makeup of its board to include two African-Americans because the company needed to change not only its image but its leadership philosophy. However, the members of the board would not listen to me. There wasn't enough groundswell for them to do it. There wasn't any pressure from investors, and they were reluctant to break up their exclusive fraternity.

What they didn't realize then was that a commitment to diversity and inclusion in the workplace is essential to any company's long-term success. Because this usually involves changing the mindset — and not just the face — of a company's culture, the commitment involves an ongoing process over many years. To cultivate a truly diverse and inclusive environment, it is important for leaders to clearly understand what constitutes workplace diversity and to boldly support inclusion. To cultivate a diverse workplace, leaders must proactively encourage the hiring of talent from a variety of backgrounds. More than just a black and white issue, diversity within the workplace should embrace differences in race, gender, ethnicity, age, religion, sexual orientation, military service, disabilities, mental and physical conditions and other perceived differences.

Attitude and actions must then extend from leadership to every employee in the company. D&I must become the new culture of the company; otherwise, the effort will fail. Window-dressing in the form of superficial D&I activity to improve the company's image or to please onlookers, may approximate an immediate result, but it won't do anything to create a "new normal" or accomplish sustainable results.

As I continued my research into this topic, I began to get useful feedback. I reached out to Mike Paul of New York City, whom I have known for a number of years. As the president of Reputation Doctor® LLC, Paul is a crisis communicator, a senior PR guy and a media presence regarding current issues and D&I topics. He believes "those who are racist and prejudiced in leadership must be fired with zero tolerance."

Following one of our conversations Paul remarked that actor Jesse Williams, of *Grey's Anatomy*, is calling for tech industry bosses to diversify America's Silicon Valley. Williams's commitment aims to help minorities get fair chances of landing tech jobs. Citing 2018 research, Williams noted that a *USA Today* article pointed out that only three percent of Facebook employees are black, and Google's numbers are even lower, at just two percent. "Stop excluding black people," Williams was quoted as saying, also noting that many diversity initiatives are full of hot air.

Similarly, Paul urges corporations and PR firms to start their diversity programs at top leadership positions, rather than at the bottom tier, as has been typical since D&I became an initiative.

Paul's ideas also include corrective action. He believes diversity should be built into every aspect of an organization's talent management and integrated into its internal and external global brand, with proper marketing and communications. To ensure accountability, Paul recommends that diversity goals and objectives should be made part of performance appraisals and compensation. "This is critical for success," Paul emphasizes. "If you don't live diversity, you can't own it."

Paul commended Hewlett Packard for setting the right example. He praised HP's decision to demand that its communications agencies become more diverse and inclusive — or risk losing HP's account.

In September 2017, *Ad Age* reported that Antonio Lucio, who was then chief marketing and communications person at Hewlett Packard, "tasked HP's global agencies — BBDO Worldwide, Fred & Farid, Gyro, PHD and Edelman — with including more women and minorities in their ranks, specifically in senior and creative leadership roles." Likewise, Dion Weisler, the president & CEO of HP, reiterated Lucio's position in a statement posted on the company's website: "HP Inc. creates technology for everyone, everywhere, making diversity and inclusion a vital part of who we are. We embed diversity and inclusion into everything we do. We started by creating the most diverse board of directors of any tech company in America. And we'll continue by attracting and growing diverse talent and by building the most innovative products, services and solutions. Diversity and inclusion matter not only in the communities where we live and work, but also in the bottom line of our business."

Rudyard F. Whyte, a civil litigation attorney with The Cochran Firm in New York City, shares similar views and is concerned about the lack of meaningful diversity and inclusion programs within the contemporary corporate culture and the legal field. Whyte and I are elders at the same church and have discussed this topic many times. "In the last 15-to-20 years, things have gotten worse instead of better regarding diversity and discrimination," Whyte told me recently. "What we are seeing now is window dressing when it comes to diversity programs being developed and implemented by companies and service organizations. Early on in their careers, young black lawyers are visible in the courtrooms and at meetings with clients. But they never seem to make it to the top at the prestigious law firms, and they disappear in about five years. They don't survive in the big, white-shoe law firms."

Whyte advocates for authentic D&I programs that will help blacks, women and other minorities rise to the levels of their potential. "Diversity & inclusion programs in the public and private sectors are what will save America," Whyte contends. "Let's go for it now."

Another outspoken advocate for diversity and inclusion is Dr. Rochelle L. Ford, who has served as dean of the School of Communications at Elon University in Elon, North Carolina since June 2018. Previously, she held senior administration and faculty positions at Syracuse and Howard universities and was the former public relations chairperson at the S.I. Newhouse School of Public Communications at Syracuse University. According to Ford, "The public relations industry could be considered the tortoise from the children's story 'The Tortoise and the Hare' when it comes to diversity and inclusion. We have not won the race, but we are still in it. I believe we are making solid strides and are ahead in some meaningful ways, but we still have a way to go. We can't quit, and we must learn from those industries that have moved faster. Now the pressure for change must be an economic one coming from the brands and clients forcing agencies to change. New contracts and subcontracts should go to women and minority businesses."

PRSA LEADERS SPEAK UP ABOUT D&I

Members of the Public Relations Society of America and its New York chapter are actively talking about the importance of diversity and inclusion, to identify critical areas for advancement. According to analysis posted on the PRSA website: "While the practice of public relations in the United States has undergone dramatic changes, a lack of diversity in communications management positions persists. Many studies indicate that the industry still struggles to attract young black, Asian and Hispanic professionals to pursue public relations as their career of choice."

Anthony D'Angelo, national chair of Public Relations Society of America and a professor and director of the executive master's program in communications management at Newhouse who has served in PR leadership roles in the corporate and agency sectors for more than 25 years, says, "Diversity and Inclusion is a professional imperative for public relations as a function that must engage diverse publics and lead by inclusion in order to succeed." Taking a proactive initiative, PRSA has developed the annual Paladin Event, which, in 2017, raised more than $185,000 to support scholarships for diverse populations. PRSA is also exploring partnerships with communications associations in allied disciplines to arrange a "Diversity Summit" aimed at advancing diversity and inclusion on a greater scale and with enhanced efficiency.

Sharon Fenster, president of Fenster Communications and current president of PRSA-NY, led an effort to honor the PR industry's most diverse agencies. She created PRSA-NY's inaugural Big Apple President's Diversity Data Award and announced the honorees at the Big Apple event in New York City in June 2018. Awards were based on data documenting agencies' gender and ethnic demographics. HP was the sole sponsor of the award, and winners were Hunter Public Relations, Finn Partners and Zeno Group.

In addition to these agencies, others should also be applauded for making appropriate changes in 2018. Ketchum appointed Barri Rafferty as the agency's first woman global CEO. Edelman promoted Lisa Ross to be the first black president of the company's Washington D.C. office. WPP named Donna Imperato the new CEO of the merged agency, Burson Cohn & Wolfe, which made her the executive leader of the world's third-largest PR agency by revenue. Karen van Bergen, CEO, Omnicom Public Relations Group, continues to lead the group that includes Fleishman Hillard, Ketchum and Porter Novelli since its formation in 2016.

In February 2018, Judith Harrison, president of the PRSA Foundation and senior vice president of Diversity & Inclusion at the PR firm Weber Shandwick, said in an article in *PR Say*: "With the dramatically changing political, cultural state of play in the United States and 47 percent of millennials believing that CEOs have the responsibility to speak up about important societal issues, it will be more important for companies to articulate their points of view with courage and authenticity."

Harrison's perspective shapes her company's philosophy. Diversity, Equity and Inclusion (DEI) are at the core of Weber Shandwick's business culture. Speaking on behalf of WS, Harrison asserts, "We believe that diverse backgrounds and perspectives make our work stronger, our workplaces richer and more interesting, and better connects us to clients and our communities. We appeal to diverse talent by evolving our workplace, and our work is evolved when we have the benefit of diverse teams."

In October 2018, Harrison was credited as being instrumental in the development of an important book, *Diverse Voices: Profiles in Leadership*, edited by Shelley and Barry Spector of PRMuseum Press and supported by numerous leading PR entities. Featuring interviews with more than 40 corporate and PR agency leaders and educators of diverse backgrounds, the book aims to help communications professionals better understand the challenges faced by minorities in the field.

Angela K. Chitkara, an active PRSA-NY member and PRSA national committee member who serves as a PR track director in the Branding & Integrated Communications program and a CUNY Mellon fellow at City College of New York, has also been actively researching this topic. She surveyed 18 CEOs of leading, top-100 global PR agencies, and her findings were summarized in the April 2018 issue of the *Harvard Business Review.*

Chitkara said, "One of the biggest risks to a company's reputation is a tone-deaf advertising campaign. PR practitioners need to be keenly attuned to what their brands' strategies are and how their campaigns can be perceived, but they'll be hard-pressed to do so if they don't become more diverse and inclusive themselves."

In addition, Chitkara's research revealed a marked difference between diversity and inclusion. She said, "The majority of the CEOs conflated inclusion with diversity — only six of them addressed inclusion specifically. While many recognized the importance of changing recruitment to create more diverse workforces, only a few recognized that hiring a diverse staff would not guarantee a sense of inclusion among those hired. For example, Padilla CEO Lynn Casey told me that inclusivity is 'where the rubber meets the road, not only checking the box and getting x people of color, but also making them feel welcome and making sure we understand and celebrate each other.'"

This is an important clarification to realize and support — because, without inclusion, diversity is just a hollow numbers game. As such, it will invariably fall flat. However, on the contrary, inclusion holds the power of change. Inclusion is where we can realize our similarities, feel our shared humanity and energize our common purpose. Inclusion also creates a safe space in which to learn about each other's cultures and traditions, mindsets and experiences — and to recognize all the wonderful variety that "difference" brings to the rich, multitudinous whole. Inclusion is the mechanism that normalizes diversity and works to equalize power dynamics — so that one day we will stop thinking about creating "diversity" and instead recognize all differences as equal parts of our one vast and beautiful human tapestry.

A DIVERSITY LEADER SPEAKS OUT

Michelle Gadsden-Williams, whom I know from our mutual work with the Jackie Robinson Foundation, has been living with issues of gender and race her entire life. She personally and professionally understands the need to be fearless in the face of adversity. In an interview with *Diversity* magazine in 2017, Gadsden-Williams said, "Diversity and Inclusion is important to me. I am a woman. I am a person of color. Both of my parents were born and raised in South Carolina during Jim Crow and segregation, and it was always a topic that was discussed in our household — and not just diversity necessarily, it was more about inclusion — how are you going to immerse yourself in a society that may not accept you for what you are? So, naturally, it's work I gravitated toward."

Today, Gadsden-Williams is an award-winning global diversity expert, activist, philanthropist and the managing director of North American Inclusion and Diversity lead at Accenture. In her book *CLIMB,* Gadsden-Williams characterizes her journey as a process of taking every step "with conviction, courage, and calculated risk to achieve a thriving career and a successful life." She reminds readers that "from a corporate standpoint, diversity is strategically important for several reasons: it provides organizations with the opportunity to attract, develop, promote, and retain the best talent; creates an inclusive culture for employees to thrive; and most importantly, addresses the needs and wants of a diverse customer base."

Gadsden-Williams notes the challenges that African-American women must overcome: "Sitting at the intersection of biases around race and gender, African-American women must labor to overcome both. While white women speak of shattering a glass ceiling, women of color describe their barriers to advancement differently. Many women of color who have made it to the executive suite describe the process as breaking through a *concrete* ceiling."

The same holds true for Andrea Stewart-Cousins, who on November 26, 2018, became the first woman — and the first black woman — to lead a majority conference in the New York State legislature. Officially starting on January 1, 2019, her achievement will succeed in breaking the normal order of things. I have known Stewart-Cousins for several years and admire her ability to build consensus while helping politicians on both sides of the aisle do the right thing.

JACKIE ROBINSON FOUNDATION

Just like the Royal Wedding, I think of the Jackie Robinson Foundation as a positive example of natural diversity and inclusion. JRF not only perpetuates the memory of the great American hero who broke the color barrier in Major League Baseball in 1947; it also works to carry the message forward by addressing the achievement gap in higher education. For over 45 years, JRF has provided higher education scholarships and leadership development opportunities for highly motivated students of color with limited financial resources. The Foundation is distinctive for the depth of its mentoring program and the nearly 100 percent graduation rate among students served. Rachel Robinson, Jackie's widow, founded the organization in 1973, while sitting at her kitchen table in Connecticut, to honor her husband and provide scholarships and mentoring for students. I know this for a fact since I served on the foundation's board of directors for 22 years.

In nurturing the development of each scholar, JRF ensures that Jackie Robinson's commitment to equal opportunity and humanitarianism will live on as JRF scholars assume leadership roles in society. JRF scholars are encouraged to carry Jackie's often-quoted message forward — by service, example and advocacy: "A life is not important except in the impact it has on other lives." Sharon Robinson, Jackie Robinson's daughter, an author of children's books for Scholastic Books, vice chairwoman of JRF and director of the Breaking Barriers Program for Major League Baseball, recalled her father's famous quotation, on the occasion of the April 15, 2017 annual Jackie Robinson Day: "This is the way he lived his life, on and off the field. His legacy in baseball and beyond reflects the power of this statement."

As JRF president and CEO, Della Britton Baeza adds her perspective about JRF's impact on D&I objectives: "The goal of the Jackie Robinson Foundation's scholarship program is to create a pipeline of well-prepared, highly competitive, minority college graduates who will go on to add value to the global workforce, while carrying on the commitment to community service and humanitarianism that define the lives of Jackie and Rachel Robinson, JRF's founder. And our impact is clear from our consistent 98 percent graduation rate, employment placements, and the numerous testimonials from our scholars, alumni, corporate sponsors, and organizational partners, whom we track through both surveys and focus groups.

"With more programs like JRF's that provide hands-on mentoring and exposure over a number of years, it's clear that we as a society can create an authentically diverse workforce that reflects at all levels the talent of *all* members of our society."

THE NEW NORMAL

Of course, diversity and inclusion must be recognized as the norm in all institutions, workplaces, organizations, neighborhoods, social clubs, media representations and every aspect of society for real change to occur. Leadership and decision making should include input from diverse voices, and power should be collectively democratic — rather than based on exclusive hierarchies and closed doors. This will take time and require conscious corrective effort until diversity and inclusion become the new normal. When that happens and is sustained, there will no longer be a need for specific D&I programs guiding people to do the right thing in business, education and other organizations.

It's time to break up the "old boys' club" mentality that has permeated many social organizations. This includes country clubs, where African-Americans were often silently barred from joining and where women were denied the voting rights, weekend tee times and equity interests that their husbands enjoyed.

Following the publication of *The Unplayable Lie: The Untold Story of Women and Discrimination of Golf*, by sports journalist Martha Chambers, in 1995, it took more than 15 years for discrimination at those clubs to be seen as unacceptable and for meaningful corrective action to be taken. In 2012, when the long campaign to admit women at the Augusta National Golf Club in Georgia, home of the Masters, was finally realized, her book was thought to be an important ingredient of that success. Former U.S. Secretary of State Condoleezza Rice and South Carolina financier Darla Moore became the first women members of Augusta National. Other clubs followed the example.

Here in Westchester County, where I live, women in multiple numbers are now being elected to country clubs' boards of directors. At Scarsdale Golf Club, Betsy Broyd became the first woman president in 2015, and five other women were elected to the board that same year. Other country clubs have also opened their leadership to women, such as Scarsdale's Quaker Ridge Golf Club, where Beth Post was elected president.

EDUCATION AND ACCESS TO OPPORTUNITY

Because of their role as a gateway to opportunity, educational institutions should take steps to make diversity and inclusion the norm. Looking at my own alma mater, Colgate University, the recognition of this need for diversity and inclusion is a very self-conscious goal at the moment.

Colgate President Brian W. Casey made a point to discuss diversity and inclusion during his remarks in "Colgate University's Third Century: A Vision Statement, February 2018," included in a booklet mailed to alumni and other interested parties.

He said: "In America today, a great institution is a diverse institution. It is one that brings students of different socioeconomic backgrounds, races and ethnicities and religions to campus."

While Casey's words seem to state a clear and obvious fact, I know from experience it wasn't always that way on college campuses, including Colgate. When I arrived as a freshman at Colgate's idyllic campus in Hamilton, New York, I was a 17-year-old public high school graduate from 30 miles down the road in Utica, New York. It was 1955, and I wasn't familiar with the concept of diversity and inclusion or what it could have possibly meant for the 1,300 male students and their educational experiences over the next four years.

Unlike my hometown of Utica, almost all the students in my freshman class at Colgate looked like me — clean cut, American and white. Looking through my 1959 college yearbook, *Salmagundi*, the exceptions could be counted on one hand. They were Fred Davis, of Omaha, Nebraska, who was African-American; Arnie Quiros, from San Jose, Costa Rica; Anis Khan Satti, from Pakistan; and Pedro Jorge Carrus, from Buenos Aires, Argentina. Looking back in that yearbook, I also realized that the Jewish population, which included at least five members of my fraternity Delta Upsilon when I graduated in 1959, was also not well represented.

Back then, when I was a student, I'm not sure we knew what to think of the lack of diversity. As young people often are, we were probably more absorbed in ourselves, our studies and our preoccupations to really take notice. As silly as it may sound, the main distinguishing differences observed among classmates involved physical size. The basketball players were tall. The track stars were long-legged. And the football players, with perhaps the exception of the quarterbacks and running backs, were bigger than everyone else.

Otherwise, we felt we were all pretty much the same — at least from appearances. Although we came from different communities and regions in the U.S., we had the same goal — gather new knowledge about a variety of subjects, get good grades and graduate in four years. We were there to study hard, pass exams, memorize both verses of the alma mater, wear the freshman beanie our first year and attend chapel three times a week as required, even if it didn't always involve praying or religion.

Today, with a student body of just under 3,000, which includes 55 percent women to 45 percent men, Colgate, which adopted co-education in the early 1970s, is more diversified. This is also true for other educational institutions. According to the U.S. Department of Education, women currently comprise more than 56 percent of all students on U.S. college campuses, and that number is expected to increase to 57 percent by 2026.

However, while eliminating the gender gap, Colgate could still be more diverse. President Casey sent a clear signal that during his tenure he will champion this goal: "Colgate must attract a body that reflects the vibrant diversity of our nation."

However, inclusion must also be made a priority, and discussions must take place to address potential issues of implicit bias. This is because stereotyping unfortunately remains a problem in our culture. In May 2017, Colgate University made news because of the way campus security reacted to a student of color holding a glue gun for a school project. Another student saw the black student holding the glue gun, mistook it for a real gun and reported it. The report triggered a lockdown of several hours and prompted a campus-wide email notification of an "active shooter" before campus police were able to determine the facts — that a student working on an academic project was no threat to the community. Many people viewed the incident as an overreaction, and students immediately gathered at the college chapel to discuss the unfortunate situation until about 2 a.m. As reported in local news media, students questioned the role that racial bias might have had in the matter. Although the university argued that its reaction followed protocol, the incident provoked campus-wide conversations about the experience of black students on campus.

Similarly, Harvard, the well-known Ivy League university in Cambridge, Massachusetts, was also at the center of a race-related controversy in April 2018. At that time, three Cambridge police officers were called to calm down a student who was allegedly high on LSD. The situation escalated when they took down the student during his arrest. In a follow-up article on May 5, 2018, in the *New York Post*, entitled "Harvard vs. the Cops," Harvard President Drew Gilpin Faust was quoted as saying: "This profoundly disturbing arrest comes during a period of increasingly urgent questions about race and policing in the United States." The event provokes people to think critically about implicit biases so that, in the words of Faust, "people from all backgrounds and life experiences can come together confident in their ability to do their best work in a safe, supportive, and constructive environment."

Like Faust, I believe our society must actively enact change, rather than wait for change to occur. We must examine our thinking, the implicit beliefs that inform our world view and our assumptions — because these are the things that shape our actions. We must also do more on all levels, individually and as a nation. And it should start with the elected officials in Washington, D.C.

GOOD FOR BUSINESS

Doing the right thing and making diversity the new normal is good for so many reasons — including business.

In the January 22, 2018, edition of *Black Enterprise,* editor Derek T. Dingle, writes, "Studies have confirmed that diverse environments bolster corporations, promoting greater innovation and sharpening competitiveness. In fact, for years the New York-based Center for Talent Innovation has found that inclusive leadership produces the 'diversity dividend' that results in greater market share and a competitive advantage in gaining access to new markets as well as a 'speak-up culture' that values and stimulates new ideas."

Yet, as Dingle points out, "Even with undeniable evidence, diversity continues to be one of the today's most challenging organizational issues."

As such, we need to seek out good examples and follow them, particularly in the area of leadership.

One of the most highly recognized and esteemed corporate leaders is Kenneth C. Frazier, the chairman & CEO of Merck. Frazier, who is black, says on the company's website, "At Merck we believe there is strength in differences. Our ability to continue delivering on our mission of saving and improving lives around the world relies on having globally and locally diverse teams of talented employees at all levels. ...Diversity is woven throughout our business practices and training strategy. ...Leaders are accountable for specific objectives related to Diversity and Inclusion. Results are measured in terms of individual, division and company-wide performance."

Frazier was commended for resigning from President Donald Trump's presidential advisory council "after Mr. Trump's equivocating response to the outburst of white nationalist violence in Charlottesville, Virginia," in 2017, according to reporting in *The New York Times*. Frazier was quoted as saying, "The most important role of a leader is to safeguard the heritage and values of the company."

Frazier's decision and Merck's support demonstrate that it is necessary not only to enact principles of diversity and inclusion within your own structure, but also to stand up for diversity and inclusion everywhere and to call out injustices. The voice of change must become the voice of reason.

Likewise, Jon Iwata, former chief brand officer and senior vice president at IBM, was quoted in *Diverse Voices: Profiles in Leadership* as saying, "There are many reasons to make a commitment to diversity and inclusion. It may be the 'right thing to do.' It's also the smart thing to do."

John Lewis, a vocal civil rights leader and Georgia Congressman, is optimistic that we are indeed moving in the right direction. His commitment was quoted in the June 15, 2018, edition of *Time* magazine: "The next generation will help make this society less conscious of race. There will be less racism, there will be more tolerance. Dr. [Martin Luther] King said we must learn to live together as brothers and sisters. ...You have to be hopeful. You have to be optimistic. If not, you will get lost in despair. When I travel around the country, I say, 'Don't get down — you cannot get down.' I'm not down. I got arrested, beaten, left bloody and unconscious. But I haven't given up. And you cannot give up."

I am convinced he is right. We cannot give up. We must keep trying. We'll have a much better world if we do.

DOESCHER LESSON: *Borrowing from an Oprah Winfrey comment, "Real integrity is doing the right thing, knowing that nobody's going to know whether you did it or not."*

32.
MENTORING A MUST

Bill with mentees (pictured left to right) Christina Siekierski and Carolyn Siekierski, Colgate University sophomores, 2018

"Good leaders need to listen as much as they need to talk."

— Lee Iacocca

Find a mentor — or two or three or more.

That's been my advice to numerous high school and college students, Jackie Robinson Foundation scholars, attendees in my courses and lectures, and children of friends who have told me they were looking for "wisdom and contacts my parents said you had." Experience is probably more to the point, but I'll take "wisdom" from those fresh-faced, earnest kids.

Mentoring is a two-way street as far as I'm concerned, and I am fortunate to have experienced it from both sides. I've benefited from mentors along the way — and from being a mentor myself.

Obviously, being a mentor means a lot more than just sharing wisdom, contacts or experience. It's a long-term relationship focused on supporting the growth and development of a mentee, as well as providing the guidance to help them become leaders.

Above all, as a mentor, it is important to show the mentee that you believe in his or her potential. It is even more important to cultivate within the mentee the belief in oneself. Confidence, after all, is one of the greatest ingredients of success. My Aunt Elsie was my first mentor, and one of her strongest and most enduring gifts was that she always let me know she believed in me.

Mentorships bring a few challenges and many rewards. Keeping the mentees on a schedule and ensuring that they show up for meetings and conference calls are the greatest challenges. Some overwhelming benefits, however, other than the personal satisfaction gained by helping another person, are mentees' outward enthusiasm, obvious appreciation, gigantic smiles, and those moments when a mentee cares enough — and is brave enough — to speak up and share meaningful advice. One of my mentees even inspired an idea for this book, which was later developed into an essay considering the future of communications. In many cases the mutual respect shared with mentees has cultivated lasting friendships.

Some mentors think of themselves as coaches, but I never have. I think of coaching as the process of teaching proven techniques for immediate results. Coaching brings success, for example, to an athlete in a game or to a writer on deadline. Mentoring, on the other hand, requires a much longer commitment and focuses on personal development. It may last from high school, to college, to initial career, or it may endure for a lifetime. Mentoring should always be approached as a relationship for the long haul, and if productive, it will almost always advance one's professional goals.

Harold Burson, one of PR's most influential figures, was one of my mentors. Although I never hired his firm, Burson-Marsteller, for public relations advice for any of the companies I worked for, Burson and I talked often — and not just in New York City where we had lunch occasionally at one of his favorite restaurants within walking distance of his office. There was always room for conversations, no matter the venue. These included meetings of the Arthur W. Page Society, PRSA and Wisemen events, as well as happenings at the Scarsdale Golf Club where we were both members and the Scarsdale Woman's Club where our wives were active. Probably most impressive was the fact that Burson never missed returning my phone calls. I was most pleased to be in the mix with his client calls to various CEOs who relied on him for advice. Like them, I knew Burson's advice was always on the money.

Among other skills that he transferred, Burson set an example by being a strong proponent of networking and mentoring. He knew the value firsthand because he had learned from a number of mentors himself. Since Burson was famously free-thinking, some mentors even included his competitors — George Hammond, CEO of Carl Byoir Associates; Farley Manning of Manning Selvage & Lee; independent consultant G. Edward Pendray; and John W. Hill, founder of Hill & Knowlton.

According to a story memorialized in *PRWeek*, Hill called Burson after losing a pitch to Burson's agency and said: "Are you Harold Burson? I'm John Hill, and if you're going to take business away from us, I'd like to see what you look like. Come over and have lunch with me." It was the first of a series of lunches that forged a strong friendship between the two business rivals. The two respected each other and learned from each other, and eventually their firms ended up being part of the WPP empire, which was one of the world's largest advertising agencies at the time.

No doubt, Burson and Hill's relationship worked so well because it was based on mutual respect and trust. These two ingredients are essential in any relationship, including mentorships. They are what enables open communication and an easy transfer of advice.

There's no question that having a mentor makes a positive difference in one's career. A mentor can be a sounding board or provide reality checks when you're considering a new job or a career change. A mentor can also help navigate strategies when you're having difficulty with your boss, colleagues or higher-ups.

In my own case, Joseph T. Nolan and Chester Burger always provided me with reasoned lists of assets and liabilities relating to situations with which I was struggling. Each of these mentors was always there for me, on the phone or across the table at a working lunch, ready to discuss my options.

While I worked for Nolan at my first PR job with The Chase Manhattan Bank in my 20s, I never worked for Chet Burger. Nevertheless, Burger and I became close when he once floated the idea that I could become the CEO of his company as he neared retirement. It never happened, because his company was bought by another group that nominated its own executive for the top spot. Later in his life, Burger continued to support my career as a mentor, and no matter what he was doing, he never failed to answer my phone calls. Whether he was teaching at an Episcopal church near his home in the Big Apple or taking photos for his book, *Unexpected New York*, he always made time for me. In particular, I recall that he saved me from making two decisions that would have been disastrous for my career. Both of these decisions would have involved the possibility of changing jobs, industries and locations.

After discussing the different scenarios, Chet convinced me, each time, that staying in my current jobs was the correct thing to do at the moment. His sage recommendations proved to be right, and I'm glad I could rely on him for that advice and mentoring.

The recollection of these mentors' generosity with time and authentic support is part of the reason why I have become a mentor to others. It's called giving back.

Many of my mentees have started out as students. I have met them through my role as an alumni-interviewer for Colgate University and the S.I. Newhouse School of Public Communications at Syracuse University. Other mentees came to me through my work as a board member of the Jackie Robinson Foundation. Sometimes, too, the beginning has been less formal. On more than one occasion, a casual piece of advice uttered during a conversation has led to interested follow-up and a mentorship — and later to a seat at my mentee's college graduation.

Although a mentorship may start with advice, its true value lies deeper. The belief of the mentor in the mentee's potential is paramount — and the communication of this kind of cheerleading and support is immensely powerful. Such a projection of confidence can dismantle the barriers of self-doubt and the limiting thoughts that people often have. This opens the potential for achievement and starts to make dreams into realities. This, I believe, is worth more than all the collected recommendations together.

I am proud to say that my mentees have gone on to graduate from esteemed programs at schools including Harvard University, Yale University, Newhouse at Syracuse University, Spelman College, Bentley College, Penn State University and others. Many have followed their educations with successful careers in finance, law, healthcare, marketing, advertising, public relations and other specialized fields. They have worked in the United States and abroad, fulfilling their ambitions and forging new paths to success.

Heather Holloway Moore was one of the JRF mentees who completed a superb internship in my department at Dun & Bradstreet in the 1990s. She showed promise and ambition, which earned her the opportunity to write a speech for CEO Terry Taylor. While still a scholar with JRF, she received the Ralph E. Ward Achievement Award for being the graduating senior with the highest GPA. She went on to graduate from Spelman College and Duke University School of Law. Later, in 2005, she was honored with a national Outstanding Student Award from the Clinical Legal Education Association for her work in the Children's Education Law Clinic, where she successfully represented a high school senior who was facing permanent expulsion from school. After receiving the award, Heather expressed sentiments that recalled Jackie Robinson's own philosophy. She said, "I have come to realize why I have wanted to be a lawyer since the age of eight and what exactly I can do to make a difference in the lives of others." She is now a product policy manager at Facebook headquarters in Menlo Park, California.

It is rewarding to receive feedback from mentees and learn about their ongoing success and engagement in new environments. Recently, my email inbox lit up with news from Jordana Kaller, of Scarsdale, a recent mentee who started her freshman year at Colgate University. "I am genuinely having the best time of my entire life in school," she wrote. "I have made many amazing friends, love my professors, love my classes and just feel so at home here. ... I have gotten involved in campus — I am a greeter in admissions; I am on the board of Hillel; and I am in Challah for Hunger, a club called Colgate Buddies and a mentorship club."

I am particularly pleased that Jordana is carrying the torch of mentoring further, sharing her knowledge and giving support to others through Colgate's student mentorship club. In today's culture, where human-to-human interactions are increasingly being replaced by virtual scenarios, face-to-face mentoring is more important than ever. I'd like to believe that, like Heather and Jordana, all of my mentees are making a difference in the world.

DOESCHER LESSON: *Finding a mentor ... or two ... or three ... or more ... is a necessary ingredient for success. You won't regret it.*

33.
A PIPELINE TO TALENT

"It is every man's obligation to put back into the world at least the equivalent of what he takes out of it."

— Albert Einstein

As a proponent of mentoring and giving back, it was a natural choice for me to become involved with developing the Communications Career Academy program, sponsored by the Public Relations Society of America Foundation, in 2000. The program focused on the potential of bringing minorities into the public relations profession and was an incredibly satisfying achievement in my 57-plus-years career in public relations and marketing communications.

The idea was born from a goal to promote diversity within the field of public relations by increasing awareness about communications professions in inner-city schools. The program sought to inspire talented minorities who might not otherwise be exposed to such careers. It was the dawn of the 21st century, and as members of the philanthropic PRSA Foundation board, we reasoned that the face of public relations must mirror that of America. Our plan involved developing and supporting a number of Communications Career Academies located in predominantly underprivileged neighborhoods in different geographic areas. Our plan was to test the program with seven pilot sites and keep going.

David Grossman, a principal thought partner of David Grossman & Associates in Chicago, and the then president of the PRSA Foundation, professionally produced the program's attractive brochure. He implemented unusual graphics and an appealing sell that focused on how the curriculum would engage students in "real world" learning by bringing them together with teachers and public relations professionals. The magic we hypothesized would lie in connecting students to a career by involving them with working industry leaders.

It was a great idea, first introduced by Jean Farinelli, who at one time was chairman and chief executive officer of the PR firm Creamer Basford. She brought the idea to the Foundation while serving as its president, one year before Grossman held the position. She called a meeting in New York City to propose her plan of "introducing high school students to public relations as an exciting college major and fulfilling career." In order to accomplish her vision, she recommended utilizing the nationwide resources of 113 Public Relations Student Society of America (PRSSA) chapters, the 6,000-member-strong university student society of PRSA and sponsors who could provide financial wherewithal.

As members of the Foundation board, David and I were at that meeting. We listened to Jean's ideas and enthusiastically endorsed her plans. We became officers of the program, and at different times, each of us served as Foundation president. We were a good, rational, dedicated, business-like team — absolutely simpatico on the potential value of the program.

We were sure we knew what the Communications Career Academies could mean to motivated minority students and the future of PR, if we could only expose those high school students to the public relations profession. We also felt our program was needed, as we suspected that high school students' knowledge of the public relations field was basically nonexistent. As we forged ahead, we learned that we were right. Public relations was not previously on the radar screen for any of the students we encountered, not even for their teachers.

Nevertheless, with the backing of the national PRSA organization, which is the largest public relations organization in the world with 21,000 members, we rolled up our sleeves, raised funds and found satisfactory high schools to take on the academic role in seven U.S. cities. We developed an extensive and professional curriculum for the program with the help of Dr. Shirley Serini, a seasoned college professor who has held PR teaching positions at Morehead State University in Kentucky and Ball State University in Indiana.

When I later started teaching courses in investor relations and public relations-related subjects at the S.I. Newhouse School of Public Communications at Syracuse University, Columbia University and other colleges — I looked back on Shirley's curriculum and realized how thorough a job she had done. Her lessons for the Communications Career Academy provided breadth and depth on the subject.

The first Communications Career Academies were partnered with seven schools and linked to seven local PRSA and PRSSA chapters. They were located in Baltimore, Maryland; Dallas, Texas; Newark, New Jersey; Oakland, California; Philadelphia, Pennsylvania; St. Louis, Missouri; and Tampa, Florida.

In order to oversee the academic operation of the program and handle on-site visits, we then hired Sandy Mittelsteadt, a former high-school English teacher from Bakersfield, California. She brought valuable experience from having worked as the executive director of the National Career Academy Coalition, and she was introduced to us by Ray Gaulke, who served as president and COO of PRSA National for eight years in the 1990s. Sandy was particularly helpful in setting up the academies and ensuring that the curriculum was being followed to the letter. Sandy recommended we add two Communications Career Academies in Atlanta, Georgia, and one in Washington, D.C., to the original seven pilot schools, and we followed through with her advice.

As we became more organized, we concentrated on student education. We believed effort in this area would generate the most sustainable results, and we started to show success. During meetings with leaders and students, it was clear that the program's coursework was having a positive impact on the students. They were engaged in each lesson and excited to speak with guests from the PR world. The students' questions were intelligent and forward-thinking. Moreover, it was noticeable that the computers supplied by AT&T were better than any Christmas present. The kids told us so with their enthusiasm and prolific thanks.

Delighted with our initial results, we continued putting our hearts and souls into the program. We wanted the Communications Career Academies to succeed. We would have even washed dishes or waited on tables to raise money for the program if necessary, but fortunately we didn't have to. Sponsorships started coming in. Everyone involved with the program did some fundraising and made awareness calls to opinion leaders and other influential people whom we knew.

Somewhat unexpectedly, we succeeded in attracting corporate partners who believed in the program. Under the banner of the PRSA Foundation, we were able to secure sponsorships from the following corporations: American Airlines, AT&T, Bob Evans Farms, Inc., Cigna, Edelman, Fusive.com, JPMorgan Chase, Nike, PepsiCo Inc., Prudential, The Rockefeller Foundation, Sears Roebuck and Co., and Visa. I was particularly pleased that Joe Vecchione and Bob DeFillippo, for Prudential, and Richard and Dan Edelman, for Edelman, had made sure their respected companies were represented for this important cause.

The corporate generosity we received legitimized the value of our vision and our efforts. I clearly remember my delight when JPMorgan Chase presented us with a big check for $100,000 that was used for operations and a number of other important items in the program.

AT&T was also extremely supportive — but not with money. In 2002, on a personal fundraising visit to the AT&T headquarters in Basking Ridge, New Jersey, I hit the jackpot. In all my years of raising millions of dollars for charities, colleges, and nonprofits, I have to say that my appointment with Dick Martin, AT&T's executive vice president of public relations and brand management, was undoubtedly the most interesting, friendly and direct conversation. It also garnered the fastest results.

Sitting in the company cafeteria, Dick said, "How would it be if AT&T gave the academies 200 slightly used laptop computers?"

I tried to act nonchalant, but it was impossible to contain my excitement over such a meaningful contribution. "Absolutely yes!" I exclaimed. "We'll distribute them evenly among the academies."

"It's easy for us to do," Dick replied, "because we give our employees new computers every year."

I had been in the headquarters building for only 20 minutes and had more than accomplished my mission. We were now getting 20 laptop computers for classroom use at each PR academy. Just think of what the students could do with those!

My 90-minute car ride back to Scarsdale on the New Jersey Turnpike, over the George Washington Bridge, up the Major Deegan Highway to the Cross County and Bronx River parkways seemed like a helicopter ride. I had known Dick only casually from industry meetings, but I had an instinct that AT&T would be a good company to approach, especially since Dick was also chairman of the AT&T Foundation. Obviously, I was right.

The addition of PR professionals in our academies' classrooms was integral to the program's initial success. One of those people was Dave Imre, CEO and founder of Imre Communications, located in Maryland. The 25-year-old firm is today an $18-million marketing communications agency with expertise in social media, creative public relations and paid media. In 2003, I witnessed, firsthand, as Dave shared his extensive knowledge with students at the Baltimore academy. I saw how he was able to light up the room and how students responded with electric enthusiasm. Dave was a dedicated supporter of the program who made many inspiring visits to the classroom.

In November of 2002, David Grossman was quoted in *Public Relations Tactics*, a PRSA publication, about the future of the PR academies. As president of the PRSA Foundation, he said, "We're looking at continuing to strengthen the existing pilot program through additional curriculum and best-practice sharing. This is a 20-year journey to make the face of public relations different. It's going to take us a long time, but we're thrilled to be taking a step in the right direction."

When I took over as president of the PRSA Foundation in 2004, it made sense that David and I would continue to work closely together to attract the brightest and the best participants into our program. We shared a vision of diversity and talent for the future of our field, and we wanted to preserve our program's continuity and integrity. So we left our personal agendas and egos at the door and simply focused on this essential program. It absolutely had to succeed so we could show the world — the PR world and the entire world — what was possible.

In many ways, it was like having a baby, and we were just as excited. You couldn't take the smiles off our faces — or those of the students and PR professionals who volunteered their time — if you tried. All of us could already see the future in what we were doing, and it was brighter than ever before.

David and I had hoped to expand the curriculum and the program to other start-up Communications Career Academies in the U.S. But for some reason it didn't happen. Without much explanation, in 2005, PRSA, which held the purse strings for the PRSA Foundation and therefore the academies, pulled the plug on a minimal budget for the PR academies. As a result, the momentum and the program itself were lost. I was deeply disappointed by that decision — not only because it precipitated the program's demise, but moreover, because it closed important doors that were opening to underrepresented people, whom, I believed, had the power to reinvigorate our field.

Is it time for PRSA and the PRSA Foundation to resurrect the Communications Career Academy program? My vote is a resounding yes.

DOESCHER LESSON: *Sometimes when you give your all and a project fails, you should take solace in the fact that some benefit went to those for which it was intended. Half a loaf of bread is better than no bread at all.*

34. THE REAL DEAL

"Whatever title or office we may be privileged to hold, it is what we do that defines who we are."

— Queen Rania Al Abdullah of Jordan

Life abounds with many opportunities to learn and grow. Some occur in structured school settings or informal mentorships. Others are built around professional programs like the Communications Career Academies we tried to get off the ground in the early 2000s. And some just happen because of the people we meet.

Over the years, I have met and worshiped with a number of lead Protestant ministers. They have included the Rev. P. Arthur Brindisi of the Westminster Presbyterian Church in Utica, New York; the Rev. Gordon Sperry of the Corinth United Church of Christ in Hickory, North Carolina; the Rev. Philip Washburn of the Scarsdale Congregational Church and the Rev. Dr. John Miller, formerly of Hitchcock Presbyterian Church, both in Scarsdale, New York.

Each of these ministers was highly professional and immensely dedicated to his calling. However, they differed in how they performed their missions and how they approached issues concerning religion, God, staff management, and counseling their flock in both good times and bad. Like most members of the cloth, these ministers followed certain routines and rituals as they adhered to service schedules and monthly and quarterly themes.

While all of these ministers were excellent, their sermons were distinct. As each minister spoke about broad themes, his words revealed his individual interpretation of the Bible, his personal ideas about current events and a signature preaching style. Each minister showed his calling was more than just a job. In watching them in action, I could see their pleasure in serving parishioners, the church and the Lord.

But the minister who stands out most in my mind is the young Rev. Pete D. Jones, who at age 37, became the new pastor at Hitchcock Presbyterian Church, in Scarsdale. Upon his arrival, in 2015, Pete received immediate approval from the congregation. For some, Pete was received as the "Messiah" they had been waiting for. For me, sitting in the choir loft and serving as a Ruling Elder at the Session meetings, it was truly amazing to watch the changes that this new pastor brought. I noticed a major change of attitude in the church, a surge in attendance of Sunday services, an increase in new members, robust involvement of children, and continued diversity among church members.

Parishioners now come to Hitchcock on Sundays because they want to, not because they feel obligated to show up. As a member of the Chancel Choir, I'd like to believe that the sweet sound of our music is also a draw, but realistically, I know it's more because of Pete.

Pete briefly tried his hand in the business world after college. But it didn't feel right, and he eventually listened to his wife Annie's advice to embrace what he really wanted to do in life. She encouraged him to go back to school, complete divinity studies and follow his father's and sister's footsteps into the ministry.

Pete came to Hitchcock from a historic church in Kentucky, and the entire Hitchcock congregation is pleased he accepted the call. Pete brought his lovely family along — including Annie, their four school-age kids – Gracey, Kate, Martha and Jack — and his mother in law. They became immediately involved in the community and are now a welcoming and most visible feature of the church, both in and out of the sanctuary.

Annie chairs church fundraisers and works hands-on with whatever needs to be done. Gracey sings in the Chancel Choir and performs solos. The three younger kids are involved in the children's choir. Kate and Martha have read scripture. They are indeed the church's family, and it is heartwarming to watch them grow up before our eyes.

Pete is most definitely not a cookie-cutter minister. For openers, he's a regular guy with a favorite sports team, the Boston Red Sox, who's not full of himself and clearly understands the mission of serving his parishioners and God. He seems to enjoy every moment of his new pastoral assignment in Scarsdale, and only seems uncomfortable when church members praise him, which happens often.

On Sunday mornings, Pete arrives at church early and in shirt sleeves. Without wearing the minister's black robe, he ventures into the sanctuary to greet the early arrivals with a pastoral hug. I don't think they teach that in divinity school. Perhaps it's a topic in public relations classes or customer focus scenarios, but not at divinity schools.

Then, acting as the "CEO" of the church, Pete checks out everything to avoid any glitches that could disrupt the service. He goes over the sound system, the candles to be lit, the readings and anything special for that morning. Sometimes, he rearranges things on the altar as if he were a decorator. He then talks to anyone scheduled to participate in the service, including communion servers and the excited families of soon-to-be baptized babies. He also warmly greets any visitors he notices.

Listening to the Chancel Choir rehearse under Director John T. King, Pete always smiles. His face radiates admiration, and this inspires the singers. As he has mentioned to the congregation several times, he smiles because he "can't do that — sing well."

When it's time for the service to begin, Pete dons his minister's robe and says, "Welcome to Hitchcock Presbyterian Church. We're glad you've joined us this morning." With his sermon and notes firmly in place on the pulpit, Pete is ready to take a chance at brightening everyone's day.

Not being a cookie-cutter minister means that Pete does not stick to formulas. He often amends his prepared sermons early each morning to make them relevant to the day. His words succeed in impacting the congregation because Pete includes references to current events or timely reflections. Pete's sermons feel personal, and he is not afraid to share memories from his own life or thoughts that came to him in the middle of the night. For the attentive listener, Pete is not just giving a sermon. He speaks to open discussions, promote critical thinking, connect people through common humanity and provide an example of a life lived with mindfulness and generosity. He is also an expert storyteller who knows how to weave meaning into entertaining narrative.

As everyone at Hitchcock has witnessed, Pete removes his wristwatch while preaching. This enables him to keep an eye on the dial and better time his sermons to the 12-to-15-minute range. You'd think, by now, that giving sermons has become routine for Pete, but it hasn't. He once admitted to me that he always has a bit of nervousness about stepping into the pulpit to preach. "If you don't have butterflies in your stomach, then you should quit and go do something else," he said.

Pete succeeds at being a minister for everyone, and his charisma extends to the congregation's youngest members. Each of his services includes a "time with the children" during which Pete welcomes kids to the altar, gets down on their level and interacts with them. These conversations are classics, as Pete opens the floor to the kids and invites them to talk. While making connections between the children's lives, scripture and sermon, Pete starts the chatter by asking kids questions about school, upcoming holidays and other aspects of their lives. By now, Pete has familiarized himself with each child's name and personality. Some kids are shy; some spill stories like waterfalls. Some kids are earnest; others are comedians. But Pete involves all of the kids, encouraging participation and truly listening to what they have to say.

Because Pete moves through the service with such precision, I always find it hard to believe that 60 minutes have elapsed by the time he reaches his closing words. It's a rare talent to keep a congregation engaged and involved for an entire hour — and an even greater achievement to keep people coming back week after week. But Pete manages to do it every time. He's more than just a minister; his authenticity makes him a real person. It's a rare trait — not only in ministry, but in real life.

One church member remarked about Pete's ministry at Hitchcock: "Once in a generation."

I agree. Pete is the real deal.

DOESCHER LESSON: *"If you really want to stand out, be authentic. Be real."*

35. EVERYTHING IS CONNECTED: A DIFFERENT KIND OF RABBI

"The job of the rabbi has always been to nurture a conversation between the generations."

—Rabbi Jonathan Blake

In Scarsdale, New York, Jonathan Blake, the senior rabbi of Westchester Reform Temple since 2011, is a different kind of rabbi. He's a regular guy with a sense of humor and a talent for music that could have taken him onto the Broadway stage had he chosen to go that route.

But he didn't.

He majored in English literature at Amherst College and graduated in 1995. While there, he was active in the college's chapter of Hillel International, the largest Jewish campus organization in the world, and he often tutored professors' children to recite portions of the Torah for their bar- and bat-mitzvahs.

It was in his freshman year at Amherst that Jonathan realized he wanted to be a rabbi. Therefore, it was no surprise that, after graduation, he immediately pursed this goal by enrolling at Hebrew Union College in Cincinnati, Ohio.

And what happened to his love of music? He satisfied it by marrying the love of his life — Kelly McCormick, who for years, has starred in many Broadway musicals around the country. Jonathan happily promotes her performances on stage, announcing upcoming performances and posting ticket information online.

Kelly was born to Christian parents — a Hungarian mother and an Irish-Catholic father. She grew up in a Presbyterian church outside Detroit, Michigan. It was at that aforementioned Hebrew Union College, where she sang, that she met Jonathan, then a rabbinical student. In 2000, Kelly converted to Judaism. A few months later, Jonathan graduated and was ordained. Two years later, the couple married.

Jonathan, who was born in Allentown, Pennsylvania, to an anesthesiologist and an accountant, has a great love of the Torah and an outward passion for Reform Judaism. His sermons on Friday evenings are friendly, intelligent, colorful and interesting. With a smiling face and a youthful energy, Rabbi Blake emerges — and never disappoints his congregants. To their delight, he sometimes even plays the guitar.

Rabbi Blake is well known for always having something meaningful to convey. Sometimes, he communicates with a song pertinent to that evening's religious lesson. Or he might share an important message related to a contemporary debate with the town, the nation or around the globe. His bar- and bat-mitzvah services are simultaneously joyful and significant. His gravesite services are sensitive and sincere. He is an active participant in ecumenical activities and services in the Scarsdale and New York Metropolitan areas.

When I asked for his help, Rabbi Blake graciously accepted to deliver the benediction at an annual luncheon hosted by the Cancer Support Team, an organization that provides free services to cancer patients in southern Westchester County. These include nursing, counseling, transportation to medical treatment facilities and other services.

In his temple, Rabbi Blake is modest, but he shines like a star. During the part of the service in which the Torah is carried through the temple, Rabbi Blake holds it proudly in his hands. You can tell he loves this part of the service. His smile, all the way around, says it all.

Rabbi Blake also teaches courses in continuing education, which draw large crowds of enthusiastic learners of all ages. These topics include the history of Interpretation, biblical and rabbinic literature, Jewish-Christian relations and the history of Reform Judaism.

Above all, Rabbi Blake is a good teacher because he is a good storyteller. In his role as rabbi, this gift of storytelling enables him to reach members of the congregation and help them understand their own, individual stories about being a part of the Jewish people.

Rabbi Blake is thought of as an unconventional and conventional rabbi at the same time. He satisfies what people are looking for, yet he always gives more. He goes beyond what is expected. As a result, his congregants love and respect him as a brother, as a member of the family so to speak.

When he was selected to replace Rabbi Richard Jacobs in 2011 as the senior rabbi at Westchester Reform Temple, Jacobs told the local *Scarsdale Inquirer* that he was "thrilled" by Blake's appointment: "He's a brilliant teacher, gifted preacher, caring pastor and creative thinker who is greatly loved by our whole community. To put it simply, Rabbi Blake is a gem."

When selected from a national search that drew 18 applicants for the position, Rabbi Blake, a noted orator and singer, was already serving as the temple's beloved associate rabbi. It was a perfect choice.

If you have ever met Rabbi Blake, you quickly learn that his devotion to work and his capabilities are givens. But his immense talent doesn't stop there. His creativity continues to flow. All the time, it seems.

"Episodes – Everything is Connected" is the name of a series of podcasts that Rabbi Blake has developed. He describes them as "connections between the world outside us and worlds within us." As the podcasts' host, Rabbi Blake guides participants to connect with guest artists, creators, and thinkers — in order to learn how to "live with purpose."

The first episode featured a reverend and a rabbi, discussing the relative merits – and demerits – of organized religion. Their conversation took a deep dive into the question: What good is religion anyway? Rev. Wayne

Francis, pastor of Authentic Church in White Plains, New York, and Rabbi Jonathan Malamy, director of spiritual care and religious life at the New Jewish Home in New York City, were the featured authorities in the lively, thought-provoking conversation.

Other podcast guests have included Michele Lowe, a playwright, librettist, lyricist and coach for speaking and writing; Abigail Pogrebin, author of *The Spirituality of Marking Time*, and a former broadcast producer for Fred Friendly, Charlie Rose, and Bill Moyers at PBS, as well as for Ed Bradley and Mike Wallace at *60 Minutes*; Tara Stiles, founder of Strala Yoga, a revolutionary approach to healing through movement, and Rev. Dr. Katharine Rhodes Henderson, president of Auburn Seminary, a multi-faith leadership development and research institute in New York City, who talked about "Do Politics Belong in Religion?"

In a talk titled "Are You Paying Attention?" Rabbi Blake addressed his temple's confirmation class of 5778 on May 23, 2018. He encouraged members of the class to speak out on issues of concern and to do so by paying attention to their surroundings. Driving the point home, Rabbi Blake urged young people to speak out "because the world is on fire, and God — so to speak — is waiting for you to pay attention, to speak up, to demand a response."

Using his storytelling verve, Rabbi Blake told the confirmation class about a burning palace in a parable. He cited Abraham in the Bible who "walks with eyes open, that he pays attention, that he notices the fire; but it is also

Abraham who wonders aloud why this is happening, why is no one else paying attention, why is no one doing anything; and then he demands a response. What makes Abraham special is that he sees things not only for what they are, but for the way they ought to be, and he roars out his objection."

Blake continued his talk with a quotation from Sir Jonathan Sacks, former chief rabbi of Great Britain, who explained, "Judaism begins not in wonder that the world is, but in protest that the world is not as it ought to be. It is in that sacred discontent that Abraham's journey begins."

With those words, Rabbi Blake had everyone's attention. With those words, he not only connected them with history, but also instilled conviction to make a difference in the world.

DOESCHER LESSON: *When looking to connect to a synagogue, church or community, you should pay close attention to the surroundings, what the people and clergy are saying, and what messages are being delivered. If you are comfortable in that environment, you have most likely found a good home of faith — and, likewise, that community will have found you.*

36.
NEARLY THE DEAN OF THE CORNELL BUSINESS SCHOOL

"Always wear a smile because you never know who is watching."

— Gracie Gold, American figure skater

Sometimes the things we remember most are the things we least expect to happen.

One morning in 1997, Happy Cuthill, my highly-organized and most efficient assistant, came bursting into my Dun & Bradstreet office in Murray Hill, New Jersey, instructing me to pick up the phone.

"Now," she said.

I usually obeyed her orders, as many intelligent bosses did back then. So, without much hesitation, I picked up the phone.

When Happy first received the call, the person on the other end had not only identified himself and his reason for calling. He also correctly pronounced my last name with a silent O (the umlaut over the O) when asking for Bill Doescher. This meant he knew me and was certainly not a new vendor trying to sell something I didn't need.

The caller was a Colgate University friend with an urgent message. His name was John E. Gillick, Colgate class of 1967 and an attorney from Washington, D.C. He greeted me with an excited voice as I put the phone to my ear.

He said, "You may not know this, but you are one of three finalists actively being considered to become the dean of the Samuel Curtis Johnson Graduate School of Management at Cornell University. I don't know if you are interested, but I wanted to give you a heads-up because the executive recruiter's next call about your background and capabilities will be to Harrington 'Duke' Drake." Drake was a former Chairman and CEO of Dun & Bradstreet and a former chairman of the Colgate board of trustees. We often traveled to Colgate together for alumni meetings.

Completely shocked, I blurted out, "What? I certainly didn't know, and besides I don't have a PhD. I only have a master's degree. Why would they want me?"

John followed with an explanation: "The reason you don't know is because they check you out first for academic positions, and then, if they believe you are a viable candidate, they contact you. You should immediately call Bill Bowen in the Chicago office of Heidrick & Struggles to get the details. He's handling the search, and I just got off the phone with him."

Taking a deep breath, I shut the door to my office so there would be no interruptions. I allowed myself some quiet time for deep soul searching.

Was this my dream job? How would I relate to professors, the majority of whom were sure to have PhDs? Did I really want to move back to an upstate environment and live in Ithaca? Would my wife Linda, a Manhattanite for most of her life, want to move there? What about my current D&B job, a very good one I reasoned, and the stock options?

I called my wife to discuss the situation. The phone rang, and I got the answering machine. She wasn't there. "Oh boy," I thought. I was on my own for this one.

Approximately 15 minutes had passed, and I called Bill Bowen, as recommended. He confirmed I was indeed a real candidate.

"Why me without a PhD?" I asked.

"They like your communications skills, fundraising capabilities and corporate experience. They're not at all concerned that you don't have a PhD," he said.

"Do the other candidates have PhDs?" I asked.

"Yes," he said. Unsurprised, I already knew the answer to that question.

"How did the committee even find me?" I asked.

Bowen explained, "A student group at Cornell got together, and we gave them one vote. You were it."

"What group was that, and who was the leader?" I asked.

"Can't tell you," he said, leaving the source of my recommendation a secret.

I then told him I was deeply honored to be considered for the position, but I was passing on the offer to be in the competition with the other two candidates.

I had thought about my family and what would happen to them if I left D&B. I also didn't want to lose my stock options. I nervously thought, if I would take the Cornell position, I would have to leave a lot of money on the table, and that didn't seem like a smart idea for the long term. In addition, I wasn't sure I wanted to move back to upstate New York. Also, I imagined Linda would veto the move.

While overjoyed with the possibility of an offer, it was not anything I had sought. I thought back to a previous career change when I accepted the VP position at Drexel Heritage and relocated to North Carolina. That was the right decision because it provided me with more business management experience at a time while I was building a resume. I was not actively building one when Gillick called.

I reasoned that I already had the best job ever, with a recognizable blue-chip company and a great boss whom I liked — the CEO, Terry Taylor. So why would I ever want to leave?

Bowen was disappointed by my decision to withdraw, because he felt I had a legitimate shot at being hired. The phone call to Duke Drake was thus averted.

I never thought I would find out who recommended me for the dean's position. I had already called Mike Ligas, the son of my friend John Ligas from Utica, since he was an MBA candidate at Cornell. But when I asked if he had recommended me, he said no.

Then, somewhat later, at a meeting of the Colgate University Alumni Corporation, one of the attendees opened his comment with a curious statement: "As an MBA student at Cornell ..." he told the group.

Immediately, a light bulb illuminated in my brain. Just maybe I finally had the answer to who recommended me for the position of the dean of the Johnson Business School at Cornell. Maybe my answer was right across the table. I couldn't wait for the meeting to be over so I could speak with him.

While others were collecting their things and making small talk, I hurried over to the young man. Shaking his hand, I asked him — Paul Lobo, Colgate Class of 1989, "Perchance, did you recommend me a few years ago as a candidate for dean at the Johnson School of Management at Cornell?"

He smiled and confirmed, "Yes. I watched you in the meetings here and liked the way you carried yourself, your communications skills and ideas about fundraising." Lobo added that he recommended me to members of the student group and they agreed with him. He, too, thought I had a good chance at getting the job.

For me, the mystery was solved, and I had Colgate to thank for it.

In 1997, Lobo received his MBA in marketing and operations from Cornell's Johnson Graduate School of Management. Today, he is a government affairs and marketing professional with 20 years of leadership experience working with Fortune 200 companies on Capitol Hill and with New York City government and politics. In

July 2012 he founded Policy Integration Partners, LLC, to provide government affairs and management consulting services.

I am still honored to have been nominated and considered for such a prestigious position. Nevertheless, I am happy that I withdrew my candidacy and remained at Dun & Bradstreet for the rest of my corporate career. So is my wife Linda.

DOESCHER LESSON: *You never know when someone is listening and watching, so always put your best foot forward.*

37.
AND, THE MOST POPULAR IS ...

Honoring Caddie Master Jimmy Rocco at Scarsdale Golf Club. Pictured left to right: Jimmy, SGC member Fred Riccio, Bill and locker room attendant Peter Kane, 1999.

"Do not desire to be famous; be loved."

— C. JoyBell C., author

Send the election machines back to the barn.
Turn out the lights.
The vote is in.
Jimmy Rocco is the winner.
Nobody else got any votes.

The most popular person over many decades at the Scarsdale Golf Club is none other than the affable Jimmy Rocco, a legend in his own lifetime. He was the club's longtime caddie master and manager of the bowling alley during the winter months. Jimmy started working at the club as a caddie at age 14 and retired in 1999 after an incredible service of 72 years. He passed away in November 2011 at the age of 97.

As a member of the club for 36 years, I appointed myself the judge and jury in this popularity contest, and it was Rocco in a runaway. Nobody else had a chance. Jimmy was an easy choice for this selection. Everybody at the club loved and admired him, and nobody ever said a bad word about him.

Honest!

In reality, there wasn't any real competition. Had there been, the following people would have been considered a close second: Noel Flagg, Sr., a SGC member for 50 years and a past president; Marina Unis, women's golf champ multiple times; Sandy Morrissey, the queen of birdwatching; Anne Lyons, a tennis and paddle tennis devotee; Linda Fiorentino, a versatile athlete and tough competitor in many sports; Steve Joynt, former CEO of Fitch Ratings who found time to play more golf after his workload lessened; Ed Howard, Wilson Cup chair and golf club member since 1968; popular men's golfers Michael Cha, Mitch Kahn and Chris Unis; Bill Minard, the current general manager; Matt Brennan, the club's finance guy; Matt Severino, the most knowledgeable golf course superintendent in the area; Dan Daly, the affable caddie master since 2000; and Fred Riccio, a 43-year-long member, who encouraged me to add a piece about Jimmy Rocco for this book. Like me, Fred was one of Jimmy's devoted fans.

The one negative about selecting Rocco at this time is that the new members since 1999 never had the opportunity to meet or associate with the friendly guy. He was one of a kind, a teddy bear sort of fellow that you could feel absolutely safe inviting to your family's Thanksgiving Day dinner. If he accepted, he would try to go unnoticed until the small children in the crowd or your grandmother would ease over to him and start a conservation that would seemingly never end. His stories would unravel, to be enjoyed more than the meal, and he'd invariably attract a crowd. You might even have to blow a whistle and call a timeout in order to get everybody back to the table for the turkey dinner.

Hundreds, if not thousands, of past and current SGC members are better off for having met Jimmy or worked with him. Everyone knew him as a courteous and most gracious person. Not many people in today's world can have those words attached to their names. Jimmy treated everybody the same — no matter your age, your golfing ability or your bowling skills. There will probably never be anybody quite like Jimmy Rocco. At least not in my lifetime.

I'm still looking for that somebody.

DOESCHER LESSON: *Never forget those people who have had an impact on your life. They have added value and deserve recognition.*

38.
BUILDING A HOMETOWN WINNER

"I view real estate as the most intriguing opportunity that I've seen in my business lifetime."

— Richard Rainwater, a self-made billionaire

It's never too late to try something new. Moreover, you'll never know the reach of your potential unless you try. After my retirement from what others have called a legendary PR career, and after some time as a communications consultant, executive recruiter and merger-and-acquisition associate in the PR field, I decided to explore the world of real estate.

Why the transition from a corporate and consulting career to real estate? First, real estate offered the flexibility I was looking for in semi-retirement. Second, the idea of working with buyers and sellers appealed to my interests in communications and working with people. Presenting and selling the best aspects of homes were not too distant from the spirit of public relations. Third, my wife Linda, affectionately known as the decorating doyenne of Scarsdale, thought I would be good at it. So, with her encouragement, I signed up for the licensing course, studied the material for five weeks and passed the test on my first attempt.

In 2014, I joined Platinum Drive Realty, in Scarsdale, New York. It was a company that had grown from a local startup with a big ambition, a dedicated work ethic and a client-focused ethos. Since that time, I've helped clients purchase and sell houses in the community, and I've been successful at it. I'm not the stereotypical real estate agent. I take time to really listen to my clients and understand their needs so I can connect them with properties that will truly satisfy their lifestyles.

I enjoy the interaction with buyers and sellers. The interpersonal skills I've gained as a communicator work well for this profession, and I understand the philosophy of putting the client first. In one case, I had the perseverance to continue working with a couple who made an offer on a Tudor and changed their minds within 24 hours. After a few more weeks of looking, they eventually bought a ranch, which is what the wife wanted in the first place.

When I joined Platinum Drive Realty, I was the oldest agent in a company of much younger people. Perhaps they wanted a gray-haired person with whom younger clients would feel comfortable, and that makes sense. With all my professional and life experiences, I am able to do more than just sell; I also advise. Whenever needed, I share my wealth of knowledge on all areas related to buying or selling a house, such as heating and plumbing systems, the financing process and the construction and rehabilitation of homes. I am honest, straightforward and treat people the way I would want members of my own family to be treated if they were finding a new place to call home.

My work at Platinum Drive Realty has afforded me another pleasure — experiencing the development of a new company and the exciting transitions related to Platinum's acquisition by Compass, the fastest growing real estate brokerage firm in the world, in 2018. I was present at the internal announcement of the acquisition and experienced the electric optimism of participating in something that felt like the future.

Even before the acquisition, however, Platinum Drive Realty possessed all the ingredients of success. It was founded by Scarsdale High School sweethearts, Zach and Heather Harrison, in 2006. From the start, the couple dedicated themselves to the endeavor and steadily grew their business. Within only 10 years of negotiating real estate transactions full-time, they had carefully and methodically built Platinum into one of Westchester County's most competitive real estate firms.

In 2017, Platinum sold $238.7 million worth of real estate and became Scarsdale's highest-grossing real estate firm, based on selling price. The company was also receiving national attention. *Inc.* magazine auspiciously named it one of the fastest-growing companies in America in 2014, 2015, 2016 and 2017.

Zach and Heather's long history together and their deep involvement with the community supported their success. The couple first met in seventh grade at Scarsdale

Middle School when Zach invited Heather to his bar mitzvah. Their young attraction held while they grew up, and they started dating seriously when they were seniors at Scarsdale High School in 1990.

Heather and Zach finished high school and continued their educations. Zach went on to complete a master's degree in government administration at the University of Pennsylvania and a law degree at Fordham Law School. Prior to founding Platinum with Heather, Zach worked during college summers at Goldman Sachs and also as an attorney for the Reed Smith law firm.

Following her graduation from Penn State, Heather, a broadcast journalism major, worked as a television news reporter and anchor for TCI 10 News Westchester and News 12 Westchester. She also worked for West Glen Communications, a broadcast consulting firm.

Although both Heather and Zach were successful in their respective careers, these lifelong Scarsdale residents wanted a change. So in 2006 they obtained real estate licenses and incorporated a business to sell real estate. That year they were involved with selling three or four houses. The next year, they gave up their regular day jobs to devote all of their time to real estate. They were working seven days a week, sometimes around the clock, to build their business.

Their first hire was Seth Keslow, a former classmate and high school friend. Seth had enjoyed an earlier career in television and motion picture production but quickly developed his skills to become an award-winning licensed real estate salesperson. Mairin Mara and Dana Goldman, two other high school friends, soon followed Keslow to Platinum.

In addition to its Scarsdale and Chappaqua offices, Platinum quickly grew to include another office in neighboring Larchmont. By capitalizing on deep roots in the area, Platinum was able to grow while maintaining its hometown advantage. Soon, Heather and Zach's firm distinguished itself by the catchy slogan: "We grew up here; we live here; we sell homes here."

When it came time to announce the acquisition of the company by Compass, Zach and Heather called their agents into the office under the guise of a "meeting and photo shoot," scheduled for Valentine's Day morning, 2018. Set in a crowded conference room at Platinum's home office in Scarsdale's Golden Horseshoe Shopping Center, at least 40 licensed Platinum sales agents and seven representatives of Compass attended the meeting. Zach was the first to make the announcement, "Twelve years ago, Heather and I set our goal to change the face of real estate in the suburbs. We've done that, and we're now moving on to the next level and a new chapter. Joining with Compass is an exact cultural alignment. We wouldn't have done this acquisition with any other company."

Tipping her hat to the agents in the room and those who were joining remotely, Heather added, "We couldn't have done it without all of you."

According to Compass, the acquisition was part of a larger plan to open 70 offices nationwide. It followed the opening of three Compass offices in Chicago, as well as the launching of a Dallas operation. Due to its integration of technology, Compass has positioned itself to become the future of real estate. Compass is building the first modern real estate platform which pairs the industry's top talent with technology to make the search and sell experience intelligent and seamless.

Experts agree. In 2016, *Forbes* called Compass "one of the most innovative startups in the real estate space today." Analysis by *Business Insider*, in 2017, contended that "while Compass functions like a traditional broker, the company's promise is using technology to reduce the time and friction of buying and selling a house or apartment."

As a self-proclaimed "real estate company with a purpose," Compass identifies its mission "to help everyone find their place in the world." Apparently, the philosophy is working. At the time of Platinum's acquisition, Compass was valued at $2.2 billion, a number bolstered by a $450 million investment from Softbank.

At the announcement meeting of Compass's acquisition of Platinum Drive Realty, Rob Lehman, chief revenue officer of Compass, said, "Reputation is everything, and we found in our research that Platinum's reputation in the marketplace is excellent. It was one of the reasons why we have acquired the company." Lehman noted that

Compass had opened 50 different markets in the last three years.

"We play to win," he continued, "and we want to become No. 1 and the dominant real estate company in the Westchester marketplace. Platinum's high ethical standards will help us get there. We are humbled and honored to be part of Platinum's next chapter."

In an article published in the local *Scarsdale Inquirer* newspaper, two days after the announcement, Heather and Zach said, "Working with Compass to empower our agents with their world-class technology and support is the best thing we can do to continue to grow our business and better serve our clients. The national network of Compass will allow our agents to reach markets and expertise that no other brokerage could. We can't wait to help everyone in Westchester find their place in the world."

Lehman said, "Zach, Heather and the rest of the Platinum Drive team share our desire to go beyond what most believe is possible. Their track record of client-centered brokerage and persistent growth makes them a great addition to the Compass family."

Most Platinum agents were caught by surprise when the announcement was made. They thought they had been called to the office for a meeting and photos, rather than to hear news that would impact their professional lives. Even a pre-meeting email announcing a party at the nearby Fig & Olive restaurant in Eastchester, New York, ostensibly to celebrate the new sales season that same evening, did not seem to raise any eyebrows.

I, however, was not surprised by the sale of the company — just the timing of it. As a licensed real estate agent for Platinum and someone who has been a visible citizen in Scarsdale for nearly 40 years, I knew the company had been attracting general interest for a while. Over the past few years, I had been asked by interested parties if I thought the firm could be bought, and some acquaintances even asked for an introduction to Zach and Heather. Such interest in Platinum's potential was no surprise. As stated on announcement day, Platinum's reputation in the marketplace — and acknowledged by local competitors — is in the A-plus category. Furthermore, Heather and Zach are well respected as smart, honest, hardworking, friendly and collaborative business people.

Platinum's stellar reputation is what any company would want. As a homegrown business that only seriously started selling homes 10 years ago against daily competition from well-established companies like Sotheby's Julia B. Fee, Houlihan Lawrence, Coldwell Banker, Douglas Elliman and Berkshire Hathaway, Platinum's achievement is great. It has not only survived. it has thrived.

If you add all the good words heard in the marketplace to the fact that during one 48-hour time period in February 2018, Platinum closed on a combined $20 million-plus worth of business, you'd have to say that the firm is certainly "one tough customer to compete against." Over the years

Platinum has closed on deals ranging between $150,000 to $7,000,000, as well as rentals.

Heather and Zach, lifelong Scarsdale residents, smile when they say, "We never minded being known as the upstarts or new kids on the block. In fact, our-own-age customers represent an important part of our base in the marketplace."

It is obvious that Zach and Heather love the real estate business. They seemingly never stop working except to take care of their two children or their dog, Chase, a cockapoo. Each of them has often said that the Platinum office is never closed.

Some of the couple's pride and passion, as well as sound strategic planning, came from Heather's grandmother, Sunny Dubbs. Sunny was in the real estate business for 50 years and sold countless houses in Hartsdale and Scarsdale. She knew all the tricks of the trade. She introduced Heather to the profession, shared her secrets and was an important member of Platinum's first team.

Sunny said she always wanted to have an office close to a railroad station so clients, especially those from New York City, could easily reach her from the train. When Heather and Zach started their business, they knew it was more important to have access to easy parking. Now, as they move into the future with Compass, what counts may be the client's ability to navigate an app on a smartphone. Nevertheless, home will always be home.

DOESCHER LESSON: *Don't be afraid to try something new, and when you do, go for it with your best effort and a mindset of success. Particularly, if you want to own your own business, don't wait too long. And don't be afraid of where that business takes you, especially when you find yourself crossing unexpected horizons. Admiration, success, and money in the bank may be just around the corner.*

39. A LIFE-CHANGING MOMENT AT THE THIRD TEE

Bill with Hale Irwin, three-time U.S. Open champion, at a Dun & Bradstreet golf outing in Chicago, 1983

"There it was again, that aching pressure in his chest. Love, or a heart attack."

— Kristan Higgins, author

Parred the first hole.
Birdied the second.
Should have called 9-1-1 on the third.

I love golf. For me, it's a game of relaxation and mind-clearing that includes light competition among friends.

I've been a member of the Scarsdale Golf Club in Westchester County, New York, since 1982. I've played hundreds of rounds there, too many to count. With the help of former head pro Bill Smittle, fellow amateur golfer Fred Riccio, senior caddie Tony Cox, and others, I have honed my skills and become fairly accomplished at the game.

When I was younger, my best scores were in the mid-to-high 70s, which is considered an accomplishment on the SGC layout. An old scorecard from September 1996 says I shot a 75, my best ever, and my playing partners from back then — Riccio, Scott Robb and Jack McCaw — can confirm. Now I welcome scores in the mid-to-low 80s. But I'm happy with most games where I can stay below the low 90s, avoiding the dreaded 100 mark.

But never mind the score. All of my golf games, wherever played, have been most enjoyable. Pleasant is the word I'd choose to describe them, with the exception of a few special golf outings that have been truly memorable.

The first highlight was when my stepson Marc Blair and I won low net in SGC's annual father and son tournament in 1992. The next ones involved customer golf outings I organized in Japan and the United States with Hall-of-Fame golfer Hale Irwin, when I was a public relations and marketing executive at Dun & Bradstreet. Irwin was a three-time U.S. Open champion with 20 victories on the regular

PGA tour and 45 wins on the PGA Champions Tour. Those were definitely good times.

In fact, there has been only one bad day of golf for me. But, in fairness, it had nothing to do with the game. What occurred on the course was life changing, if not life threatening, and the day remains ingrained in my memory.

I remember the morning well. The sun was shining, and it had warmed the air to a comfortable temperature on a late summer day — Saturday, August 29, 2015. The Scarsdale Golf Club course was filled with all the regular weekend players. My foursome consisted of club friends Bob Czufin, John Lamson and Wink McKinnon. It should have been the perfect day for a game of golf. Only I made a mess of it. While the others in my group completed the round, my experience was similar to a prize fight. I was knocked out in the third round, which in this case, was actually the third hole.

But it didn't start out that way. At the beginning, I had high expectations that this was going to be a good game. I parred the first hole. I birdied the second. I approached the third tee brimming with extreme confidence for a possible low round. However, it didn't happen. When I teed off on No. 3, I felt a twinge of pain in my left shoulder and arm. I thought it was a muscle pull and kept playing. I hit one more shot, contemplated another and then called it a day. I was concerned I would collapse on the course, as I was suddenly feeling nauseous and weak. I was also experiencing chest pains. I did not call 9-1-1, and this was my first mistake.

Without telling my playing partners I was experiencing all the symptoms of a heart attack, I vaguely said I wasn't feeling well and decided to go home. I had our caddie for the day, Tony Cox, call the caddie master, Dan Daly, to come get me in a golf cart, and he did.

At my request, Dan drove me to the men's locker room, where I got my cell phone and car keys. I then drove home, which was a short distance away. This was my second mistake.

When I arrived home, my wife Linda, whom I now think of as "my doctor in residence," asked why I was home so early. I said, "Let's go, you need to drive me to White Plains Hospital, because I think I'm having a heart attack."

As mistake number three, we got into the car and headed to the hospital. During that short ride, I felt safe but wondered if, please God, could we only hurry up and get there so the doctors could save my life. When I arrived in the emergency room, I said I thought I was having a heart attack. The doctors and nurses quickly moved into action, skipping the routine of first asking for my insurance card. My blood pressure was rising for sure.

From the first sign of a heart attack on the golf course to my arrival at the hospital emergency room, approximately 18–20 minutes had elapsed. This was all wasted time.

Later, I realized how lucky I was to make it to the hospital. If I had waited any longer or played a few more holes, I might not be around today to write these words.

I should have called 9-1-1. There's no question about it.

I had three chances to do so, yet I didn't. I'm not sure what made me so reluctant, but I think I was initially hoping my condition would improve. When it didn't, I felt hesitant to bother anyone with my health problem, whatever it was.

Even though the eventual outcome was successful, and everything turned out OK, I feel foolish for not calling an ambulance at the start. A good recovery, I'm told, is possible after a heart attack, but so much depends on quick treatment.

When I arrived at the ER, the hospital staff wasted no time in assessing my symptoms. They immediately attached me to an EKG machine, began monitoring my heart and checked my blood pressure. Their findings confirmed my suspicion that I was indeed having a heart attack.

I was quickly brought to the hospital's catheterization lab, where I met my new doctor, Mark Greenberg, a truly caring professional, who identified the problem that precipitated my cardiac condition. I had 100-percent blockage in a vital artery, thus limiting the supply of oxygen-rich blood to my heart.

Greenberg and his team found the source of the blockage during a 45-minute procedure. They inserted a stent to open the clog and restored blood flow to my heart.

The team of doctors at White Plains Hospital saved my life, and I am forever grateful.

During follow-up care, there was talk of possibly inserting more stents, which would have meant going to Montefiore Hospital in the Bronx for the procedure. But I sought a second opinion and contacted Dr. Michael J. Wolk, a longtime friend and former All-American swimmer from Colgate University who had become a prominent cardiologist at Weill Cornell Medicine, in New York City.

Dr. Wolk ordered a visit with his hospital's top stent man. He conducted a variety of tests, including a nuclear stress test and another EKG. The results led to a recommendation for no more stents. Instead I was to follow a regimen of medication and physical therapy to keep my heart healthy and reduce the risk of another heart attack.

Dr. Wolk directed me to a cardiac rehabilitation program at Burke Rehabilitation Hospital, in White Plains, for several weeks. It included supervised exercise and nutrition counseling. I began to feel stronger and healthier, and I lost 20 pounds in the process.

I have been back on Scarsdale Golf Club's course for about three years now. I regularly use the SGC gym, and at home I work out on an exercise cycle that my wife purchased. To keep me on track, I also employ a trainer I had used prior to the heart attack.

I have tried to forget that third-hole heart attack and the events surrounding it, but my mind won't let me. The experience remains ever present, as a whisper of caution. And that's a good thing because it means I won't forget to take my medicine or skip my workouts.

Of course, my red-haired "doctor in residence" is still on the case, too. She watches everything I put in my mouth, to keep my diet healthy at home or when eating out.

DOESCHER LESSON: *Don't take chances with your health. Call 9-1-1 immediately if you suspect you might be having a heart attack or suffering from any other serious condition. Your life depends on it.*

40.
THIRTEEN HOLES IN ONE: FAVORITE GOLF COURSES

"Some of us were bitten with the idea that playing golf was a necessity for a wholesome life and wholesome conscience."

— Dr. Willis E. Ford, President (1897–1899), Yahnundasis Golf Club, New Hartford, New York

I am taking a huge risk by selecting my favorite 13 golf courses. My many golfing partners and friends over the years undoubtedly have their own favorites and will argue why some of my choices made the list. Bill Kupper, former publisher of *Businessweek* and one of those golfing friends, rates courses around the U.S. and has played on some golf layouts I have never heard of. He no doubt will have opinions about my selections and regret courses that did not make the list. Other friends have knocked that little white ball around in Ireland and Scotland in all kinds of weather, and I'm sure they would pick a number of courses from across the ocean for their lists. Although I would love to play the Old Course at St. Andrews in Scotland, my choices are all based in the U.S. and represent courses that I have played at least once.

It should be noted that my list excludes four courses I have played numerous times as a club member and the one I often played at Colgate University. To be fair, I disqualified them. They are: (1) the Scarsdale Golf Club in Hartsdale, New York, an A.W. Tillinghast course, where I have been a member since 1982; (2) Bear's Paw Country Club, a Jack Nicklaus signature golf course in Naples, Florida, where I spent 12 winters; (3) the Yahnundasis Golf & Country Club, a course designed by famed architect Walter J. Travis in New Hartford, New York, on which I grew up as a golfer; and (4) Seven Oaks Golf Club at Colgate in Hamilton, New York, designed by Robert Trent Jones, which I frequently played as a loyal volunteer alum.

Square footage and the par have been omitted from the list because some of the courses have more than 18 holes, and golfers — depending on their abilities — can choose to play from different tees.

1. PEBBLE BEACH GOLF LINKS,
PEBBLE BEACH, CALIFORNIA

The views are out of this world and definitely worth the price of admission. My two favorite rounds there came at a conference of the PR Seminar for top global PR executives, now called just the Seminar. Playing with Charlotte Otto (then of P&G), her husband Bob and Bob DeFillippo (then of Prudential), I shot an 83. Two days later, I shot an 82 playing with Bob Feldman, co-founder of Pulse Point Group, a management and digital consulting firm with offices in Los Angeles and Austin. Bob was also a transplanted New Yorker and a graduate of Utica College, where I served on the board of trustees even though I wasn't a graduate. Even with those good scores, the draw for me still remains the views.

2. AUGUSTA NATIONAL GOLF CLUB, AUGUSTA, GEORGIA

Any golf devotee would pick this course as one of his or her favorites, especially after having the opportunity to play it. Watching the Masters tournament with the infamous Amen Corner on TV — and then actually being there — would do it for most golf junkies. I only played the course twice at the invitation of the Augusta golf lords there when I was affiliated with Drexel Heritage Furnishings and the Heritage Golf Classic PGA tournament. Knowing the course's wonderful history gave me goosebumps each time I stepped on the hallowed ground. I was in such awe of being there, I don't even remember my scores. But I think I broke 100 each time.

3. RIVIERA COUNTRY CLUB, PACIFIC PALISADES, CALIFORNIA

A D&B customer golf outing with three-time U.S. Open champ Hale Irwin initially brought me there. I was just as pleased as the customers to play this course, the site of many PGA events. My big news on one of the many times I played there was missing a hole-in-one on the 6th hole by inches. But, as they say, a miss is as good as a mile. Since my friends will ask, I made the birdie putt.

4. PEACHTREE GOLF CLUB,
ATLANTA, GEORGIA

John Imlay, then CEO of D&B Software, invited me to be his guest several times there, and every time we were the first ones on the course at 9:15 a.m. You could see our spike marks in the dew on the grass. It's truly a private club. Reminiscent of Augusta, the course was in tip-top shape every time we played. As per John's recommendation, I followed the caddies' advice, and it enhanced my play and lowered my score immensely. Later, over the years, John took me to some of his 11 other golf clubs, including the Atlanta Athletic Club, in John's Creek, Georgia.

5. HARBOUR TOWN GOLF LINKS,
HILTON HEAD ISLAND, SOUTH CAROLINA

When you have the chutzpah to recommend that your firm, then Drexel Heritage Furnishings, replace Chrysler as one of three sponsors for a PGA tournament with "Heritage" in its name, in the 1970s, for marketing and promotional reasons, you just have to select that tournament's course for your list of favorites. Moreover, having played the course many times, I continue to like it despite its treacherous postage-stamp greens. I always dreamed of making a birdie on the par-4 18th at the lighthouse to win the Heritage Classic, but obviously that never was going to happen. The honor of winning the title belongs to the pros — Arnold Palmer, Jack Nicklaus, Bernard Langer, Hale Irwin, Johnny Miller, Tom Watson,

Davis Love III, Fuzzy Zoeller and others. No matter how many times I played the course, I never birdied the 18th hole. Par was my "birdie." However, walking down the fairway was always thrilling for me. Dreams are good even when they don't become reality.

6. THE TPC SAWGRASS (PLAYERS STADIUM), PONTE VEDRA BEACH, FLORIDA

The permanent home of THE PLAYERS Championship with the "sink or swim" par-3 17th hole. Jack Nicklaus is the only 3-time winner of the event. It was quite an honor and pleasure to play this course. I parred the 17th. Don't ask me what I scored on the other holes because it was ugly! Thanks to Bob Beauregard, a longtime friend and guru in advertising and publishing for many years, hosted me the first time I played there. I thank him for introducing me to this famous course.

7. CYPRESS POINT CLUB IN THE DEL MONTE FOREST, PEBBLE BEACH, CALIFORNIA

When the man who spontaneously greeted you by the tiny clubhouse just happens to be the actor Clint Eastwood, you know you're going to have a good day. "Hi, I'm Clint Eastwood," he said, as if we didn't know, and then proceeded to tell us what we could expect on the course. "Pay attention to the caddies; they know the course like the backs of their hands," he said. We followed Clint's advice and enjoyed the round even though Cypress is a most challenging course. It has a series of dramatic holes that play along the Pacific Ocean: the 15th, 16th and 17th. The 16th is a long par 3, 219 yards, that plays over the ocean. With the wind in my face on my first visit, I used my driver and aimed a little left so as to avoid the ocean. I bogeyed the hole on my first try and never did better on subsequent visits. Nonetheless, I had had the opportunity to take Cypress off my bucket list.

8. NATIONAL GOLF LINKS OF AMERICA, SOUTHAMPTON, NEW YORK

It's a prestigious links-style golf course on Long Island between Shinnecock Hills Golf Club and the Peconic Bay. If you don't lose a ball during your round, consider yourself lucky. There are no weak holes, and sometimes the wind can stir your ball in the wrong direction. The views at 17 and 18 are spectacular. No. 1 can be a relatively easy hole if you don't 4-putt the tricky green. A par there can give you a false sense of security of what may follow. I still have a vision of my D&B friend, the late Don Durgin, searching a long time for his ball in the tall grass on one of the holes. With a smile on his face the Princeton grad would say, "Play on, gents," every time he lost his ball. Durgin, a former president of NBC, became famous when he made the call to switch from an Oakland Raiders–New York Jets game in 1968 to a Heidi movie with 65 seconds left in the game. The Raiders scored two touchdowns in the last nine seconds to win the game. Also to be noted, the lunch prepared by the club is worth playing every shot of the 18 holes. Charlie Moritz, a former chairman and CEO at D&B, hosted me on my first visit.

9. WINGED FOOT GOLF CLUB (WEST COURSE) MAMARONECK, NEW YORK

I have played in many charitable tournaments on this course. I also have played a few rounds on the club's East course. I prefer the West course although some friends prefer the East course. Famous golf course designer A. W. Tillinghast put his imprint on both courses. There's lots of history there, including the time rainbow came out at the 18th hole when Davis Love III won the PGA championship in 1997. Winged Foot is a very serious golf club with dozens of low handicap golfers as members. Once, I was told by a member that golf caps weren't allowed under the awning on the terrace.

10. LOS ANGELES COUNTRY CLUB (NORTH COURSE), LOS ANGELES, CALIFORNIA

Nestled between Beverly Hills and Santa Monica on Wilshire Boulevard, the course offers a most wonderful experience for those who are lucky enough to be invited to play there. Michael Meyer, one of the U.S.'s most prominent leasing attorneys and a fellow Jackie Robinson Foundation board member, made arrangements for me to have this opportunity. We teed off on a weekday as the sun was rising, and I was welcomed to the club by being assigned former U.S. President Ronald Reagan's locker. The north course is hilly and challenging, and I played my usual game — some good holes and some not so good. I'd play it again.

11. PINEHURST RESORT (COURSE NO. 2), PINEHURST, NORTH CAROLINA

A recent post on Facebook from Hilary Howard Heieck, Scarsdale native, All-ACC basketball player and Newhouse master's grad, said, "Escape to Pinehurst, where golf is more than a game — it's a way of life." Well Hilary, I've done that — but not recently. On a July 4th weekend in 1990, Congressional Country Club member Ron Sappenfeld and I dragged our wives to North Carolina for a golf bonanza at Pinehurst. We played four of the Pinehurst courses on four successive days. We liked all four and settled on the world-famous No. 2 as our favorite perhaps because of its storied history and the fact that it has been the site of more single golf championships than any course in America. About No. 2, Jack Nicklaus, once said, "I've always thought Pinehurst No. 2 to be my favorite golf course from a design standpoint. I've enjoyed going out on No. 2 and seeing a totally tree-lined golf course without a tree coming into play."

12. BALTUSROL GOLF CLUB (LOWER COURSE), SPRINGFIELD, NEW JERSEY

Friends Len Coleman, Jim Rutter, and Bill Bak invited me to be their guest at this magnificent course a number of times. I enjoyed the rounds each time, remembering the likes of Jack Nicklaus, Arnold Palmer and even my Utica hometown touring pro, journeyman Ed Furgol, who won the U.S. Open there in 1954, marching around the course as if they owned it. Rutter, a D&B executive who was the senior champ there at least once, gave it his all during one customer golf outing in order to better 3-time U.S. champion Hale Irwin's score. It didn't happen, but nice try, Jim.

13. GARDEN CITY GOLF CLUB, GARDEN CITY, LONG ISLAND, NEW YORK

Bill Dwyer, former mayor of Garden City, president of Moody's Investors Service (twice) and president of D&B Japan, was always proud to have his business brethren as guests at his club. Originally designed by Walter J. Travis, Garden City is a course that looks very natural and could be easily classified as a links-style course except it's not located by water. The first two holes look easy unless you find your ball in the bunkers. All the greens are small in nature so be careful with your "up-and-down" routine. The 18th finishing hole, a par-3, 159-yards, is a great way to conclude a friendly match. Over the years, I played on many different courses with Bill, including three times in Tokyo, Japan, at the Chiyhoda and Seve Golf Club courses. The other two players were Mike Armacost, U.S. Ambassador to Japan, who had a body guard following his every step, and Hale Irwin, 3-time U.S. Open champion. I am happy to report that I had the second lowest scores all three rounds.

DOESCHER LESSON: *If you've read this far to ascertain what courses I selected and why, you may wonder what conclusions, if any, you should draw from this list or about golf in general? Here are some additional thoughts about the game of golf:*

1. *With an average golf game, I was fortunate to have the time and energy to have played so many interesting and dynamic golf courses with some very nice people. Golfers by and large are nice people unless proven otherwise.*
2. *For years people have been drawing comparisons between the game of golf and the game of life. How a person acts and reacts on a golf course can usually portend how they will act in the real world.*
3. *A long time ago, someone told me that playing a decent game of golf can be an asset in the business world. That person was right. The many customer golf outings I planned for D&B certainly proved that scenario was 100 percent accurate. Also, I've been told that verbal agreements on important business deals have been made on the golf course.*
4. *John Feinstein, author of 35 books, described golf as* A Good Walk Spoiled. *He was wrong. Dead wrong!*

41.
THE NEXT 20 YEARS

"Every generation imagines itself to be more intelligent than the one that went before it, and wiser than the one that comes after it."

— George Orwell, author

What will life be like in 2030?

While the future is impossible to predict, contemporary tendencies and trends may help anticipate possible directions. No matter what may occur, it is important to keep an open mind with regard to change so that we may stay in tack and steer our success within the forward-moving river of time.

In 1949, George Orwell wrote *1984*. At that time, the year that gave the book its title was still almost 40 years away. Nevertheless, Orwell's portent about the future, which included aspects of a totalitarian government and the use of media manipulation and advanced technology to control people, has some relevance in today's world.

Orwell's book predicted something called a "telescreen," a TV that observed those who were watching it. Orwell was ahead of his time. In 1987, Nielsen Media Research invented a technology to measure the viewing habits of TV audiences. It was called the People Meter.

More recently, it has been revealed that the government, smartphone apps and hackers have the ability to spy on people through the camera and microphone functions of smartphones and computers.

Orwell's future also predicted a world of three "megastates" rather than hundreds of countries. These megastates had different names, but they can be roughly compared to modern day mega-powers such as China, the collective European Union, the United States and its allies, or Russia and its allies.

Looking back on my career, much has changed since I received my master's degree in public relations from Newhouse in 1961 and ventured out into the field. In addition to the constant flux taking place in business styles, consumer preferences and PR strategies, we have also experienced an exciting roller-coaster ride of new product ideas, mass marketing techniques, consumer data configurations, tailored content, different advertising models and creative retail concepts. We have also seen new startup companies that have developed unusual but exceptionally useful products. Some of these products have succeeded in pushing back against the status quo of the blue-chip companies that our dads told us to work for and to add to our stock portfolios. Just look at what Amazon has become — selling everything to everyone online.

According to the April 24, 2018, edition of *The Guardian*, "What makes Amazon so frightening for rival businesses is that it can use its expertise in data analytics to move into almost any sector." As a result, the big news in the marketplace and on Wall Street is that some well-known past and current U.S. business leaders are becoming increasingly threatened by Amazon and its founder Jeff Bezos, who has been identified as the world's richest man with a net worth of $158 billion. Bezos and his company are even being talked about in "corporate war rooms" where competitors, CEOs and marketing gurus are strategizing about how to compete. Even the White House has voiced concern about Amazon's impact on the expense borne by the U.S. Postal System in delivering Amazon packages.

When my father, in the 1950s, advised me about a safe direction for my future, companies like Amazon weren't even on the radar. His favorite line, which he repeated on numerous occasions, was: "You should go to work at the New York Telephone Company and retire after 40 years. And while you're at it, buy some of their stock." Today, the New York Telephone Company no longer exists, as it was merged into a larger conglomeration. General Electric was another stock my dad recommended and bought for himself. Like New York Telephone, it is no longer what it used to be. While in the process of selling off parts of its business to improve earnings, GE fell from grace in the eyes of investors, and it was removed from the Dow Jones Industrial Average list of 30 stocks in June 2018, a spot it had held continuously since 1907.

Amazon, and companies like it, are successful in today's market because they are experts in data analytics and big data. Amazon and Bezos are expanding their reach into many different sectors with acquisitions and startups including Whole Foods, the Washington Post Company and Blue Origin. In the *Guardian* article, Tuck School of Business Professor Vijay Govindarajan said, "[Amazon's] obsession with knowing its customers means that, while feared by almost every business, Amazon is beloved. It's viewed as cheap, convenient and reliable."

Proficiency in using data analytics and customer information, as exemplified by Amazon, will continue to be a key to a company's operational success as we move into the next decades.

This is one of the lessons that today's students of business, PR and advertising are learning. Many of them are entrepreneurial. Julia Haber, one of my mentees, a 2018 graduate of the Newhouse School of Public Communications at Syracuse University with a major in advertising, is in the process of seeking venture capital for her company, Wayv Experiential, which "brings the heart of brands to college campuses ... through experiential, data-driven pop-up shops." She started the business in college.

While still on campus, Julia conducted an informal poll with some of her professors in public relations and advertising. The professors were asked to predict what might be happening in their fields in 2030. Julia shared her findings:

1. The projected increased use of collected personal data will use Artificial Intelligence to create a mass-market

technique in the management of personal in-depth data profiles.

2. Algorithms will perform calculation, data processing and automated-reasoning tasks.
3. Heart-rate sensors or other biological factors will provide a more reliable way to explain how you are "feeling."
4. The growth of more tailored content will continue.
5. Traditional mass market advertising will disappear altogether.
6. Artificial Intelligence will affect the way consumers make decisions and interact with brands.

To me and many others, Artificial Intelligence is the new buzzword. But the term was actually first discussed at a conference at Dartmouth in 1956. It is only within the last decade, however, that "we've seen the first truly substantive glimpses of its power and application," according to the November 2018 issue of *Fortune* magazine. Although we are now encountering this terminology everywhere, few of us fully understand what it means and how it functions within practically every field.

For starters, AI describes the use of low-cost, digital technology for prediction and discovery. It exploits the vast amount of available online data to identify patterns and learn from them. One of the benefits can be seen in science and medicine. Already in practice, AI is being used to reduce the amount of time and cost spent on traditional methods of drug development and testing. In agriculture, the technology is being used to optimize cassava crops in rural villages in Tanzania. Engineers at Google, working with the International Institute of Tropical Agriculture, have programmed smartphones to act as diagnostic tools when hovered over plants. The installed software is able to identify botanical disease and pest blight, as well as recommend low-cost solutions. In the commercial sector, AI logarithms are increasingly being used to give companies insight into customers' buying preferences and spending habits.

According to a *New York Times* article by Steve Lohr, published on October 19, 2018, "Much of what AI does today can be thought of as a prediction. What product is recommended, what ad to show you, what image is in that picture, what move should the robot make next — all are automated predictions." Lohr muses that AI logarithms may become so efficient that retailers may someday ship desired products even before the purchase transactions have been completed. But, then again, this may be a little too far-fetched — or not. Lohr said, "Just where artificial intelligence is taking us, at what pace and along what trajectory is uncertain."

After all, we're human. We're not robots.

Looking at the future of AI and the world today, I hope we don't ever lose sight of our values. I pray that someone like Fred Rogers, and his signature children's television program, *Mister Rogers' Neighborhood*, will appear again in 2030 and make our world a better place. Mister Rogers utilized an understated, soft-spoken manner that made children feel special, loved and safe. The program ran for more than 30 years and touched many hearts.

I was reminded about Rogers and his show by the documentary, *Won't You Be My Neighbor*, released in 2018. It demonstrated that Rogers did a lot of good and changed many lives. Importantly, the closing line of the signature song "Won't you be my neighbor," which Rogers sang during every episode, reminded viewers to always respect one another.

We should remember Rogers's attitude now — and in 2030 and beyond. Everyone is indeed special, no matter what accomplishments they achieve — or don't achieve — in the world. This belief is what will make the world a better place to live.

DOESCHER LESSON: *Tomorrow is a matter of choice and opportunity. Take an active role in shaping it. Make it "a beautiful day in the neighborhood."*

AFTERWORD

Writing my first book has been a blast.

For some, writing a tome creates a sense of nervousness and sleeplessness. Sometimes, it causes migraine headaches that are hard to eradicate. Constant thoughts of failure are usually the culprit.

For me, since I had been thinking about writing a book for several years and contemplating various themes, failure was no longer in my vocabulary. The process of writing was nothing but joy, and I enjoyed applying the storytelling craft I have practiced all my life. As this was to be a memoir about my life and career, including lessons learned, I was determined it had to be nothing short of perfection.

In my career, I learned that you sometimes need to do serious research — quantitative and qualitative — if you are going to be any kind of writer. I needed to do the same for this book as well. While my memory is strong, I found myself reading and re-reading textbooks, autobiographies, online documents, website posts and a whole lot of newspaper clippings that my wife of 41 years kept feeding me in order to gather "Just the facts, Ma'am." That was what Joe Friday used to say to victims and witnesses in the *Dragnet* TV series I watched as a kid in the 1950s.

I even convinced a reference librarian at the Utica Public Library to help me dig up details about how and when my father "the superhero" saved three people's lives. I remembered a lot of the story on my own, but since I was only in third grade at the time, I needed additional research to make sure my recollection was accurate.

Now that the writing is complete, I am pleased — not just because I finished the book but because I have been able to share a lifetime of memories, reflections and lessons learned. I know members of my family and friends, in particular, will enjoy reading it — as they will anticipate a quiz at the end of the exercise.

I hope you enjoyed reading this book as much as I did writing it. Thanks for paying attention.

Bill Doescher
January 2019

ACKNOWLEDGMENTS

The idea for this book came about in the spring of 2011. Its chief cheerleader, then and now, has been public relations guru Gary Grates. Gary and I connect on a variety of professional levels — we are both Newhouse alums and adjunct professors, and have served together on the Utica College board of trustees — but we also share a mindset that comes from growing up in small towns in Upstate New York. Gary hails from Frankfort, a town of approximately 7,500 centered around a historic, gabled town hall building; and I was born in Utica, a formerly industrial city located approximately 12 miles to the west of Frankfort.

The first time Gary and I discussed the idea of a book was during a car ride on the New York State Thruway. We were driving back to Westchester County from the Syracuse University Carrier Dome, where we had just heard Richard Edelman deliver a convocation speech to Newhouse grads on May 14, 2011. While heading east on the long and winding Thruway, our conversation drifted from the roadway scenery, to the field of public relations, to the notion of writing a book. Piloting our rental car, Gary brought it up with a simple statement.

"Bill, you should write a book about your experiences," he said.

"A book? And what would it be about?" I asked him. Intrigued and excited, I was already playing with the idea, but not in a serious way.

Then, about four months later, on September 20, Gary encouraged me again. Following a lecture I had delivered to a crowd of 400 at Newhouse's Joyce Hergenhan Auditorium, "Embracing Change: 50 Years in Public Relations," Gary came up to me in the hall where we were waiting for dessert and coffee. He clasped my hand and exclaimed, "Now, that's the book." His enthusiasm about the content of my lecture prodded me to take my ideas further. Of course, a book based on the contents of that lecture, would have become a textbook. Most likely, that was Gary's initial thought, and it became my starting direction too. However, like many projects, the book evolved over the years, and in its existing state, its pages are much more reflective of my life than a textbook could ever be.

Thanks, Gary, for your most positive input along the way. It was more than any friend could have asked for. Our coffee shop breakfasts in Scarsdale, the Arthur W. Page Society and PRSA meetings in multiple cities, the Newhouse gatherings, our post-Utica College board meeting conversations, and numerous phone calls were most beneficial as I was figuring out "what in the world I was going to write about."

Thanks also to Shelley and Barry Spector for enthusiastically agreeing to publish this book. Shelley is a Newhouse alumna who, along with husband Barry, founded the Museum of Public Relations in New York City in order to archive the history of our industry. Knowing that my approach to this memoir would be centered on my life and career while highlighting mutual lessons learned along the way, Shelley encouraged me to include a heavy dose of subjects related to public relations. The essay, "Where is Public Relations Headed" is part of my response to Shelley's suggestion, aimed at the professional audience.

Thanks also to members of my family who supported my effort and generously shared ideas, recollections and thoughts. Our son Doug Doescher reminded me about one childhood drama, and this memory turned into my essay, "A Scare at Madison Square Garden." Our daughter Cinda Doescher Malec urged me not to forget to honor Aunt Elsie, and that essay is called "Everyone Should Have an Aunt Elsie." Our daughter Michelle Blair Hammond, an author, filmmaker and English professor at San Jose City College in California, inspired me by sending samples of her work with specific notations. Our son Marc Blair shared press releases about some of the financial deals he's worked on over the years to remind me of some of my past experiences in financial and investor relations. In turn, I have included some of these recollections in the book. And, what seemed like a daily routine, my wife, Linda Blair Doescher, left hundreds of notes and newspaper clippings on my desk chair about her ideas of what should be included in the book. I considered all of the family's suggestions seriously, and in the end, I did it my way.

Thanks also to all those leaders in their respective fields, such as Roger Bolton, president of the Arthur W.

Page Society; Anthony D'Angelo, chair of PRSA National and professor at Newhouse; Mike Paul, senior PR guy who calls himself The Reputation Doctor®; and Della Britton Baeza, president and CEO of the Jackie Robinson Foundation, who patiently answered my many questions and agreed to comment on a plethora of subjects. For all the others, whose relevant comments I found in the public domain — in books, articles and on the internet — and are quoted in this book, I sincerely say "thank you."

Thanks also to the individuals profiled here. They include Scarsdale's Rev. Pete Jones and Rabbi Jonathan Blake, and former chairman and CEO of Champion International Andy Sigler. I also had the pleasure of sharing the story of Heather and Zach Harrison's success in real estate. Each of these people reviewed what I wrote, liked what they saw and offered favorable comments with very few changes. That's called batting 4-for-4 or 1,000 in any league. That never happened to me in sports or in my corporate endeavors, although I got close a couple of times. The fifth profile is about Jimmy Rocco, the former longtime caddie master at the Scarsdale Golf Club who passed away and therefore had no chance to read what I wrote. But I always had his back; so, I'd like to think his review wasn't necessary.

Thanks also to Sarah Schultz, digital literacy librarian at the Utica Public Library, who provided me with important archival information from the *Utica Observer-Dispatch* and *Utica Daily Press* about the heart-thumping criminal incident where my father saved three people's lives in our Utica neighborhood called Ridgewood. That essay is called "My Father the Superhero," and he certainly was.

And last but certainly not least, a huge bouquet to Traci Dutton Ludwig, my editor, a superb wordsmith and amateur dancer of note, who pushed me hard with a smile to always do better and to consider different subjects for the essays. A sensitive and inquisitive reader, she encouraged me to provide more detail in order to make the stories more vibrant and interesting for the reader. During one of our many editing sessions, usually held at the Starbucks coffee shop near the Scarsdale railroad station, she said, "That's a nice story about your father. Now, where's the one about your mother?" Paying attention to her question, as I did for all her questions, I penned two about Mom. It was through my wife Linda, once called the Scarsdale Decorating Doyenne by the editor of the local *Scarsdale Inquirer* newspaper, that I met Traci. At the time, Traci was interviewing Linda for a special design supplement. Following the interview, Linda introduced us and suggested I consider Traci as the editor for my book. It was an excellent suggestion that led to a great working partnership, and the prose before you is proof positive of that.

My life has been blessed with many lessons along the way — some personal and some professional. In paying attention, each of these lessons has made me a better person, and I hope you will find value in them too. As a final thought, here's a bonus lesson: Listen to your wife's (or husband's) suggestions; they certainly contain winners sometimes. Recommending Traci to be the editor of my book was one of those ideas. Thank you, Linda and Traci — a dynamite duo, with plenty of opinions to go around.

Bill Doescher
January 2019

INDEX

C

I

J

N

O

P

Q

R

S

T

U

V

W

CPSIA information can be obtained
at www.ICGtesting.com
Printed in the USA
FFHW020415091218
49810747-54325FF

9 780999 024577